The New Radicals

'In the dark days of the early seventies, when the news filtered through to Robben Island of a campaign to release political prisoners, waged by a small group of left-leaning, white students, it buoyed our spirits immensely. This book provides invaluable and illuminating insights into how the next generation of activists took up the struggle against apartheid under very difficult conditions, a story that has not often been told.'
– Ahmed 'Kathy' Kathrada, Rivonia trialist and Robben Island prisoner

'A much-needed and engrossing personal account of the embryonic student and black trade union movements of the early seventies, and how this younger generation of activists, both black and white, battled to wage struggle at a time when apartheid was at its height, and the liberation movements at their weakest. Through their actions, the radicalism of this generation defined a new politics of opposition.'
– Barbara Hogan, former Minister of Health and Minister of Public Enterprises, and a political prisoner under apartheid

'Fascinating and important insight into the emergence of a brave young radicalism of the early 1970s embracing white campuses, Black Consciousness and trade unionism which raised questions and challenges not only for the apartheid-capitalist nexus but also for the mainstream liberation movement.

'Those in exile and in prison strove then to discern what was new and possible. While hope for change was reinforced by these developments, there was also a degree of concern and prejudice. This was compounded by lack of clarity from afar, as to whether such emergent forces would be loyal to the ANC–SACP alliance and how to provide leadership to them.

'Looking back there is much need for honest reflection and the author does us a service with his well worked research and writing. It leaves one with tantalising thoughts as to whether the incipient democratic left challenges from civil society and trade union circles in South Africa today might fundamentally change our political landscape.'
– Ronnie Kasrils, chief of intelligence for Umkhonto we Sizwe and a government minister from 1994 to 2008

THE NEW RADICALS

A Generational Memoir of the 1970s

Glenn Moss

For more information about this book, see www.thenewradicals.com

First published by Jacana Media (Pty) Ltd
First and second impression 2014

10 Orange Street
Sunnyside
Auckland Park 2092
South Africa
+2711 628 3200
www.jacana.co.za

© Glenn Moss, 2014

All rights reserved. No part of this book may be reproduced or utilised in any form and by any means, electronic or mechanical, including photocopying, without permission in writing from the publisher.

ISBN 978-1-4314-0971-6

Cover design by publicide
Set in Sabon 10.75/15pt
Printed and bound by Creda Communications
Job no. 002249

See a complete list of Jacana titles at www.jacana.co.za

Contents

Preface vii
Abbreviations x

1 Trading places 1
2 Radical challenges to liberal politics 32
3 Rejecting the Republic – and a detainee dies 50
4 The student left takes charge 75
5 The rediscovery of resistance 105
6 Release all political prisoners 121
7 Students, intellectuals and worker organisation 147
8 Unravelling the Industrial Aid Society 174
9 Unavoidably detained 189
10 Trials and tribulations 212
11 Bookends 247

Notes 267
Index 274
Picture credits 283

Preface

> I need to return briefly to a few incidents that have grown into anecdotes, to some approximate memories which time has deformed into certainty. If I can't be sure of the actual events anymore I can at least be true to the impressions those facts left. That's the best I can manage.
> – Julian Barnes, *The Sense of an Ending*

A story usually has a beginning and an end. This one does not. Reflecting on the past, evaluating its influence on the present and predicting its effects on the future involve a never-ending and often-changing narrative.

But a story, like political history, needs to be framed, to have some structure. That is the function of the background and historical detail which appear in some of the chapters. This builds the pillars within which political history and memoir are held up. If the pillars move, then the shape of the story will alter.

This book charts a slice of political history. It also reflects the first phase of my own political involvement. Much of the writing is based on memory – mine as well as that of other participants. I initially wrote each section from what I could remember, and only then checked and verified my recall against other sources, written as well as oral.

Based largely in Johannesburg in the first half of the 1970s, the narrative tells of the political, ideological and organisational journey undertaken by a group of students. It records how they moved from the relatively insular liberal protest and symbolic politics of an elite university to help in creating the preconditions for a radical challenge to the society which had formed them.

It also chronicles some of the embryonic initiatives which moved

South African resistance politics from its historical low point at the end of the 1960s to the organisation, mobilisation and rebellion evident by 1976.

* * *

Tony Webster, in *The Sense of an Ending*, warns about the limits of memory: 'What you end up remembering isn't always the same as what you have witnessed.' A number of people functioned as my informal 'memory group', doing their best to insert greater accuracy and detail into the way I recalled events. My special thanks to the following, all of whom have been close friends for 40 and more years: Cedric de Beer, Richard de Villiers, Alan Fine, Barbara Hogan, Kally Forrest, Gerhard (Gerry) Maré and Elaine Unterhalter. Steven Friedman was particularly generous in sharing memories and information, especially on early initiatives to organise workers.

Atlantic Philanthropies' Gerald Kraak supported research, travel and editing costs of this project, while Deborah Posel of the University of Cape Town's Institute for Humanities in Africa (Huma) was unfailingly generous in her support and offers of institutional assistance.

Ivan Vladislavić has been much more than a reader and adviser. Long before I had started writing, he encouraged me to record the stories I sometimes recounted over lunch and wine. His comments and suggestions on drafts of the manuscript were wise, insightful and gentle in their very necessary criticism. Ivan has been a friend as well as a guide.

Russell Martin from Jacana Media has guided this book through the complex publishing process. As editor, proofreader, co-ordinator and adviser, his professionalism and experience have been a pleasure to encounter. The way he and Ivan Vladislavić collaborated to guide me in producing a better-structured and more readable book is a fine example of skill, wisdom and maturity.

Archivists at the University of the Witwatersrand were particularly helpful in finding material on the 1970s, often going way beyond the call of duty by scanning and sending copies to me in Cape Town, and answering numerous queries. Special thanks to Michele Pickover and Gabi Mohale at Wits Historical Papers, and Elizabeth Marima at the Wits Archives. Leslie Hart, then of the University of Cape Town's Special Collections, and Diana Wall from Museum Africa were both very generous with their time and assistance. Annette Gerstner compiled an index in record time, with flexibility and professionalism.

My sons, Michael and Anthony, did much to encourage the writing of this book. Passionate about needing to know what I, and my close friends, 'did in the war', they maintained pressure on me to deliver something. Michael also investigated the Nusas archives at the University of Cape Town, uncovering some remarkable documents which were vital in stimulating, confirming and amending memory.

Georgina Jaffee, life partner, wife and sternest critic, kept me at my computer when I most needed disciplining, gave me space to write and reflect, and fed me when I forgot to eat. Without her support and love I would still be talking about writing a book on the politics of the 1970s. I very much hope that *The New Radicals* will allow both her, and Michael and Anthony, to understand more about the period and events that formed me as an adult.

Glenn Moss
Cape Town
April 2014

Abbreviations

AAM	Anti-Apartheid Movement
ANC	African National Congress
Apdusa	African Peoples Democratic Union of Southern Africa
ARC	Alliance for Radical Change
ARM	African Resistance Movement
BC	Black Consciousness
Boss	Bureau of State Security
CIA	Central Intelligence Agency
CIS	Counter Information Services
Cnetu	Council of Non-European Trade Unions
Cosatu	Congress of South African Trade Unions
CPSA	Communist Party of South Africa
Fosatu	Federation of South African Trade Unions
GFWBF	General Factory Workers Benefit Fund
HRC	Human Rights Committee
IAS	Industrial Aid Society
ICFTU	International Confederation of Free Trade Unions
ICU	Industrial and Commercial Union
Idaf	International Defence and Aid Fund
IIE	Institute for Industrial Education
ILO	International Labour Organisation
IUEF	International University Exchange Fund
Mawu	Metal and Allied Workers Union
MK	Umkhonto we Sizwe
MP	Member of Parliament
MSD	Movement for Social Democracy

ABBREVIATIONS

NCL	National Committee of Liberation
NEUM	(Non-European) Unity Movement
Nudo	National Unity Democratic Organisation
Nusas	National Union of South African Students
Nuswel	National Union of Students Welfare
PAC	Pan Africanist Congress
Progs/PP	Progressive Party
SACP	South African Communist Party
Sactu	South African Congress of Trade Unions
SADF	South African Defence Force
SASM	South African Students Movement
Saso	South African Students' Organisation
SATIS	South Africa: The Imprisoned Society
SRC	Students' Representative Council
SSRC	Soweto Students' Representative Council
Swanu	South West Africa National Union
Swapo	South West Africa People's Organisation
Tuacc	Trade Union Advisory Co-ordinating Council
UBC	Urban Bantu Council
UCM	University Christian Movement
UCT	University of Cape Town
UDF	United Democratic Front
UN	United Nations
UP	United Party
WAP	Workers Advisory Project
Wits	University of the Witwatersrand
WPWAB	Western Province Workers Advice Bureau

1
Trading places

The imposing figure sitting at the fire had a laugh that came from deep within his chest. He had consumed as much cheap red wine as the rest of us, maybe more. Chortling, he moved over, put his arms around my waist and lifted me up. 'This one,' roared Steve Biko, 'this one understands.'

It was April 1970, and we were huddled around a fire at the Redacres Mission, near Howick in Natal. Blankets helped to protect us from the icy winter. A large flagon of Tassenberg, now nearly empty, rested on the ground. The group included the University of Natal political philosopher Rick Turner; Neville Curtis, president of the National Union of South African Students (Nusas); and his sister, Jeanette, the Transvaal regional director of Nusas. Biko was president of the South African Students' Organisation (Saso), which was increasingly challenging the multi-racial liberalism that Nusas had championed over many years.

I was 17 years old, having recently finished school in Pretoria and then registered as a student at the University of the Witwatersrand. The journey which had brought me from the administrative capital of apartheid to this fireside gathering had been short in time, but of tumultuous intensity.

My parents had wanted me to study law at the University of Pretoria. They were concerned that, if I went to Wits, I might become 'involved in politics'. After a number of heated discussions, it was finally agreed that I would go to Wits, and I left for Johannesburg in February 1970 under strict instruction not to 'join' Nusas.

Their concerns were well founded. I had shown some early signs of social and political radicalism while still at school. During 1968, I joined my history teacher, Clinton Harrop-Allin, in a two-person demonstration in support of a student sit-in at the University of Cape Town, called to protest against the university council's decision to rescind the appointment of Archie Mafeje as a lecturer on the grounds of his race.

The next year, I was part of a group which broke into the classroom of a notoriously right-wing teacher. We burned the South African flag he proudly displayed above his desk, leaving the ashes for his discovery the next morning. However, I had reason to question whether this sort of personal attack was legitimate when I found the teacher sitting at his desk, shedding tears as he wondered who could hate him so much. This was one of the few times I initiated action against a 'soft' civilian target.

These events took place at Pretoria Boys High, a well-known public school which had been home to a surprisingly wide range of political beliefs. The right-wing National Party and Herstigte Nasionale Party leader Albert Hertzog had studied there, as had Dennis Higgs, a member of a 1960s anti-apartheid sabotage group, who had fled to Zambia to avoid arrest and marry his black fiancée. Peter Hain had also been at Pretoria Boys. After moving to England, he went on to lead a number of boycott campaigns against South African touring sports teams. Although our time there overlapped, he was a few years ahead of me and I did not know him personally. However, I certainly became aware of his presence in fairly dramatic circumstances.

In 1966 John Harris placed a bomb at the Johannesburg station in a desperate act of anti-apartheid protest. In the ensuing blast, one person was killed and another seriously injured. Harris was convicted of murder, sentenced to death, and executed.

The Harris family was close to Peter Hain's parents, and Anne Harris stayed with them while her husband was on trial in Pretoria. The Hains were banned, and hence not permitted to speak at the memorial service for John Harris. Undeterred, the young Peter delivered a message on behalf of his family. The resulting photograph on the front page of the *Rand Daily Mail* newspaper, with Peter dressed in his Pretoria Boys High uniform at the memorial, created something of a stir. My parents and their circle of friends were unimpressed when I expressed support for Hain's courage and wondered out loud about the reasons for Harris resorting to such desperate action.

My rebellion at school probably had its origins in an intense dislike of mindless authority, although this developed organically into an interest in opposition politics.

I participated in Young Progressive Party activities, but by my final year of school was having doubts about the party's adherence to a qualified, rather than universal, franchise. Nonetheless, this was one of the few outlets for 'anti-government' activity for a middle-class white youngster in Pretoria.

During the 1960s, white school boys were subjected to a military programme of cadets. This entailed wearing a khaki uniform and cap once a week, marching up and down the sports fields, and being screamed at by older boys whose efforts to be 'officers' were undermined by their breaking voices. I soon resolved to avoid cadets as often as possible, and began arriving at sessions with notes purportedly written by my mother excusing me because of some or other health issue. By the time the school authorities realised that these notes were, in fact, written by a friend with a mature handwriting, they had also discovered that I was something of a sportsperson, setting school athletics records and playing soccer for an outside club. My cover as a perpetually ill pupil, unable to participate in cadets (or, for that matter, the hated physical training or PT sessions), was blown. However, I continued to sit on the side of the sports fields each week, watching others drilling or doing mindless exercises, without interference. Someone in authority must have decided that confronting me was more trouble than it was worth, and I slowly developed a protected status allowing me far more freedom than other pupils enjoyed.

This 'outsider' position was solidified through sport. Pretoria Boys High was one of South Africa's premier rugby schools, and participation through playing and attending matches was compulsory. Rugby symbolised all I disliked about Pretoria's culture. I saw it as boorish, the preserve of Afrikaans-speaking apartheid-supporting racists, with both spectators and players prone to violent behaviour. There was no way I was going to play the sport. I joined a private football club, and became a successful goalkeeper for both Arcadia Shepherds and various provincial and national teams.

Although the school did nothing to discipline me, my achievements as a footballer were never acknowledged. Week after week, I would sit in school assembly with another successful footballer – he went on to play professionally in England and America – listening to the sporting accomplishments of others being listed. It was not even mentioned when I was selected to play for a representative national side. There is little doubt that these experiences helped me to become relatively comfortable with being an outsider, something which was particularly helpful as I grew increasingly critical of the institutions and 'rewards' of white society.

Military service was compulsory for young white males. Most of my school friends reluctantly accepted that they would be 'called up' and spend nine months in service, probably in the army. I had decided that I was not prepared to do this. There was some political motivation involved in this decision, as my youthful rejection of apartheid included a critique of the police and military as pillars of racial discrimination. At the same time, I also knew that I would find the authoritarianism and culture of blind obedience in the Defence Force hard to cope with, and this formed another good reason to circumvent military service.

My parents had few reservations when my older brother was called up to the army. In my case, they agreed that my conscription should be avoided if at all possible. Finally, a sympathetic private medical specialist agreed to certify, on the basis of a childhood illness I had contracted, that I was unfit for military service. In those somewhat more relaxed times, medical examinations took place at school, and the civilian doctor who examined me accepted the specialist's certificate. A week later I receive a white card – which I still have – confirming that I had been exempted from military training, and 'need no longer advise of any changes of address'.

Towards the end of 1969, two friends and I hijacked the school newspaper, *The Boys Highlights*, to produce a pirate edition. We launched a scathing attack on the National Party and apartheid, and urged our co-matriculants to think seriously about supporting the Progressive Party in the upcoming 1970 general election. This escapade came close to ending my time at school, with the headmaster, Desmond Abernethy, indicating that he was only sparing the three of us from expulsion because we were about to write our final examinations.

* * *

My political awareness began deepening in the late 1960s, at a time when opposition to apartheid was in disarray, and white support for government policies and actions strong. The sabotage campaigns launched earlier in the decade had been contained and then destroyed by a rampant security establishment. The national liberation movements in exile were weak and struggling for survival. Within South Africa, organisation of the African working class into trade unions had faltered, and the limited challenges there were to the racist status quo came from within a generally ineffectual liberal fold.

At the end of the 1960s, as I was preparing to enter university, the political options for those opposed to apartheid seemed both restricted and bleak. Yet the seeds of an increasingly radical opposition were being planted and would soon produce new shoots.

Arriving at Wits as a 17-year-old from Pretoria, with my parents' injunction to avoid politics ringing in my ears, I was thrown into the milieu of a men's residence soaked in decades of 'tradition'. Dalrymple and College Houses embodied a culture of binge drinking, boorish behaviour, bullying and political conservatism. The 'initiation' of first-years was central to this system. It soon brought me into conflict with the university authorities, who seemed to condone these practices, and introduced me to the leadership of student politics.

By 1970, initiation was not as physically brutal as it once had been. However, first-year students were still subject to a programme familiar to those who had undergone compulsory military training before coming to university. Sleep deprivation, physical exercise and forced compliance with trivial rules were combined with rituals of excessive drinking. University and residence management believed this built up 'spirit'.

'Freshers' – first-year male students in residence – were compelled to wear ties and jackets at all times, together with large name cards strung around their necks. After a few days of enduring this, I decided to object. Perhaps I was less inclined to accept this sort of authoritarianism because I had not been subject to it in the military before coming to university. But the majority of first-years seemed ready to reject initiation, regardless of any previous military experience. After a few nights of my visiting first-years in their residence rooms and urging defiance of initiation, most of them arrived at breakfast one morning without ties, jackets and name cards. These actions were not without consequence, and I soon became the object of attack by other residence inmates.

I approached *Wits Student*, the campus newspaper, which agreed to expose initiation practices in a front-page story. The matter escalated further when College House diehards set fire to copies of the student newspaper, whose editor had questioned why initiation was condoned by university management.

The culmination of 'freshers' initiation' involved crawling through the sewers of Johannesburg to 'meet Phineas', the university mascot. I resolved not to participate in this ritual, which happened to fall on my birthday. That night, I joined my brother and his partner for dinner, avoiding the residence for as long as possible. When I finally returned to my room, I created a barrier between the door and my mattress, using an upturned bed. This was a wise move because, some time later that night, seniors from College House threw fireworks into the room, and drenched it using a fire hose.

Earlier that day, I had contacted the *Rand Daily Mail*, and told the news desk of the Phineas ceremony planned for that night. I think it was Tony Holiday, a political reporter, who was sent to cover the story, and the next morning the front page of the newspaper featured a photograph of students hooded in pillow slips crawling through the sewers of Johannesburg on their bellies.

The three most senior SRC members, the president, Ken Costa, and the vice-presidents, Rex Heinke and Clive Smith, lived in College House, and were critical of initiation practices. The vice-chair of Nusas on campus, David Selvan, was also in residence, and made contact with me in a much-appreciated effort to offer support. They mounted night-time 'guard duty' outside my door, escorted me to and from the communal bathrooms, and arranged for me to meet with the university's vice-chancellor, Professor G.R. Bozzoli. My first meeting with a senior university manager was disappointing. He indicated that he was loath to intervene in what he saw as an 'internal residence issue', and expressed support for 'some form of introducing students to residence life'.[1]

* * *

I was walking across the campus to Braamfontein on a Saturday morning in March 1970 when I came across the SRC president, Ken Costa, mounting a one-person poster demonstration on Jan Smuts Avenue. It was 21 March, ten years after the Sharpeville massacre, when police had opened fire on a crowd protesting against the pass laws, killing 69 and wounding many more.

Standing alone on Jan Smuts Avenue, Costa appealed to passing drivers and pedestrians to remember Sharpeville. I joined Costa for a while in this rather modest action. A few of those travelling towards the white suburbs hooted in support. Others wound down their car windows to shout abuse and shake fists in fury. '*Betoger!*' they screamed in condemnation of this minor show of dissent. In those years, this Afrikaans word for protester was a livid insult.

Passengers in the racially segregated buses that transported domestic and other workers from the suburbs to the city centre and back responded more enthusiastically. Some leaned out of the windows, and gave the thumbs-up symbol as a gesture of support. This was the first time I heard the call of *Mayibuye iAfrika* ('Come back, Africa'), a slogan associated with the campaigns of the Congress Alliance in the 1950s.

I could remember the sombre and anxious mood in suburban Pretoria at the time of the 1960 massacre, but otherwise knew little about the anti-pass campaign which gave rise to the Sharpeville shootings. On a weekend just after the state of emergency had been declared, my older brother was due to travel by train to a Boy Scout camp in Dundee, Natal. There had been some discussion as to whether it was safe for the group to attend the camp, given the politically inflammable context and the perception that black people were on the rampage. However, the camp went ahead, and I recall the Sunday afternoon car journey to drop my brother off at the Pretoria station, at the top of Paul Kruger Street in town. The streets were noticeably quiet. There were few people out and about, and I remember my parents commenting on this with trepidation. This was hardly surprising. There had been a massacre at Sharpeville, marches and the threat of 'riots' elsewhere, a state of emergency declared. Most black residents of Pretoria and its surrounding townships were staying well out of the way of fearful and aggressive white people and police and army patrols.

Ten years after Sharpeville, many had forgotten the massacre and its importance, and it would still be a number of years before 21 March became a popularly declared public 'holiday', with tens of thousands in the townships attending rallies and demonstrations, and trade unions organising work stayaways. In 1970, in Johannesburg, Sharpeville was being commemorated by one Wits student leader, demonstrating on the edge of university property.

* * *

Towards the end of April, Costa visited me in my residence room. It was the night before the general election for the all-white parliament, and Costa had been supporting the campaign of Helen Suzman, the Progressive Party's only member of parliament. Would I, he asked, be willing to join a group in protecting the Prog's constituency tent at the Houghton Primary School? There were rumours that students from the right-wing Rand Afrikaans University were going to launch an attack on the venue, and vandalise the tent and its contents.

Although I was not comfortable with the Progressive Party's policy of a limited or qualified franchise, I did have admiration for Suzman's lone parliamentary battles against the ruling National Party. In addition, the idea that proto-fascists from a neighbouring university should be able to disrupt an electoral process because they rejected one of the candidates was offensive – and I was also probably ready for a fight. Armed with a heavy walking stick, I joined the group sleeping over at the Houghton polling station. Sometime during the night, a mob did try to storm the tent. However, when they were confronted by a stick-wielding crowd of aggressive Wits students, they backed off and disappeared into the night, ending my brief contribution to Progressive Party electoral politics.

Within a few months of starting university, my parents' worst fears had been realised. I had started a rebellion in residence; argued with the vice-chancellor; and was now being befriended by SRC and Nusas leaders. I ceased going to Latin lectures, signalling that my chosen career path of law was open to question. The call of philosophy and politics was considerably stronger. I began attending talks, seminars and meetings that took place on campus. Evenings were often taken up with film club and other cultural events, where English lecturers like Barry Ronge, Robin Lee, Tim Couzens and John and Sue van Zyl were regular speakers.

Athol Fugard, Yvonne Bryceland, Fats Bookholane and Barney Simon were often to be found at Dorkay House, a run-down building on Eloff Street Extension to the south-east of the city centre. So were a range of jazz and blues musicians, poets and writers who included Nadine Gordimer and Lionel Abrahams. The 'mother of Dorkay House', Queeneth Ndaba, worried over destitute musicians like the African Jazz Pioneers saxophonist, Ntemi Piliso, and singers such as Abigail Khubeka, Thandi Klaasen and Dolly Rathebe. Some of them had nowhere to stay and would sneak back into the old factory at night, after the last rehearsals and jam sessions had ended. I began spending time at Dorkay House in the evenings, making new friends, sometimes watching rehearsals for one of Fugard's plays, listening to musicians jam or poets read.

* * *

Nusas had been founded in 1924, in an attempt to unify the white English- and Afrikaans-language campuses. By 1936, the four Afrikaans-language colleges had left Nusas and joined the rival Afrikaanse Nasionale Studentebond, a strongly Christian national organisation promoting racial segregation. At the end of the Second World War, Nusas finally admitted its first black university member – Fort Hare – although there had been nothing to prevent this being done earlier. The black section of the University of Natal followed Fort Hare into Nusas in 1947. With the decline of the Afrikaanse Studentebond, a new student body representing white Afrikaans-speaking students – the Afrikaner Studentebond, or ASB – was founded in 1948.

Following its electoral victory in 1948, the National Party government indicated that it intended restructuring tertiary education to comply with the policies of strict racial segregation. This involved establishing tightly controlled 'tribal colleges' based on 'ethnic' identity; downgrading Fort Hare to a tribal college; and prohibiting black students from studying at the historically 'open universities' without special ministerial permission. The Nusas campaigns to oppose these measures were organised under the banner of academic freedom, and represented the high point of liberal protest for both Nusas and the English-language universities, particularly Wits and UCT. However, by 1959 the government was ready to implement its apartheid policies in tertiary education, and by 1960 had taken over the administration of Fort Hare, and established four 'tribal colleges' for 'coloureds', 'Zulus', 'Sothos' and 'Indians'.

Relations between black, white English-speaking and white Afrikaans-speaking student organisations continued to dominate student government in the 1960s, with Nusas advocating multi-racial forms of organisation as a political principle, although this was not always adhered to in practice.

The state acted against a number of Nusas leaders during the 1960s. In 1966 the incumbent president, Ian Robertson, was banned. A year later, it was the turn of the past deputy vice-president Rogers Ragaven. John Sprack, president-elect, was stripped of his citizenship and deported in 1967, while John Daniel, who served as president in 1968, had his passport withdrawn. Past presidents Adrian Leftwich and Jonty Driver were detained under the Sabotage Act (the 90-day detention clause) in 1964, while Professor Raymond Hoffenberg, chair of the Nusas advisory panel, was banned in 1967. By the late 1960s, it was fairly common for Nusas leaders to be deprived of their passports.[2]

When Neville Curtis assumed office as Nusas president in 1970, the organisation comprised 14 affiliated Students' Representative Councils and 12 branches, representing 30,000 students.[3] Most of these were drawn from five mainly white English-language campuses: Wits, UCT, Rhodes and the two Natal campuses (Pietermaritzburg and Durban).

Nusas policy was based on a commitment to the United Nations Universal Declaration of Human Rights, and emphasised the importance of both 'free education in a free society' and 'the realisation of full human rights in South Africa'.[4] The majority of anti-apartheid students at the affiliated institutions were centrist-liberal, committed to political gradualism and moderation, and a charitable approach to welfare involving assistance to those 'in need'.

By 1970, students at many of the black campuses had withdrawn from Nusas to form the Black Consciousness-supporting Saso, which had been established in 1968 under Steve Biko's presidency. However, over the next few years some black students, including Saso leaders, continued to attend Nusas events.

Racial integration of residential, meeting and eating facilities at Nusas conferences and seminars remained a priority, even though most black students had withdrawn from Nusas. This had been a point of major conflict at the 1967 Nusas national congress. In this case, Nusas had failed in its efforts to ensure that congress facilities would be fully integrated, after management at Rhodes University retreated from its earlier agreement that all Nusas delegates could use its residences during the congress.

> Despite months of planning, the [Rhodes University] Acting Vice-Chancellor Professor J.V.L. Rennie bowed down at the last moment to government and Security Police pressure to announce that no black students would be allowed to stay in the university residences. Although the accommodation of black students was always an issue at Nusas congresses, this was the first time a 'liberal' university had taken such a stand … The black students demanded that the congress be adjourned but most of the white delegates decided that they would continue under protest. The black students felt this demonstrated a lack of commitment in the fight against apartheid and the compromise position of 'liberals', particularly white liberals.
>
> One of those black delegates was Steve Biko. He and his colleagues effectively resolved then that a separate black student body was needed and by the following year they had decided to establish the South African Students Organisation (Saso).[5]

Nusas could be legitimately criticised for continuing with a congress where delegates were expected to accept segregated facilities. This was a clear violation of the credo of multi-racialism which united liberal opposition across racial boundaries. However, it was becoming increasingly difficult to find facilities where white and black students could stay together, especially now that university management on Nusas-affiliated campuses had capitulated to state pressure.

Nusas began investigating the use of self-catering rural facilities, often on farms or linked to religious bodies, for its national gatherings. Some of these institutions were more flexible than the universities over the use of their premises for multi-racial gatherings.

* * *

Each April, Nusas held a national seminar as part of its ongoing education and leadership training programme. Senior office-bearers and younger delegates from different campuses met at these events, in which leading anti-apartheid figures often participated. After a fairly rigorous interview process, I was accepted as a Wits delegate for the 1970 seminar.

The Natal Province of the Oblates of Mary Immaculate had purchased the 56-acre Redacres dairy farm in the 1960s. This was the venue for the April 1970 seminar. The stables had been converted into dormitories, and the milking shed had become an ablution facility. The old farmhouse was now a place for meetings, and contained a large communal dining room and kitchen. The caretaker in charge of the premises was invariably accompanied on her rounds by a phalanx of dogs and cats, as well as a parrot called Martin, whose language was something of an embarrassment on a Catholic mission station.[6]

One of the Wits delegates attending the seminar was Renfrew Christie, subsequently sentenced to ten years under the Terrorism Act for providing information to the ANC on South Africa's nuclear programme. A legendary but reluctant commerce student, clearly unsuited for the study of accounting, Renfrew became more and more active in Nusas, and was elected deputy president in 1972. Apart from his status as a recalcitrant commerce student, he was famed for his voracious appetite, and the rumour was that he could identify a student house where dinner was being cooked from miles across Johannesburg. On the first night of the seminar Renfrew, true to reputation, broke into the kitchen, and ate the whole week's supply of biscuits.

Nusas had been running its April leadership seminars since 1963, and it was traditional for the president to open proceedings. Curtis was not in the mould of previous Nusas presidents. He had attended a government school, not one of the more elite private institutions which had produced so many student leaders. His hair was long, his glasses unfashionable, and his clothes often baggy. Although remarkably articulate when the mood took him, he sometimes mumbled and muttered his way through inordinately complex sentences.

The opening address to the seminar was a brutal assessment of Nusas's failures.[7] Late in 1969, Curtis had committed Nusas to a radical reassessment of its activities and goals, and indicated that one outcome might entail closure of the organisation. He would have approved of Amilcar Cabral's dictum 'Tell no lies, claim no easy victories'. 'We are confused and unprepared,' he told the delegates assembled in the old farmhouse at Redacres. 'Our morale is low, our image bad and our impact and effectiveness limited.' To change this, argued Curtis, 'we must reach agreement on basic goals, values and priorities ... we must work and plan effectively'. But in doing this, 'we must deal with more than just Nusas ... We must deal with things political and things philosophical. We must test, evaluate, criticise, formulate, accept and reject.' This was the only process through which students could establish conditions to 'realise their full potential, and provide a vehicle through which they can assert their responsibility to society'.

That responsibility, Curtis told the young delegates gathered, had three elements. It was an intellectual exercise in 'gaining knowledge and information and distributing it, formulating opinions and ideas, and distributing them'. There was a personal responsibility, 'formulating and evaluating a sense of morality, ... trying to see it achieved and living by it'. The third responsibility involved a commitment to implement the ideas derived from the first two responsibilities, and increasing their currency by working in projects and campaigning.

None of this would be easy. Apartheid society had shaped 'the people in it, and shaped them to accept and conform to values, behaviour and a situation which robs them of their basic humanity'. It would take 'conscious effort' to change this socialisation.

The liberalism that was the ideological hallmark of the universities affiliated to Nusas came under scrutiny too. Liberal values and systems could shape and condition people in the same way that apartheid society did, and there was a danger that the 'liberal ideal of "how to think" has become ... just another "what to think"'.

There were striking parallels between Curtis's views and Steve Biko's early formulation of Black Consciousness. Apartheid society had structured and socialised people into passive roles, which undermined their humanity and ability to act on an ethical basis. Breaking these shackles involved enormous individual and collective efforts to change individual consciousness and to reject the effects of socialisation through rational reflection and active participation in initiatives to change society. Almost as an aside, both student leaders had reached the conclusion that current forms of liberalism did not advance efforts to change consciousness or society.

Curtis was not the only political figure dominating this gathering. His sister and fellow Nusas executive member, Jeanette, short in stature but massive in commitment, was another. So was the political philosopher Rick Turner, as well as Mewa Ramgobin, just released from a banning order. It was Mewa who introduced us to the philosophy and practice of Satyagraha (passive resistance against an immoral order). Turner, who was to become so central in the development of non-Stalinist and new left Marxism in South Africa, set out the relationship between capitalism, exploitation and apartheid – the first time some of the delegates present had been exposed to this form of analysis.

However, it was the presence of the two student presidents, Biko and Curtis, that loomed largest. Saso still retained contact with Nusas, especially at leadership level. The two student organisations were in the process of defining their respective roles and relationships, and the rigid racial separatism that preoccupied some of the later Saso leaders was not yet in evidence.

It was a time of intense talking and political exploration, and one night Biko sat up with a group of the younger delegates, wrapped up in blankets against the cold of the Natal Midlands winter. This was my first experience of serious political discussion and debate involving articulate black leaders. One of the younger white delegates asked Biko about multi-racialism: how could Saso and Black Consciousness set themselves against the principles of multi-racialism in their opposition to apartheid? Surely BC was being just as racist as the apartheid government in this approach. For the first time, I heard criticism of the liberal obsession with multi-racialism, with Biko arguing that insistence on this form of organisation disempowered and undermined black identity and assertiveness. Confusingly for me at the time, Biko suggested that racially separate forms of organisation could facilitate the longer-term goal of a non-racial society. For many of those present, non-racialism and multi-racialism were synonymous and could be used interchangeably. There were, however, important differences between the two. Multi-racialism involved efforts to organise distinct 'racial groups' in the same bodies and through joint activities. Because apartheid sought to separate the races, multi-racialism was seen as a central principle in opposing segregation. Non-racialism, on the other hand, questioned the centrality of race in the construction of a common identity, opening the way for other collective identities such as class and gender. Confronting the difference between the two was one of BC's important contributions to anti-apartheid strategies.

The debate turned to liberalism. Why was Biko so critical of what he called 'white liberals'? Surely liberals were opposed to apartheid and the government, and were to be supported and admired. The discussion went back and forth, with Steve arguing that liberalism was compromised by its relationship to a total 'system' of oppression, that it was patronising of black people, and that the multi-racialism of South African liberalism inhibited the development of black self-sufficiency and leadership.

The ideas of Black Consciousness dominated the seminar, with Nusas being called on to respond to the critique of multi-racialism that Saso was developing. Sitting round the fire one evening, Biko threw out a challenge: how did the young white delegates from Nusas feel about being in a multi-racial environment, interacting with black people at the table, over wine and in discussions on a supposedly equal basis?

Naively, I responded with what I saw as 'the truth', admitting that I was not comfortable. I explained that I had grown up in white Pretoria, that I had been at Wits for only a few months, and that I had rarely had the opportunity of meeting black people as anything other than domestic workers and gardeners. (I did not know at the time that Biko's mother, Alice, worked as a domestic in the Eastern Cape.) I suggested that apartheid had been largely successful in making it difficult to interact comfortably and honestly with people of other colours.

This was the moment when Biko unleashed his enormous laugh and lifted me up into the air.

* * *

Neville Curtis was part of the group sitting round the fire that night. Like Biko, he was a large man, although he tended to shuffle rather than stride because of the early onset of arthritis, which affected him his whole adult life. The 'Curtis shuffle' was part of his charisma, reinforcing his powerful and brooding personality.

As the most senior office-bearer of Nusas, he faced what appeared to be an insurmountable contradiction. Whatever strength Nusas had lay in its multi-racialism, and its history of membership on both black and white campuses. Its international standing was largely based on a long-term commitment to multi-racialism and liberalism. However, the most articulate and influential leaders on the black campuses were arguing for racial separation, both in organisational terms and in ideology. This would weaken Nusas numerically, and remove its right to be viewed as the legitimate representative of students who rejected apartheid.

Curtis was noticeably quiet at the seminar. He listened much of the time, occasionally asking probing questions as he got to know the younger delegates better. He was often seen in private discussion with Biko. Later that night, he told me that he admired my honesty for what I had said about black–white relations, and that I had no reason to feel embarrassed at my admission. Nusas, he explained, had collaborated in a façade for some time, in which many of its leaders acted as if relations between black and white within the union were equal and harmonious because of a shared belief in multi-racialism. He and Biko, as presidents of the two student bodies, were committed to confronting this, both ideologically and organisationally.

I left the seminar awestruck at having met intellectuals like Turner, and inspired by the commitment of Biko and Neville and Jeanette Curtis. Soon after, I was co-opted onto the Wits local committee of Nusas as treasurer, and began attending its weekly executive committee meetings.

The seminar in Natal marked a critical moment in my political development. I began to reconsider my adherence to liberal multi-racialism, developed at some price in the conservatism of white Pretoria, as the only credible opposition to apartheid. Within a few months, I had become part of a younger group of white defenders of the Black Consciousness initiative, arguing heatedly with horrified liberals, who held multi-racial organisation as an unchallengeable mantra of anti-apartheid opposition.

* * *

While still at school, I had been deeply affected by what became known as 'the trial of the 22'. During May 1969, security police detained a group of supporters of the banned African National Congress (ANC). They used the provisions of section 6 of the Terrorism Act to do this, in terms of which any police officer of the rank of lieutenant-colonel or above could detain a person for interrogation. The period of detention was unlimited, and no detainee could be released until the Commissioner of Police decided that they had answered all questions satisfactorily, or that there was no further point in continuing to detain them. Detainees were held in solitary confinement, without access to reading material, family, friends or legal representation. Courts were excluded from ruling on the validity of any detention or the conditions under which a detainee was held.

The Terrorism Act had been passed by the all-white parliament in 1967, with only Helen Suzman of the Progressive Party opposing it in its entirety. The official opposition – the ineffective and compromised United Party – voted for the Act.

Once the security police had these powers, torture and abuse of political detainees became commonplace. The security police's chief interrogator, Theuns 'Rooi Rus' Swanepoel, had developed a reputation for particularly sadistic forms of torture of political detainees in the early 1960s. It was under interrogation by men like Swanepoel and 'Spyker' van Wyk that Suliman 'Babla' Saloojee, James Lenkoe, Ahmed Timol, Imam Haron, Steve Biko, Neil Aggett and more than a hundred others died horrific and lonely deaths.

The systematic use of torture to extract information from detainees corroded the humanity and integrity of law-makers, police, prosecutors, district surgeons, magistrates and judges. It compromised those private medical practitioners, lawyers and journalists who collaborated with the system. Opposition to detention without trial was an important part of my politicisation and the political awakening of many of my generation.

The 1969 detentions targeted a group which the state believed was trying to revive ANC structures in the Transvaal. Prominent among those detained were Winnie Mandela, at that time the wife of Nelson Mandela; the *Rand Daily Mail* photographer Peter Magubane; and Shanti Naidoo, who came from a well-known Congress Alliance family and whose brother, Indres, was serving a ten-year sentence on Robben Island for sabotage. Those detained also included Samson Ndou, 'Snuki' Zikalala, Elliot Shabangu, Joyce Sikhakhane and Rita and Lawrence Ndzanga. Towards the end of 1969, while I was studying for my matriculation examinations, 22 of the detainees were charged under the Suppression of Communism Act. Others continued to be held as potential state witnesses.

Their trial was held in the Old Synagogue, north of Pretoria's Church Square, which had been expropriated by the government for use as a court in 1952. Soon the focus of proceedings moved from the activities of the accused to security police interrogation techniques. The *Rand Daily Mail* newspaper, delivered to the front door of my parents' Sunnyside flat every morning, as well as our local *Pretoria News*, covered these events in some detail. As my final matriculation exams ended, I became more and more influenced by the drama unfolding in court.

Witnesses in political trials were often brought to court by their security police jailers directly from their cells, sometimes after months of solitary confinement and interrogation. This created intense pressure on them to testify according to the requirements of interrogators and prosecutors. Refusal to testify usually resulted in further imprisonment; and testimony which deviated from what was required could result in the witness being detained again and tortured, pressured or punished in other ways. Despite this blatant coercion, most judges and magistrates accepted the truth of evidence given under these circumstances.

Shanti Naidoo had been detained in June 1969. When she was brought from her cell to testify, she had been in solitary confinement for six months. However, she told the court that she could not testify against her close friends Winnie Mandela and Joyce Sikhakhane. She held steadfastly to this decision, even after the presiding judge advised her that he would be compelled to sentence her to a further term of imprisonment if she refused to give evidence.

Advocate Jack Unterhalter, who represented Shanti, asked her to explain what had happened in detention: 'I slept on the floor in the cell,' she told the court. Prison regulations prescribed that she should be allowed a minimum of 30 minutes a day of exercise outside her cell. However, on many occasions she was not even allowed this brief respite from solitary detention in a confined space. During security police interrogation, she was made to stand 'for hours and hours. I lost track of time and there were periods when my mind went blank ... The interrogation went on for five days during which I was not allowed to sleep.'[8] Ms Naidoo was sentenced to two months' imprisonment for refusing to testify. Other witnesses who had been in detention gave similar accounts.

On 16 February 1970, the Attorney-General of the Transvaal arrived in court, and advised that he was stopping the trial by withdrawing charges against the accused. The publicity around the proceedings was beginning to embarrass the government as the trial of the 22 evolved into an examination of security police methods of interrogation.

When charges are withdrawn after an accused has pleaded not

guilty, acquittal is automatic, and so the presiding judge declared the 22 not guilty and free to leave court. Freedom, however, was short-lived, as security police moved into the dock and redetained them, again in terms of the Terrorism Act. They were returned to solitary confinement, in the hands of those who had been exposed as their torturers during their trial.

* * *

Neville Curtis was a graduate from Wits University, where he had served as vice-president of the Students' Representative Council before taking office as Nusas president at the end of 1969. He soon joined the many voices raised in protest against the treatment of political detainees, and called on students to protest against the continued detention of the 22.

Legal action was launched in an effort to protect those back in detention. Relatives of detainees, including the sister of Winnie Mandela, applied to the courts for an urgent interdict restraining security police from assaulting or unlawfully interrogating their prisoners. While on trial, some of the detainees had made statements to their attorney describing what had happened to them in detention, and these were now presented in support of the application. Detainees described how they had been made to stand on bricks for extended periods of time, deprived of sleep, and assaulted if they fell off or stepped down from the bricks.[9]

Despite these details, the presiding judge refused to grant the detainees the protection sought. The statements submitted, he ruled, dealt with allegations of torture dating back some months. There was therefore no urgency to the matter. Just because someone claimed to have been tortured in the past, reasoned the judge, this did not mean that protection from being tortured at a later stage was a matter of urgency.

Following Curtis's call for intensified action on detentions, students began campaigning for the release of the 22. The campaign garnered some international support, with a United Nations committee protesting against the continued incarceration of the detainees.

Joel Carlson, defence attorney for the 22, undertook a tour of the Nusas-affiliated campuses to highlight the situation of his clients, as well as the ramifications of section 6 of the Terrorism Act. Over a thousand students packed into the Wits Great Hall to hear Carlson explain why solitary confinement was a form of torture, and how the Terrorism Act had created a context for the systematic abuse of political detainees.

Carlson had recently represented the family of James Lenkoe, who had died in detention. Evidence at the inquest showed that security police interrogators had tortured Lenkoe by means of electric shocks before his death. 'Rooi Rus' Swanepoel, implicated in torture during the trial of the 22, had been Lenkoe's main interrogator.

Demonstrating how security legislation had corrupted judicial processes, Carlson described the conduct of the presiding magistrate during the inquest. David Soggot, an advocate representing Lenkoe's wife, had attempted to introduce evidence from ex-detainees confirming they had been tortured with electric shocks. Without hearing the application, the presiding magistrate tried to close the inquest.

> Soggot: I want to make an application for the witnesses to be called.
> Magistrate: That is being refused.
> Soggot: Well, your worship hasn't heard me.
> Magistrate: I don't want you to address this court.
> Soggot: I want to make an application, which is my right.
> Magistrate: Yes, and that is refused.
> Soggot: Before your worship will hear what my application is? I can't understand how your worship can refuse an application before understanding its contents.

Shortly after this, the magistrate returned to court to find that 'No blame was attached to any person' for Lenkoe's death.

A separate inquest was under way into the death in detention of Imam Abdullah Haron in Cape Town. A highly respected religious and community leader, he had been detained on 29 May 1969. Four months later, he was dead. His interrogators had included Sergeant 'Spyker' van Wyk and his brother Andries. Through the cases of Lenkoe, Haron and the 22, security police treatment of detainees was receiving more attention than before.

The mood on the Wits campus was becoming angrier, as students became more conscious about the consequences of the Terrorism Act. They had learned, over the first few months of the year, that a large number of people had been detained, incommunicado, indefinitely, in solitary confinement, with access to no one but their interrogators and jailers. Joel Carlson argued that solitary was, in itself, a form of torture, and that security police were also employing physical torture as part of their interrogatory methods. The fate of the 22, who had been released and then redetained, aroused particularly strong feelings.

Activity intensified on campus. There were talks, seminars, posters and pamphlets, initially under the guidance and leadership of the SRC and the local Nusas branch. Internationally, it was a time of anti-institutional radicalism on many campuses. American student politics, especially anti-Vietnam war protests, had their resonances at universities like Wits. Criticism of the genteel liberalism that had dominated anti-apartheid activity at the university was growing, and radicals began arguing that structures of student and university governance served to moderate, co-opt and weaken spontaneous and direct action. Lectures evolved into teach-ins and sit-ins, as radical challenges to liberal processes gathered momentum.

Demands for more direct forms of action became increasingly strident, and radicals outside the institutions of student government began assuming leadership roles. Critical of the liberal forms of protest that had dominated the white English-language universities, they were often well read in contemporary politics and philosophy, and posed a direct challenge to the SRC's centrist-liberal leadership. Agitation grew for 'action' rather than 'words' over the situation of the 22.

Under this pressure, the SRC president, Ken Costa, usually identified by his blue university blazer and tie, applied for permission to stage a protest march from the university to security police headquarters at John Vorster Square. The aim of the demonstration was to call for the 'charge or release' of security detainees, including the 22. This was, in itself, controversial. Some students argued that campaigning for the charging of detainees under laws like the Terrorism Act, which clearly failed any human rights standard, was unacceptable. The demand, they argued, should be for the unconditional release of all detainees and the abolition of all laws allowing for detention.

Permission to undertake a public demonstration had to be sought from two different authorities: the local City Council and the city's chief magistrate. The first application was approved by the City Council, at that time run by the opposition United Party. The night before the planned march, students gathered on campus to prepare for the next day's events. In an open area at the top of the Students' Union building, we worked late into the night, painting slogans on large calico banners and cardboard sheets. Flagons of red wine were passed around, cigarettes shared, the sweet smell of marijuana was in the air. Radical politics and protest, youth and the counter-culture combined to create an atmosphere of solidarity, excitement and anticipation.

* * *

Early the next morning, the chief magistrate of Johannesburg, Oliver John Gush, issued a notice prohibiting the gathering. Groups of students congregated throughout the morning, discussing how to respond to the banning. Some argued that defiance was an appropriate response, and that the march to John Vorster Square should take place regardless of the prohibition. Consequences could be grave, including the violence of police baton charges, arrest, and criminal trials under one or more of the many laws governing public demonstrations. There was particular concern over a section of the Criminal Law Amendment Act of 1953, passed to increase punishment for civil disobedience in the Congress-led Defiance Campaign of 1952. This made it a specific offence to break a law while campaigning for the repeal or modification of any other law. It allowed for severe penalties: up to three years' imprisonment, and flogging. If charged under this law, there was a presumption of guilt, with an accused having to establish innocence. This law also prohibited newspapers from reporting on any incident where people were incited to break a law, and there was concern that this might stop newspapers from covering protests against the Terrorism Act if they involved illegal actions.

Just 18, recently out of a conservative schooling system, I had a 'commonsense' view that 'obeying the law' was generally a self-evident good. Now I had to confront the strategic, ethical and personal implications involved in deliberately breaking the law.

By lunch-time the Great Hall was overflowing, with students sitting in the aisles, on the stage, in the corridors along the sides of the hall, and spilling out of the back doors into the foyer area of the Central Block. Not all of those present supported protest action. The Wits student body was divided, with conservatives tending to support authority and the status quo. But the majority of the thousand-plus students attending the meeting seemed to endorse protest action.

The SRC president set out the history of the issue. He explained the processes involved in applying for permission to stage a protest march, and updated students on the decision of the chief magistrate of Johannesburg to ban the march. Costa was critical of that decision, and indicated support for the 'rule of law' and opposition to 'arbitrary decision-making' – very much the hallmarks of principled liberal opposition to an authoritarian state. He counselled students against defying this ban, setting out the potential consequences.

Calls to 'march' came from some sections of the crowd. Speakers from the floor argued that it was time to stand up to the forces of apartheid rule, to 'act rather than talk'. Some of the conservative students present heckled these speakers, trying to shout them down. Finally Ian Margo, one of the informal leaders of the 'radicals', took the microphone. He could not, he explained, incite students to break the law. That was a form of authoritarian leadership with which he did not agree. Personal decision-making, commitment and responsibility needed to govern political action. He had made his own decision and was going to walk downtown to John Vorster Square. Anyone who wanted to join him was welcome to do so.

Margo's approach was not only an effort to circumvent laws on incitement. It reflected the radicals' critique of conventional leadership and structures, and the preoccupation with individual-centred questions about freedom and responsibility.

The chants of 'March, march, march' became stronger as about half of the students present began moving out of the hall towards the piazza in front of the Central Block. I was uncertain what to do. Fearful of the consequences, yet believing that it was right to join the protest, I linked up with a small group of first-year students uncertainly hovering on the edges of the crowd. They included Barbara Hogan, Elaine Unterhalter, Pat Horn and Susan Brown, also first-year students who were becoming close friends and political colleagues.

As a crowd of around five hundred set off down Jan Smuts Avenue, towards the city centre, I joined it. Those in front held placards and a banner reading '22 Detained. Charge or Release'. Those of us further back held hands or joined arms as we marched along.

Office workers along the route rushed to the windows of high buildings, astonished by the sight. Pedestrians stopped to gaze at the phalanx of students and a few university staff, including the philosophy lecturer Ian Thompson. That morning, he had delivered a challenging first-year lecture on Socrates and moral responsibility, which I had attended. Quite a few of his students joined the march. Some bystanders indicated support, others deep hostility. Most seemed bemused by this public display of dissent.

As we reached the middle of town, police on foot and in vans began appearing. Dressed in the characteristic blue uniforms of the time, peaked caps prominent, most carried batons. Marchers linked arms and moved on. I held the hands of the marchers to my right and left as we moved forward. We turned into Commissioner Street, location of security police headquarters at John Vorster Square. As we neared the police station, a senior police official appeared in front of the procession, and began addressing marchers through a crackling megaphone. He instructed us to disperse within a specified time period, and threatened arrest if we did not. On we marched, getting ever closer to Vorster Square. Marchers began singing 'We shall overcome'.

Just outside Vorster Square, police made their move, charging at the marchers, swinging their batons and dragging off the first rows of students. However, the next rows of marchers did not disperse, as police hoped, but sat down in the middle of Commissioner Street. Police began dragging students off. No one resisted, and nobody tried to flee.

Police arrested the protesters as they sat in their neat rows on the warm tar of Commissioner Street, dragging them into Vorster Square. Male and female protesters were separated, finger-printed and photographed. Police became particularly agitated when some of those arrested smeared ink from the finger-printing exercise across the walls and basins of Vorster Square's bathrooms. Then we were moved into large communal holding cells and a courtyard enclosed with wire netting – my first experience of police cells.

Spirits were high. There was singing, shouting, joking, calling across to those held in the cells for women. Some of us were also afraid. Would we be held overnight, perhaps refused bail? Might security police start separating out perceived leaders for special attention?

Ian Thompson, the philosophy lecturer who had joined the march, still had his notes from his lecture on Socrates delivered earlier that day. Worried that, if security police found these, he would be seen as an instigator of the illegal march, he began chewing and swallowing them. He proudly announced the moment when he finished his 'meal'.

Later that evening, the cell doors opened to admit the lawyers Raymond Tucker and Jack Unterhalter, who had appeared for Shanti Naidoo when she was brought from her detention cell to testify in the December 1969 trial of the 22. They had negotiated our release with police, and we would be allowed out in small groups, without having to appear in court or post bail.[10]

When I arrived back at Men's Residence, and entered the dining hall fairly late for supper, I was met with a mixed response. Some of the students started booing and hurling verbal abuse. However, a few – including a number of the first-years who had joined me in opposing initiation practices – called out encouragement. One or two made a point of joining me at the long table where I had sat down to eat.

* * *

The next morning, sitting down to breakfast, I was horrified to see my parents walking through the residence's front entrance and stopping at the porter's lodge. Soon a message boomed over the public address system: 'Would Glenn Moss please come to the porter's lodge, Glenn Moss to the porter's lodge.' I had not told them of my arrest, but they read about it in that morning's *Rand Daily Mail.* Long before the days of cellphones or e-mail, without any easy way of contacting me, they did what many concerned parents would do: took the day off work and drove to Johannesburg.

A heated exchange followed, with my parents demanding that I cease engagement in politics, and me responding that this would not happen. I lacked the maturity or empathy to understand that these were simply frightened parents expressing concerns for my safety and couching these in the anger that relief sometimes engenders. A few years later, in rather more serious circumstances involving long-term detention and an onerous trial, my parents were to be strongly supportive of my political involvements, even though it cost them most of their friendships in the conservative social milieu of white Pretoria.

* * *

Shanti Naidoo's case continued to disturb me greatly. After serving a two-month sentence for refusing to give evidence, she was again detained under section 6. She was still in solitary, without access to anyone apart from jailers, interrogators and state officials. Her mother brought a habeas corpus application, only to be told that the Terrorism Act excluded the courts from any jurisdiction over detainees. Finally, after 369 days in solitary confinement, she was released from custody on 18 June 1970, and returned to the banning order which had curtailed her life before detention. On the same day, 19 of the original 22 who had been charged in 1969 again appeared in court, this time indicted under the Terrorism Act.

One of the group charged in 1969 had suffered a severe mental breakdown after his redetention in February 1970. He had been transferred from prison to a psychiatric facility outside Pretoria. Neither his family nor lawyers had been informed of this. This exemplified the horror of long-term solitary confinement and its effects. A person had been taken into custody in 1969, held in solitary confinement, charged, acquitted, detained at the moment of acquittal, again interrogated and held in solitary – and then released from a psychiatric facility. Nobody, apart from his jailers and state doctors, knew that he had been admitted to mental care, nor what had led to this.

When the accused appeared in court, Benjamin Ramotse, who had not been in the first trial, was charged as the first accused. Few apart from security police had known he was in detention. It transpired that Ramotse had been in custody since 16 July 1968, when he was handed over to South African police by their Rhodesian counterparts. Ramotse had been one of the first Umkhonto we Sizwe (MK) saboteurs. He subsequently formed part of the ANC's Luthuli Detachment involved in the Wankie Campaign, when the ANC attempted to infiltrate guerrillas through Rhodesia and into South Africa. Captured by Botswana forces, Ramotse was handed over to the Rhodesians, who passed him on to 'Rooi Rus' Swanepoel.

At the opening of this new trial, Advocate Sydney Kentridge applied for all of the accused, apart from Ramotse, to be discharged because they had already been acquitted of the charges brought in their first trial. In the case of Ramotse, Kentridge argued that he had been unlawfully detained by Botswana authorities, handed over unlawfully to Rhodesian security, who then compounded these breaches of international law by transferring Ramotse to the custody of the South African security police. A South African court, argued Kentridge, did not have jurisdiction to try Ramotse, given that he now appeared in court as a result of these violations of international law.

Accepting Kentridge's argument in respect of the accused who had previously been acquitted, the judge discharged them from further prosecution, and they were released. Soon after, all 19 were served with banning orders severely limiting their abilities to work and prohibiting them from engaging in political activity. They were also not permitted to write anything for publication, attend any gathering, or communicate with other banned people.

The presiding judge ruled that Ramotse had been legally arrested and therefore brought before the South African courts lawfully. After a short trial, he was found guilty and sentenced to 15 years' imprisonment.

* * *

Students at Wits protested against the banning of those acquitted, with a legal and orderly march through the centre of Johannesburg in which university management participated. A meeting before the protest, held on 8 October 1970, was addressed by the university's acting vice-chancellor, Stanley Jackson, and the Progressive Party MP, Helen Suzman. The radicalism of the first wave of student protest in May had receded, and liberal support for the 'rule of law' dominated both the form and content of this protest. Many participants wore academic gowns, while placards seemed to suggest that judges were the victims of repressive laws. 'Insulting to our judges' and 'Humiliation for our courts' read some. 'Free the judges' was the message of a large banner prominent in the march.

University management was clearly relieved by this retreat from the 'dangerous radicalism' of those who had marched in defiance of the law just a few months previously. The second march 'demonstrated once again that it was possible for students to protest in a dignified and orderly manner', crowed an official organ of the university, *Convocation Commentary*. 'Critics had often argued that student protests are the work of an unrepresentative, extremist fringe,' continued the report. 'That charge cannot be levelled at this demonstration.'[11]

Wits students and their leadership had retreated into the relative safety of symbolic protest action.

2
Radical challenges to liberal politics

During the 1960s a liberal worldview had dominated Nusas's largely reactive politics. Individual voices were on occasion raised in criticism of this. At a 1965 conference in Dar es Salaam, Martin Legassick, a South African student leader, suggested that Nusas should position itself as the student wing of the liberation movement. John Daniel, in his presidential address to Nusas in 1968, noted that the student organisation usually 'reacted to ... bannings and deportations with protests and then ... settled back and waited for the next time we will have to protest.' Nusas, he argued, must become 'more aggressive, positive and militant on the campuses'.[1]

The election of Duncan Innes as Nusas president for 1969 was something of a victory for the more radical elements in the student organisation. Although black student leaders were becoming increasingly critical of the union for what they perceived as its patronising and multi-racial liberalism, Steve Biko had proposed Innes as president, and they worked together to keep open lines of communication between Black Consciousness supporters and Nusas.[2]

This uneasy tension between liberalism and radicalism in the anti-apartheid student movement continued into the early 1970s, with radicals and liberals locked in an ongoing contest for influence and ascendancy on the Nusas campuses. Fluctuations in support for these different political approaches were particularly pronounced at Wits University during this time, as student politics lurched from the symbolic and reactive protest criticised by John Daniel to a more radical and proactive confrontation with the issues of society.

Student defiance of the law, such as the actions of the May

1970 demonstration demanding the release of political detainees, represented a new stage in anti-apartheid radicalism on the largely white campuses. But the pendulum soon swung back towards the sporadic protest politics criticised by radical opponents of Nusas's liberal policies and strategies.

* * *

A more radical politics on the university campuses continued to develop within this contested environment. Youthful activists began to find their own paths and strategies independently of what had gone before, and their rejection of multi-racialism as a principle and liberalism as a goal initially left them politically adrift in uncharted waters.

This had both its dangers and advantages. On the one hand, there was little guidance from a credible older political generation, thus limiting the younger generation's capacity to build on any collective institutional knowledge passed down through the prism of experience. The successes and failures of earlier political strategies and programmes, the decisions to launch various forms of armed and violent struggle and their consequences, disputes between Africanists and non-racialists, nationalists and communists – none of this history was available to the new generation of 1970s political activists.

On the other hand, the absence of established political leadership opened up space for the development of new and uniquely 'internal' initiatives and approaches, largely independent of the organisations that had dominated the politics of the 1950s and the first half of the 1960s.

Black Consciousness mounted one of the central challenges to the liberalism of the Nusas-linked campuses in particular, and to the small community of political liberals in general. Paula Ensor, a radical activist from the University of Natal and a member of the Nusas executive until her banning in 1973, has described how BC confronted both the form and content of the liberalism espoused by Nusas in the 1960s:

> For many white male student leaders, involvement in SRC and Nusas politics was a stepping stone to an Abe Bailey Scholarship, or a Rhodes Scholarship to Oxford. That these scholarships were not open to women or blacks caused no greater concern than the fact that Nusas conferences were held on white campuses which obliged blacks to find accommodation elsewhere. Nusas in the late 1960s was largely a debating forum ... Liberal ideals were energetically defended, but hunger, oppression and transformation were not placed seriously on the agenda.
>
> Biko, and the leadership that formed around him in Saso, identified the moral vacuum within Nusas and challenged the white student body to question itself.[3]

Liberalism was also subject to critique from the evolving forms of Western, or new left, Marxism. This questioned the relations between apartheid, the state and capitalism, and sought to place the interests of the working class high on the agenda of anti-apartheid struggle. Support for meritocracy and individual rights as the basis for a political programme was increasingly called into question. In their place, the relations between class and race, the 'national' question and socialism, and the position of intellectuals in working-class and multi-class popular organisation began to inform political debate and planning.

* * *

Three figures presided over the changing political landscape on the campuses and the challenges to liberal thought and activity which this involved. They embodied different, but in some ways complementary, approaches and represented the intellectual and organisational leadership of this new politics.

Steve Biko was Saso's first president and the most prominent of the pioneers of Black Consciousness in the late 1960s. In challenging the multi-racialism that dominated internal opposition to apartheid, BC broke the political logjam, smashed a dead-end liberal consensus, and opened the way to new forms of thinking, organisation and action.

Neville Curtis served as Nusas president in 1970 and 1971. His fundamental radicalism guided students on both black and white campuses in their confrontations with apartheid and racism. He led white students in finding progressive responses to the challenge of BC, playing a massive role in constructing a politics of transformation. Curtis gave content to these responses through his tactical flexibility and strategic insight, linking these to solid principles of planning and organisation, which had often been absent in the student movement.

Rick Turner taught political philosophy at the University of Natal from 1970. He guided a generation of student activists to become critical and strategic thinkers, helping them to understand that there were systems of participatory democracy which provided real alternatives to formal and representative democracy. Turner emphasised the centrality of utopian thinking, by means of which the ability to imagine a world based on different social relations became a precondition for transformative politics. He insisted that individuals could make ethical choices, even in authoritarian environments. This inspired a generation to seek new identities, values and ways of acting, based on the rejection of both apartheid and capitalist socio-economic relations.

Turner was a central influence in the development of a body of socialist thought that rejected Soviet Marxism, drew on the varied traditions of Western Marxism and existentialism, and blended these into an analysis that addressed the specifics of South African conditions. This had a strong impact on students and other intellectuals who formed the Wages Commissions in 1971, and who took the first steps to establish the new trade union organisations of the early 1970s.[4]

All three of these figures were banned in February 1973. Turner and Biko were killed by state agents within a short space of time, the one in an assassination, the other assaulted so brutally under security police interrogation that he died from his injuries. Curtis escaped from South Africa in 1974, using the passport of an American acquaintance to board a ship in Cape Town harbour. This enabled him to live longer than Biko and Turner, but he died in 2007 in what had become self-imposed exile, never fully acknowledged for the central role he had played in the formation of a new South African politics.

* * *

Criticism of symbolic protest politics intensified on both the Nusas and Saso campuses in the early 1970s. Black Consciousness intellectuals were particularly scathing of what they called 'white liberalism', linking this to privilege, hypocrisy and paternalism. At the same time, the new radicals on the Nusas campuses launched a sustained attack on the edifice of liberal ideology and organisation that dominated opposition politics.

There was, of course, no single liberal orthodoxy. However, the many forms of liberalism associated with opposition to the policies of the National Party government had common elements. There was an assumption that 'Afrikaners' were responsible for apartheid, and that the 'civilising' tendencies of English-speakers might slowly erode the worst aspects of socio-political policy. Liberalism assumed that gradual assimilation of people of colour into English-language culture would have a positive impact on society as a whole, eroding the worst manifestations of racial inequality and prejudice.

Anti-apartheid liberal orthodoxy was based on a value system that included adherence to the rule of law, a belief that charity given to the less fortunate was politically progressive, and that politically motivated violence should always be condemned and rejected. Additionally, there was an insistence on multi-racialism as an act of faith, even when this was based on token incorporation of small numbers of black people into organisations and events. Multi-racial activity was viewed as a political act of opposition in and of itself. Not even the vast disparities in wealth, access to resources, skills, experience and confidence, coupled to geographical separation and differences in language use, were sufficient to challenge this liberal principle.

Liberals had failed to distinguish between multi-racialism and non-racialism. Multi-racialism involved a non-negotiable principle about what constituted desirable forms of organisation and racial representation, and identified challenges to racial segregation as the bedrock of opposition politics. Non-racialism challenged the primacy of race as the basis of identity, economic interests and social explanation. It opened the door to other ways of analysing society, which used the prisms of class, gender, structural inequality, access to resources and economic location to understand the fault lines in South Africa. A non-racial interpretation generated strategies to challenge relations in all those areas, rather than just in the domains of racial inequality and prejudice. Non-racialism also had a view of the future in which race would cease to be a central element in self-definition and identity. Multi-racialism, on the other hand, aimed for a society where people from different racially defined groups would relate on a more equal basis.

Part of the BC challenge to liberalism was founded on a long-term vision of non-racialism and the rejection of multi-racialism and racial categorisation. 'We see a completely non-racial society,' wrote Biko. 'We don't believe in ... guarantees for minority rights, because [that] ... implies the recognition of portions of the community on a race basis.'[5]

The challenge to liberal orthodoxy went beyond the questioning of multi-racialism as an immutable principle. Liberal ideology embraced free enterprise, unfettered market forces and economic growth, and asserted that these features of capitalism would inevitably erode apartheid and racially based inequality. Armed with the conceptual framework of Marxism, the new left questioned this, identifying the broadly functional relationship between existing capitalism and the apartheid state, especially in respect of labour recruitment, control and allocation.

Most students attending the almost exclusively white English-speaking universities at the beginning of the 1970s would have understood apartheid 'as the consequence of racial ideology imposed on the society by Afrikaner nationalism. The new radicalism insisted that all of white society – in particular English-speaking business – derived benefit from racial domination and so had a stake in its survival.'[6]

Liberals argued that there was an inherent contradiction between capitalist development and apartheid. Radicals understood the relationship as largely symbiotic. The unfettering of free-market capitalist relations might involve superficial changes to the policy and administration of apartheid but would not challenge the core elements of that system. These included migrant labour, low wages, a rural–urban divide based on the maintenance of a reserve army of labour at lowest possible cost, and the use of rural subsistence production to maintain artificially low wages. The contemporary extension of the 'native reserves' into a system of bantustans, with the grinding poverty, destruction of family life and forced population removals associated with 'homeland consolidation', drove the real wages of migrant workers even lower. Employers could pay workers as if they had no dependants, for these were consigned to the bantustans to fend for themselves.

If apartheid and capitalism fed off and strengthened each other,

> this implied that structural change would need to tackle not only society's racial hierarchy, but its social and economic pecking order. This was attractive to radical white students whose interest in moving beyond liberalism was fuelled by the rise of the Black Consciousness movement led by Steve Biko, which challenged them to see the collective action of the black majority, not the polite entreaties of white liberals, as the only viable threat to apartheid ... And so it helped to provide a context in which white radicals could make sense of their belief that the suburban homes in which they were raised were as much a part of the problem as the Afrikaner nationalism which was blamed for it.[7]

* * *

The understandably cautious liberal agenda of opposition politics in the late 1960s and early 1970s was a consequence of the destruction of radical politics almost a decade earlier. The banning of the ANC and PAC in 1960 had been followed by massive state repression, which smashed the embryonic underground structures of organisation and resistance. Working-class leadership, especially through the unions affiliated to the South African Congress of Trade Unions (Sactu), had been similarly crushed through bannings, detentions and imprisonment. Surviving trade union leaders were often incorporated into clandestine political and sabotage activities, weakening worker organisation further. This ushered in a period of political quiescence, underpinned by a combination of economic growth, draconian security actions, high levels of social control, and fear of savage bureaucratic authority.

The conclusion of the Rivonia trial, in which senior ANC, Communist Party (SACP) and Umkhonto we Sizwe (MK) leaders were jailed for life, had inaugurated a period of organisational and ideological weakness in the opposition to apartheid, which endured well into the 1970s. The ANC president, Oliver Tambo, acknowledged that, as late as June 1976, the organisation was still 'too weak to take advantage of the situation ... We had very few active units inside the country. We had no military presence to speak of. The communication links between ourselves outside the country and the masses of our people were still too slow and weak.'[8]

While there had been a number of brave efforts to intensify resistance to apartheid rule in the second half of the 1960s, most had failed and few, if any, involved efforts to organise and mobilise a mass-based constituency. The politics of the period were largely based on individual initiatives and heroics, on symbolic protest founded on liberal notions of the rule of law, and on principled multi-racialism.

A 1970 draft ANC strategy proposal acknowledged that organisation within South Africa was 'almost dead'.[9] The few remaining pockets of radical opposition existed in a state of permanent fear. 'A sullen silence descended on black political life, broken only intermittently by the barely audible verbal protests emanating from liberal whites.'[10] Informers seemed to be everywhere. Detention and imprisonment, banning, house arrest and torture at the hands of security police interrogators often awaited those who tried to organise opposition to apartheid outside the confines of white electoral politics. The state had a massive array of administrative weapons to deal with dissenters, including banishment, endorsement out of urban areas, withdrawal of passports and deportation. 'Discussing politics, even amongst close friends, became a high-risk activity ... Parents warned their children to avoid trouble with the police ... Most Africans felt "an overwhelming sense of the inevitability of white power and ... the ethos of a conquered people" prevailed.'[11]

Steve Biko argued that apartheid had succeeded by instilling a sense of fear and defeat in black people. 'The central theme about black society is that it has got elements of a defeated society ... This sense of defeat is basically what we are fighting against,' he noted, adding that the 'point about conscientisation and Black Consciousness' was to help people escape from this sense of hopelessness.[12]

Gradually, below the radar, new forms of resistance, opposition politics and organisation began developing from the ashes of these defeats. Students, academics and other intellectuals linked to the university campuses began exploring different ways to respond to the situations they faced. How, they wondered, could they best develop challenges to a society based on capitalist relations of exploitation, apartheid systems of control and repression, and racist institutions and assumptions in all areas of life?

* * *

The organisations of national liberation took some time to realise the significance of the new radicalism developing on both black and white campuses within the country. The Communist Party and the ANC shared some of the assumptions of the liberal interpretation of apartheid society. There was common ground in the understanding of race and the belief that apartheid was an irrational racist policy forced on society by Afrikaner nationalism. They agreed that apartheid was a constraint on capitalist economic development. A critique of these views implicitly challenged ANC–SACP thinking at the same time as it threatened South African liberals.

The ANC and the Communist Party were initially ambivalent about, and sometimes hostile to, the emergence of Black Consciousness, as were most white liberals. Marxists schooled in the rigours of Soviet communism referred to BC as 'false consciousness', and some within the Alliance argued that BC was a tool of American foreign policy.

Few in the ANC and SACP acknowledged or understood the new dynamics developing within the country during the first half of the 1970s. Nowhere was this more apparent than in their rejection of Black Consciousness and its leadership as a CIA initiative, and in the way in which the exiled leadership was caught unawares by the student rebellion of June 1976. Neville Alexander once told Xolela Mangcu of the 'contemptuous' way in which the ANC and SACP's Mac Maharaj viewed the Black Consciousness Movement in the 1970s, and how he described Biko as an agent of the CIA.[13] It was presumably to counter this sort of hostility that Ben Turok, one of the more independent voices within the ANC, reminded readers in his 1974 booklet that 'Black Consciousness is not false consciousness'.[14]

The ANC initially vacillated between ignoring the new BC initiative and outright hostility to it. This gradually changed, particularly after Thabo Mbeki began discussions with BC-supporting students studying in Swaziland. Eventually Oliver Tambo mandated Mbeki to develop relationships between the ANC and the BC-oriented students' organisation, Saso. *Sechaba*, the ANC journal, was encouraged to change its editorial policy of ignoring Saso and its activities on black campuses.

In 1973 Tambo requested Mbeki to draft an input paper on BC for the ANC's national executive. This resulted in an ANC statement recognising that BC formed 'part of the genuine forces of the revolution', although concerns over BC's emphasis on 'national identity' and 'psychological liberation' remained.[15]

* * *

ANC strategy, at least as far as political activity within the country was concerned, concentrated on propaganda and recruitment for military training. Whether by design or default, the effect of this was to subordinate internal legal and semi-legal political organisation to the imperatives of a military strategy. As a result the ANC became distanced from the most important internal developments in the first half of the 1970s.[16]

Support for the strategies of the banned and exiled organisations generally necessitated acceptance of the use of political violence in the struggle against apartheid. Following the Sharpeville massacre, the banning of the ANC and PAC, and the declaration of a state of emergency, the most committed anti-apartheid groups and individuals endorsed sabotage and armed struggle as the core of political opposition. Some approached the use of violence from within a liberal worldview, seeing acts of sabotage as a means of changing white opinion. Others saw this as a phase towards guerrilla warfare and popular insurrection. The sabotage campaigns were also seen as a means of showing that opposition to apartheid had not been smashed, and that the violence of the state system would inevitably provoke violent reactions.

MK had been formed with a number of goals. Armed propaganda aimed to raise morale, demonstrate that the ANC was still active, and intensify mass political opposition. Another intention was to force whites in general and the government in particular to make concessions and realise the dangers involved in brutal repression of opposition. Causing substantial damage to the economy and infrastructure, including transport links between cities, might 'bring the government to its senses'. The policy set out in 'Operation Mayibuye', a document which was probably not accepted by MK but which did reflect the views of some of its leadership, saw the sabotage campaign as a prelude to a broader phase of rural guerrilla warfare. Influenced by Castro's seizure of power in Cuba in 1959, MK leaders believed that the sabotage campaign 'would serve as a detonator, provoking a more general uprising against a state they believed to be brittle'.[17]

The first efforts at infiltrating guerrilla fighters into the country, through the Wankie and Sipolilo campaigns, were disastrous. Few doubted that the ANC and SACP had more than adequate moral justification for meeting state repression with force. However, those who had argued that the conditions for armed or violent rebellion were not ripe seemed, in retrospect, to have a valid point. By 1969 it was very difficult to claim that the formation of MK and its subsequent actions had been particularly successful in advancing political opposition to apartheid.

Most committed resistance leaders believed that the turn to violence was the only option in deepening the struggle against apartheid. This was regardless of whether they were nationalists, non-racialists, communists, radical liberals, Maoists or Trotskyists. There was a broad acceptance that the era of legality had been terminated with the Sharpeville massacre, the state of emergency and the banning of the ANC and the PAC. Some debated whether an acceptance of 'illegality' was strategically identical to the sabotage campaigns of MK and the National Committee of Liberation (NCL), whose sabotage actions predated those of MK. They questioned whether there might be a strategy that combined underground organisation with use of the admittedly limited legal spaces still available for political activity.

A few within the Congress Alliance opposed the formation of MK, arguing that it would destroy whatever political and trade union organisation that still existed, and undermine the conditions for its further development. The objective conditions, they averred, did not allow for a strategy based on sabotage or guerrilla warfare. Moses Kotane, long-serving general secretary of the Communist Party and a member of the ANC's national executive, was one of the most senior voices raised against the sabotage campaign. He expressed the concern that the premature inauguration of an armed struggle would deprive the ANC, Communist Party and Sactu of many of its best people, and decimate those underground political units still operating. He also warned against underestimating the ferocity of the state's response to sabotage. 'If you throw a stone into the window of a man's house,' Kotane counselled Bram Fischer, 'you must be prepared for him to come out and chase you.'[18]

After a number of relatively successful sabotage actions, individuals within the NCL and the African Resistance Movement (ARM), which grew from it, began questioning whether they should create a 'parallel legal wing that would be involved only in legal political work'. Sabotage, argued Randolph Vigne, 'could only have limited results and some members would be better engaged in "aboveground" work'.[19] Baruch Hirson, a Trotskyist who had been involved in the sabotage campaign, subsequently supported Vigne in this view.[20] Other NCL and ARM recruits who had participated in acts of sabotage, including Eddie Daniels and Hugh Lewin, 'argued that the time had come to stop the sabotage, since it was unclear just what it was achieving'.[21]

Although there were some questioning voices, the frequent conflation of 'illegality' with 'violence' (or sabotage) limited the exploration and development of political strategies. This was to dominate the approach of the exiled opposition for many years. Developing trade unions, for example, was often viewed as a way to identify and recruit promising individuals for military training, rather than as a means of strengthening working-class interests. A militarist strategy saw the armed struggle as the central mechanism through which the apartheid state would be overthrown. Even when supplemented with international political initiatives – sanctions, boycotts, isolation – this undervalued the role of internal politics of both a legal and a clandestine nature.

* * *

Few, if any, of the aims underlying the endorsement of sabotage and armed struggle had been attained by the end of the decade. The government had initiated and then used a massive array of repressive powers, destroying opposition and breaking any spirit of resistance. The economy was thriving, military power seemed unassailable, and the state's security apparatuses appeared to have opposition to

National Party rule controlled. White support for the status quo, even when this included mild criticism of some elements of apartheid, was stronger than ever.

The younger generation of radical political activists developing on the campuses began exploring new strategies that did not prioritise either endorsement or rejection of violence as a political tool. Support for acts of sabotage or military recruitment was no longer the *sine qua non* of political commitment for these groups of students and rarely dominated discussions in the way it had in the 1960s. Nor were the issues of legality and illegality viewed as absolutes or moral principles. Rather, they raised strategic and tactical issues. Where political gains could be achieved through the exploitation of legal spaces, and where the use of those spaces could create new possibilities for political opposition, then legal strategies would be pursued.

This approach differed not only from the combination of a military strategy and international pressure which guided the ANC–SACP alliance. It was also at variance with a quasi-liberal approach which dominated so much of internal opposition politics at the beginning of the 1970s. For liberals, non-violence and legality expressed through the rule of law were principles usually cast in stone. For the new radicals, however, the issues of legality and illegality, violence and non-violence, and public and clandestine politics, were less matters of principle than of political strategy and tactics.

Intellectuals and students began to embrace the writings of Frantz Fanon and the Guinea-Bissau revolutionary leader Amilcar Cabral, and tried to reconcile them with the Marxism of a new left. The radicalisation of some Christian organisations, notably in the forms of black and liberation theology, loosened the constraints of conservatism and caution as their adherents began seeking ways to transform their current world, rather than waiting for a deity to provide a better one in the future.

The changing intellectual climate threw out different challenges and conundrums. From the late 1960s onwards, the ideology of Black Consciousness influenced and tested students at tertiary institutions. It was during this period that socialist and Western Marxist analyses took root on the Nusas-affiliated campuses, and initiatives to facilitate worker organisation grew into a set of trade unions strong enough to confront both employers and the state. In the urban townships, pupils and youths began forming organisations that were to manifest their existence in the rebellions of 1976 and 1977. The dilemmas that had dominated anti-apartheid opposition after Sharpeville were largely absent from these new initiatives. Activists pondered how to strengthen and develop the new and radical politics, rather than anguishing over violence and non-violence, legality and illegality. These issues were not posed as 'either-or' polar opposites, as abstract or moral dilemmas. They were part of broader strategic and tactical considerations, to be assessed in the light of their contribution to an emerging politics.

This involved more than rejection of the political system of apartheid. The inherent radicalism of this approach led to a critique of an economic system based on labour repression, low wages and extreme exploitation, as well as the ideological and cultural forms that expressed and reinforced political and economic power.

For some, this entailed trying to find ways of acting as 'decent' individuals in a thoroughly 'indecent' society. Radical humanism involved efforts to craft a new identity and new ways of being, based on a rejection of existing political, economic and social practices. These initiatives were sometimes linked to radical and liberation theology, as well as the idea of a 'white consciousness', which was presented as one response to the challenges posed by Black Consciousness.[22]

The anti-establishment 'counter-culture' of disaffected youth in North America and Europe also had some resonance among those seeking different ways of being in apartheid South Africa. This emboldened a number of this new generation to seek new ways of confronting the existing systems of power, authority and control.

For others, the question of how best to contribute to radical change was faced through the prism of class location and the potential roles that students and intellectuals with access to skills and resources could play. Cabral had argued that intellectuals from the petty bourgeoisie could reject the basis of their class position and privilege.

Through doing this, they could commit their skills, knowledge and resources to strengthening the revolutionary impetus of the national liberation movements. 'Class suicide by the revolutionary petty-bourgeois leadership', Cabral asserted, 'amounts to listening to its own revolutionary consciousness and the culture of revolution rather than acting on its immediate material interests as a social class. It must sacrifice its class position, privileges, and power through identification with the working masses.'[23]

Variants of this approach could be read into Antonio Gramsci's discussion of the role of traditional and organic intellectuals, and Georg Lukács's argument that intellectuals were essential to moving the working class beyond the narrow confines of 'false consciousness'. When blended with Lenin's analysis of the role of the vanguard political party, this created a powerful impetus for students to reassess their role and potential in radical and revolutionary organisation.[24]

These debates in socialist theory and practice were by no means abstract. Emerging radicals in Nusas in general, and at Wits in particular, were developing a notion of 'praxis' loosely based on Lukács's use of the term. This involved a dynamic or interactive (dialectical, in the language of the day) process combining analysis, strategy and action, with each element continually influencing and structuring the others. Debates within socialism and Marxism, especially those concerning the place of class and the role of different sorts of intellectuals in revolution, lay at the centre of strategies to develop a new generation of radical leaders and activists on the Nusas campuses. These also formed the basis for questioning how best to weaken student adherence to their class- and race-based privilege and power.

This new group of radicals had to discover Marxism and socialism, and the history of opposition in South Africa, largely without access to the collective knowledge and experience of a previous generation. However, their politics were not formed in hostility or opposition to the banned, exiled or inactive organisational traditions of the ANC, PAC, SACP, Sactu or Unity Movement. Rather, the history and strategies of these organisations had to be rediscovered and reinterpreted through a radicalism that was unable to draw on the past, consciously or explicitly.

Many of the new radicals were broadly supportive of what they assumed was a left-leaning tradition within the Congress Alliance, represented especially in the Freedom Charter and the agenda of Sactu and the SACP to strengthen working-class interests within the Alliance. In some ways, this view of the Alliance was 'manufactured'. It was as if internal and independent radicalism had 'imagined' a larger, more powerful and wiser set of influences and initiatives under whose umbrella it fell, and which could occupy the enormous gaps in experience and knowledge faced in trying to revive radical politics.

* * *

The new challenges to the existing order began developing with surprising force, despite the political defeats of the 1960s. Just three years into the 1970s, considerable numbers of Natal's workers went on strike against pitifully low wages. In the first three months of 1973 there were at least 160 strikes in Natal, involving over sixty thousand workers.[25] New initiatives to organise African workers into trade unions sprang up in the Transvaal, Natal and Western Cape. The June 1976 pupils' revolt in Soweto soon grew into a widespread youth rebellion, with student leadership calling for a number of well-supported work stayaways.

Ideologically and materially, students from institutions such as the Nusas-affiliated campuses had every reason to limit their generational rebellions and association with a new radicalism. They were linked to the interests of the ruling elite of society through family, opportunity, ideology and the expectation of a privileged future. Sustained and radical opposition to apartheid threatened their upward mobility towards the pinnacles of economic and social power.

Campus-based opposition to apartheid in the 1960s had consequences for some of its leadership. The government had withdrawn passports from Nusas leaders and, in a few cases, banned them. Leadership on the white campuses was also accompanied by opportunities for international travel and prestigious scholarships, and student leaders often moved on to the corporate and professional worlds, where their experience of student government assisted in their steady upward progress.

However, the ideological 'glue' which bound most students to the established social order began weakening on the Nusas campuses in the early 1970s. Changes in lifestyle and attitudes, criticism of white liberals from the side of Black Consciousness, socialism and new left Marxism, and the growing radicalism of student action led considerable numbers of students to question their positions of relative privilege. Many began to reject the predictable life and career paths charted for them by parents and the universities they attended, making choices that structured identity and political involvement throughout their adult lives.

3
Rejecting the Republic
– and a detainee dies

South Africa was declared a Republic, outside the Commonwealth of Nations, on 31 May 1961. Only a small majority of the white electorate had endorsed this, with just over 52 per cent of voters approving the proposal. This part of the electorate looked back to a nationalist and anti-imperialist past associated with the Boer Republics of the Transvaal and the Orange Free State, and viewed the 're-establishment' of the Republic as a victory against the British, who had conquered the Boers in war but not in spirit.

Most English-speaking white South Africans, wedded to Commonwealth and Queen, opposed the formation of a Republic. For the vast majority of the population, the new 'Republic of South Africa' represented further exclusion from the central institutions of government and administration and a consolidation of apartheid-based power.

White schools were centrally involved in successive celebrations of Republic Day. I was among the primary school children in Pretoria who were handed replicas of the South African flag and a special Republic Day coin at school ceremonies in 1961. By 1966, a few pupils and teachers at the high school I attended had become less than enthusiastic about celebrating five years of a Republic. A handful of brave boys climbed the two bell towers flanking the school's central building, erecting a Union Jack on each one in protest against what was seen as a Republic 'for the Afrikaners'. Again, small flags were handed out as part of the festivities. I was one of the group of younger pupils who expressed opposition in a way that reflected our 'pro-English' bias. We folded the flags so that only the small Union Jack showed, and displayed this, handkerchief-style, in the top pockets of our school blazers.

* * *

During the course of 1970, the National Party government announced that it was planning a massive celebration to usher in the tenth year of the Republic. This time, however, opposition among anti-apartheid students was able to advance beyond pro-colonial symbolism.

The Nusas president, Neville Curtis, was keenly aware that students at the white English-language campuses stood to benefit from both their racial and class locations, particularly in terms of access to education, jobs, resources, opportunities and material possessions, and the right to vote. However, he believed that it was possible for at least some to move beyond their immediate social and economic interests. This led him to see the value in confronting the belief system of students and working to erode the ideology which bound white students to their privileged positions in apartheid society.

Curtis also recognised the political potential implicit in the planned Republic Day festivities. These provided an opportunity to challenge the comfortable 'patriotism' of the ruling elite and to educate students and pupils in the realities of apartheid society. A campaign against the celebrations might also undermine a comfortable white English-speaking consensus that apartheid's Republic either did not concern them, because it was the instrument of 'the Afrikaners', or was something to be supported, because it was about 'the country' rather than the 'apartheid government'.

Towards the end of 1970, Curtis penned a long letter for publication, to guide student structures on the Nusas-affiliated campuses in their opposition to the Republic Day celebrations planned for 1971. He threw down a challenge to the ruling government and its supporters, and also to the Nusas constituency. 'Recent news articles', he wrote, have brought to mind the celebrations planned for the 10th Anniversary of the Republic of South Africa. It would seem that a great carnival of white patriotic joy is being planned ...

The army, the air-force and the navy will be there. The schoolchildren ... and the loyal party workers are all busily preparing ... Medals will be struck, and white mothers will be spurred on to greater fertility ... The Nationalist Party will salute their creation, the Republic, and will praise their endeavours and successes over the last 23 years, and particularly the last ten ... But what have 10 years of Republic brought us, and what have 23 years of Nationalist rule achieved?

Some of those who lived through the apartheid era without opposing it in word or deed have excused themselves by claiming that 'they did not know' what was being done in their name and interest. The censorship and propaganda, they have claimed, was so total and deep that many ordinary citizens did not know how the majority of South Africans lived. Yet the Nusas call to boycott the 1971 Republic Day celebrations set out, in stark terms, the state of the nation under apartheid rule for all willing to hear. In his November 1970 missive, Curtis listed the following indicators:

Education
0.1% of the African population have matric or school leaving certificates and the state and provinces in 1969 spent R238 million on white education and only R14.5 million on black education ...

Poverty
It is estimated that 50% of the Indian population in Natal live below the poverty datum line as do 68% of the families in Soweto. Average non-white income is R7 while that of whites is R95 per month ...

Starvation
A coloured child dies of malnutrition every thirty five minutes and two African children die during the same period. Half the African

children in a typical African reserve [homeland] die before they are five years old ...

Defence estimates, Curtis noted, had increased from R40 million in 1959 to R273 million in 1969, and by 1970 South Africa owned military equipment that had cost R2000 million. Between 1948 and 1969, the prison population increased from 294,000 to over half a million. Over two thousand Africans were arrested each day for pass offences. 'We should face the fact that there is little for the majority ... to celebrate on Republic Day ... We should face these facts and boycott the whole Republic celebration,' wrote Curtis.[1]

The Nusas National Council, made up of Nusas executive members and SRC presidents of affiliated campuses, endorsed Curtis's proposal to stage a boycott. In a detailed resolution setting out its stance, National Council, which was Nusas's highest decision-making body between annual congresses, noted

a) That the last ten years of the Republic in South Africa have seen a growing disparity in Government spending on whites and blacks in South Africa
b) That the last ten years of the Republic have seen the implementation of further restrictions on civil, human and academic rights of South Africans
c) That the majority of people in South Africa have no say in those matters which concern them, and that their material condition has declined over the last ten years
d) That the Republic celebrations are being exploited by the Government for political purposes and are segregated.

It registered its 'concern that the future of South Africa will be gravely threatened unless the fundamental inequalities between whites and blacks ... are removed, and a major effort is made to ensure full and equal rights and opportunities to all South Africans', and resolved to 'decline to participate in such celebrations', and to 'call on students and the public not to celebrate on the occasion of Republic Day'.[2]

* * *

Nusas's national leadership had prepared guidelines for the running of the anti-Republic Day campaign on affiliated campuses. These stressed the political education of students, scholars and the youth through the distribution of information on poverty and starvation, inequality, conditions in the bantustans, crime, and inequalities in education. On the basis of this data, Curtis concluded, 'many will have no reason at all to celebrate Republic Day'. What was even more striking, he argued, 'is that the situation is not getting better, it is in fact getting worse'.[3]

Nusas was able to draw a range of other organisations into campaign planning. The Labour Party, Black Sash, South African Council of Churches, South African Institute of Race Relations, Christian Institute and University Christian Movement all resolved to participate in activities drawing attention to the realities of South African inequality. A number of speakers were approached to tour the campuses. They included Joel Carlson and Mewa Ramgobin. The former US attorney general Ramsey Clark was due to speak at some of the campuses as a guest of Nusas, and the plan was that his talks would be incorporated into the overall preparation for the campaign.

During May 1971, in the days before the campaign began at Wits, Nusas local ran what it called 'Violence Week', exploring the issues of structural and institutional violence. The theme was introduced by David Thebehali, a member of Soweto's Urban Bantu Council (UBC) who was a regular speaker at Nusas events. Thebehali had become increasingly outspoken, despite his participation in compromised township administration structures, and had taken to explaining the Black Consciousness phenomenon to white audiences. He was representative of a relatively credible group of individuals who had chosen to 'work within the system's structures', using them as a platform to attack aspects of apartheid. It took another five years before the UBC finally collapsed, under attack from Soweto pupils in June 1976.

Violence Week saw the introduction of 'guerrilla theatre' into student life, with Aquarius – the cultural wing of Nusas – simulating the arrest of a black speaker for not having a pass. After this incident, I announced the launch of a planned Nusas campaign against the pass laws, including visits to the pass courts and the publication of *You and Your Pass*, a booklet produced with the Black Sash containing advice on these laws and regulations. Student leaders targeted the administration of the pass laws as one of the most oppressive elements of apartheid, and organised visits to the pass courts throughout the week as a way of educating students about the Republic, which some were celebrating.

The government must have been concerned that there might be large-scale opposition to the Republic Day celebrations, for the military began calling up national servicemen for that period. Large numbers of students who had done military service, and were now on the 'reserve' list of trained soldiers, were suddenly called up for camps and parades. Curtis wrote to the Minister of Defence, P.W. Botha, asking that students not be compelled to participate in these actions, which 'are not representative of all the people of South Africa'.[4] Botha did not respond.

* * *

Government plans were dealt a blow in the week leading up to 31 May 1971 when three military jets crashed into Table Mountain in Cape Town during a practice flight for the celebrations, killing 11 of those on board.[5]

On the Wits campus, the SRC, under Taffy Adler, and Nusas local, which I chaired, were working hard. A photographic exhibition was mounted on the piazza in front of the university's Central Block. There were mass meetings in the Great Hall, addressed by Jean Sinclair, who was president of the Black Sash; Fred van Wyk, director of the Institute of Race Relations; and Beyers Naudé of the Christian Institute. Representatives of the Coloured Labour Party, the Soweto Urban Bantu Council and the Anglican Church were also present at some of these meetings.

Part of the campaign on campus aimed to expose students to the realities of the Republic they lived in. Dr Anthony Barker, superintendent of the Charles Johnson Memorial Hospital at Nqutu, in Zululand, was becoming more and more outspoken about the conditions he encountered at his rural hospital each day. Migrant labour, forced population removals and resettlement were leading to massive increases in diseases such as malnutrition, kwashiorkor and TB. Barker was a powerful, passionate and eloquent public speaker, well equipped with facts and personal experience of the effects of apartheid. During the week running up to Republic Day, he addressed meetings in the Wits Great Hall and at Medical School.

Student leaders planned to take their campaign into the streets of Johannesburg, and sought the permission they required to do this from both the City Council and the city's chief magistrate. Application was made to the United Party-controlled council 'to stage a procession through the streets of Johannesburg ... to draw attention to certain injustices in our country'. In a bizarre response, the city's Management Committee asked the SRC to submit a supporting memorandum setting out what injustices existed in the country before the application to stage a march could be considered.

The SRC president, Taffy Adler, responded with a four-page letter. Given that they appeared to be so ignorant about the country they lived in, Adler advised the councillors to start reading newspapers and the publications of organisations like the Black Sash and Institute of Race Relations. This was widely publicised in the press. The council declared itself 'angry and offended', and accused Adler of being 'precocious'. Presumably embarrassed by its own conduct, the council then granted permission for students to stage a demonstration, but – predictably – authorisation was refused by Johannesburg's chief magistrate.

Following the mass meeting addressed by Anthony Barker and past SRC president Mark Orkin, some students moved into the city to distribute pamphlets opposing the Republic Day celebrations, while others assembled along Jan Smuts Avenue to form a picket line. Members of the Black Sash joined the picket, which carried on through the night. It threatened to turn violent when right-wing students from the Rand Afrikaans University and Goudstad College attempted to disrupt the demonstration. The all-night picket was sustained by members of the Nusas local group, a promising indication that campaign work was starting to build a political community of committed young activists on campus.

* * *

The major Republic Day celebrations in the Transvaal were scheduled for the Rand Stadium, a sports venue in the south of Johannesburg. Pupils from public schools around the city were transported to the stadium to take part in the semi-militaristic activities so favoured in youth displays of nationalistic fervour: marching, gymnastics and field exercises undertaken to the sounds of martial music.

For some years, school education authorities had been planning to introduce a Youth Defence Training Programme into the white public schools, covering topics such as 'moral preparedness' and 'national heroes' and physical activities like drilling, shooting and self-defence.[6] By 1971 this programme had been renamed 'Youth Preparedness', and was widely seen as part of a state strategy to militarise white pupils. The University Christian Movement had joined anti-Republic Day campaign preparations, and compiled its own pamphlet aimed at white pupils under the title 'Youth Awareness'. It set out the relationship between the militaristic Youth Preparedness programme and Republic Day celebrations, urging pupils to become more aware of the inequalities and injustices in their society.

On the Friday morning of the campaign, a group of Wits students set off for the Rand Stadium, with the UCM pamphlet and 20,000 copies of a separate pamphlet, in both English and Afrikaans, specially prepared for school pupils participating in the festivities. Under the heading 'What Republic Day is all about', pupils were told that half of the children born in a typical African reserve died from starvation-linked diseases before the age of five, and that government spent R285.85 annually on the education of each white child, compared to a figure of R14.48 for each African child. The pamphlet posed a question to the pupils present at the Rand Stadium: 'how can we possibly celebrate such unfairness?'[7]

As students began handing out copies of the pamphlet, teachers from some of the Afrikaans-language schools tried to assault Wits students, and a number of fist-fights broke out. Taffy Adler noted that 'one of the most disturbing aspects ... was the intolerant attitude of many of the school kids and the fact that they seemed to appreciate and approve [of] what their teachers were doing'. However, Adler also noted that 'reports reached us that some school children did object to going to the celebrations and read our pamphlet with much interest'.[8]

* * *

Taffy Adler concluded that the campaign had achieved most of its goals. The English-language press had covered the student activities well and commented editorially on the campaign on a number of occasions. After the Rand Stadium episode, the *Rand Daily Mail* devoted a full page to reports and photographs of the event; while *The Star* gave considerable coverage to the conflict with the City Council over the application to stage a march through town, and editorialised that 'the protests of the students give some cause for celebration'.[9]

The government must also have felt that the campaign had had some impact. Prime Minister John Vorster attacked students as 'unpatriotic' while the National Party senator O.F.P. Horwood – previously vice-chancellor at the University of Natal – threatened that the action of students in campaigning against Republic Day celebrations could lead to a withdrawal of state subsidies to English-language universities.

Curtis wrote to the Prime Minister, demanding that he withdraw his statement that those who had boycotted the celebrations had 'nothing to contribute', and apologise to students for suggesting that was the case. In a brief response, Vorster's private secretary wrote that 'The Prime Minister considers the attitude of Nusas, to put it mildly, so unpatriotic and such a disgrace that he is surprised that you even attempt to find an excuse for such despicable conduct'.[10]

Ten years later, a far broader alliance spearheaded an anti-Republic Day campaign. Over 55 organisations, including trade unions, community and civil society organisations, as well as a range of student and support organisations, called for a boycott of the festivities. Supporters of the exiled Sactu distributed a call to workers to stay away from work in protest against Republic Day. Over one and a half million workers were involved in this campaign.[11]

The student campaign of 1971 had been a brave initiative, at a time when there were few other organised voices raised against Republic Day celebrations. Symbolically, it marked an important milestone in a journey of radicalisation and fundamental opposition to white elites and their view of patriotism. The campaign also reflected the growing and self-conscious efforts to loosen the ties of privilege linking white radicals to those who ruled society.

* * *

Shortly after the anti-Republic Day campaign, police served a letter on me withdrawing my passport 'by direction of the Honourable Minister of the Interior'.

This sort of action was an almost inevitable but relatively minor consequence of opposition to apartheid. Nonetheless, when my repeated applications for a passport were refused, and the Minister wrote to me advising that 'I need not apply again', I felt some sort of public response was required.

I wrote back to the Minister of the Interior, sending copies of the letter to various newspapers, warning him that student leaders would 'no longer tolerate such arbitrary action'. Challenging him to reveal details of any law I might have broken which justified restricting me to South Africa, I told the minister that 'I have done nothing I will not do again. I have said nothing I will not say again.' I then challenged the authorities to charge me with any offence that might legitimate the imposition of travel restrictions. Unless they could prove anything against me, I thundered, 'I demand the return of my passport'. It took another 15 years before my demand was met, when I was issued with a passport, valid for just three months and allowing travel to only three countries.

At much the same time, two members of the security police tried to recruit a close friend as an informer. Danny Weiner and I had been at school together in Pretoria, played soccer for the same team, stayed at Wits Men's Residence in 1970, and were studying similar subjects. Although he was not politically involved, we often spoke about both national and student politics, and had a number of friends in common.

Security police had approached Danny's father to clear the way for an approach to recruit him. This was an ill-informed move, for the police did not seem to know that Danny's Hungarian-born mother was a survivor of the Bergen-Belsen concentration camp. Her camp number was still tattooed on her arm. The family was unlikely to be sympathetic to a proto-fascist division of the police.

Danny and his father discussed the approach, agreed to reject it unequivocally, and decided to warn me that police were trying to gather information about my activities. I was not particularly shocked. Although only 18 months into university, I had been arrested in 1970, and had already held a number of relatively senior positions on the SRC and in Nusas.

As my political outlook developed and matured, I learnt that the sort of liberal outrage I expressed when my passport was withdrawn, and a close friend approached to spy on me, was unlikely to gain much traction when dealing with an authoritarian state. Actions of that nature were to be expected from apartheid's administrators.

* * *

The annual Richard Feetham Academic Freedom Lecture at Wits University was a dignified and rather formal event, based on the best traditions of liberal opposition to government interference in university autonomy. Was it, I wondered, possible to inject more radical content into this occasion, challenging the university community's rather self-satisfied view of academic freedom? I applied for, and was duly appointed to, the position of chair of the Academic Freedom Committee, which organised this activity.

The lecture had been instituted after the ironically named Extension of University Education Act of 1959 had removed the right of universities to admit students of colour without ministerial permission. Universities like Wits and UCT, and students organised under the umbrella of Nusas, had voiced strong opposition to the passing of this Act, arguing that it struck at the core of 'academic freedom'. This was defined as the right of universities to admit and teach whomever they deemed appropriate, regardless of colour, and without state interference.

The opposition of Wits to this form of state intervention had gone through different phases, with the 1957 protest march of some two thousand students, academics and university management representing a high-water mark of unified opposition to government interference in university affairs.

This quest to protect 'academic freedom' was premised on the separation of state, politics and university, often leading in later years to the university being described as an 'ivory tower'. Protests over inroads into academic freedom rarely linked the issue to broader socio-political issues, although some students and academics worked tirelessly to do this throughout the 1950s and 1960s. When the government announced, in 1956, that it was going to proceed with the enforcement of university apartheid, the Wits SRC formed an academic freedom committee which aimed to involve all university constituencies in opposing this.

> In this endeavour the SRC was greatly assisted by the fact that Senate, after a famous debate in 1954, had endorsed the maintenance of 'open' admission to Wits. A key influence in this endorsement was the senior member of Senate, Professor ID MacCrone, a committed liberal who was anxious to work with the liberal student leadership

to defend Wits' open status. Together with the Chancellor, Justice Richard Feetham, he was also a key influence in persuading Council of the need for a dignified but 'emphatic' protest against legislation that would prohibit Wits from admitting black students.[12]

This was the committee I was appointed to chair in 1971, my main task being to organise that year's academic freedom lecture. By the time I assumed responsibility, an invitation to deliver the lecture had already been issued to a British Labour Party MP, Anthony Crosland. Shortly after I became chair, Cosmas Desmond, a Catholic priest prominent in exposing the consequences of forced and 'black spot' removals – notably through his book *The Discarded People* – was banned and house-arrested. Cos was well known to students through his campaigning, a regular speaker at Wits events, and a close friend of student leadership. I used my position as chair of the Academic Freedom Committee to write to Crosland, asking him to raise the banning of Cos in the House of Commons.

At the same time Taffy Adler, then SRC president, wrote to the Pope, asking him to protest to the South African government because of its banning of a Catholic priest. Perhaps the absence of a response might have had something to do with the way Taffy addressed His Holiness:

> The Pope
> Vatican
> ROME
>
> Dear Pope …

We were not a political generation deferential to authority.

To my distress, Crosland did not respond on Cos's banning, but sent a short letter indicating that he would no longer be travelling to South Africa to deliver the Feetham lecture. I did not understand why he had decided to withdraw from the lecture. Perhaps the request to intervene more directly in the politics of South Africa by raising the banning of Cos transgressed some unseen boundary between being a British MP and a political activist.

I was irritated at being let down by someone we had thought was a friend to anti-apartheid students. With little time available to find a replacement, I was relieved when John Kane-Berman, a past SRC president, proposed the name of Joan Lestor. She was, like Crosland, a Labour Party MP but was believed to be on the left of the party. A vice-president of the British Anti-Apartheid Movement and a past leader of the British Young Socialists, she had also served as a deputy minister in a previous Labour cabinet. Perfect, in my view. The South African government would be unlikely to provoke an incident with the British government by refusing a member of parliament entry to the country. In addition, her left-leaning position within Labour, allied to her position in the AAM, fitted my agenda of linking academic freedom to the broader society well.

Interviewed by *Wits Student* a week before the lecture, I acknowledged that many previous speakers were to be admired for their intellectual achievements and steadfast defence of universities against government interference. They had included Lord James of Rusholme (1967), Lord Walston (1968), Baroness Barbara Wootton (1969) and Sir Robert Birley (1970). Now we had Ms Joan Lestor, who, from a student viewpoint, was 'a far more exciting prospect'.

> She seems far more radical, far more in touch with present student thinking ... As long as the present regime is in power, our universities will not be opened ... The only way to ensure the restoration of academic freedom ... is to work for the political change we so badly need. It is for this reason that I find the prospect of the Vice-Chairman of the Anti-Apartheid Movement addressing us on academic freedom so exciting.[13]

Some members of the university's senior management were less enthusiastic. A left-wing, female, Labour Party MP, linked to the Anti-Apartheid Movement, without a senior postgraduate degree or a title – this was not the stuff that previous speakers at the Richard

Feetham lectures had been made of. But the invitation was duly extended and accepted, and the relative autonomy the Academic Freedom Committee enjoyed from the university's administration, through having its own budget, protected it from serious interference.

*   *   *

The annual Feetham lecture was one of the university's most prestigious events. The Great Hall was packed with students and staff, with SRC and Academic Freedom Committee members on stage, resplendent in (usually borrowed) academic gowns. The SRC president, Taffy Adler, introduced Joan Lestor, drawing both jeers and cheers when he mentioned that she had been involved in the 'Stop the '70 tour' campaign against the British tour of the all-white South African cricket team, which had been organised by Peter Hain. In her speech, Joan emphasised that removal of academic freedom had to be seen as part of a systematic process in which other freedoms were curtailed. All of those small losses of freedom were 'part of this filthy doctrine of racial supremacy', she argued.[14]

It was my role to thank Joan for her address and it was that vote of thanks which sparked more controversy. For I thanked her not only for what she had said, but for who she was, explicitly linking the fight for academic freedom with the anti-apartheid struggle, and suggesting that support for academic freedom necessarily led to support for the work of organisations like the Anti-Apartheid Movement. 'If we are to dedicate ourselves to the restoration of the autonomy of the university,' I stated, 'then we must be honest enough to realise that we must dedicate ourselves to the overthrow of the present system in our unhappy land.'[15]

Response from the thousand-strong audience was surprisingly good, with loud and prolonged applause. Joan leaned over and took my hand. 'Well done,' she murmured. University management was less pleased by my comments, and the vice-chancellor, Dr Bozzoli, appeared to boycott the lunch given for Joan after the lecture. (He later apologised for his absence, saying he had another appointment.)

One of his deputies, Frank Nabarro, was visibly angry and threatened that he would be taking disciplinary action against me. That did not transpire, but Joan's presence had certainly shaken up any complacency about the place of universities and their 'academic freedom'.

Relations with Joan were cemented when Taffy and I took her on a road trip around rural Zululand. This included a visit to the Charles Johnson Memorial Hospital at Nqutu, where Anthony and Maggie Barker and South African doctors like Tim Wilson were struggling to stem the tide of apartheid-induced rural disease.

* * *

Joan Lestor travelled back to England and I began campaigning for election to the SRC. I addressed a number of Medical School classes, and there met a young student, Mohammed Salim Essop. We began discussions about student and national opposition politics, and I met a group of his friends who gathered regularly in a flat in downtown Johannesburg to discuss politics. Through this group, I was introduced to activists organising non-racial sport, particularly in the coloured and Indian 'group areas'. Shortly after this, I was invited as keynote speaker to a dinner of non-racial sports organisations held at the Gandhi Hall in Fox Street. A whole new world of people was opening up to me – people who did not live in the white suburbs, who were influenced by a tradition of non-racialism, and whose symbols of political engagement were drawn from the Congress Alliance and the Freedom Charter.

I had also started meeting with young Black Consciousness-supporting cultural activists, who were organising in their communities through the use of poetry, theatre and literature. They included the former Sophiatown gangster-turned-poet, Don Mattera; Achmat Dangor and Farouk Asvat, both young writers; and a group on the left of the Coloured Labour Party who were sympathetic to Black Consciousness.

It was probably because of this range of connections that I was included in a massive set of early morning security police raids one Sunday in October. In a co-ordinated swoop, dozens of people were roused from sleep at around 4 a.m. Their premises were searched and material seized. Some were detained under security legislation.

When a team of security police, headed by a Captain Kennedy, hammered on the door of my tiny Phineas Court flat in Braamfontein, I was not in. I had decided to spend the weekend with a friend elsewhere. Steven Friedman had asked if he could stay overnight in my room as he needed some 'space' from his parents' home, where he was living at the time. He spent a difficult time trying to convince Kennedy that he was not Glenn Moss. Although he finally succeeded in this, he was subject to a search, as was my room.

Phineas Court provided basic accommodation – a small room with a basin, a communal bathroom down the corridor and, in my case, a window overlooking the kitchen of the infamous 'Pop's Café' on the corner of Jan Smuts Avenue and Ameshoff Street. Despite the absence of facilities, I cooked fairly often for friends, using a small hotplate and some pots, pans and other scavenged utensils. Cooking was one thing, but washing up was both difficult in the small hand-basin and not something which attracted a 19-year-old discovering politics. Into the drawers of my desk went dirty plates, knives and forks, waiting for an opportune moment for a major wash-up in the communal bathroom.

Steven describes how, during the search, a young security policeman opened these drawers. '*O jissus,*' he exclaimed, looking up in horror at his Captain. 'Search the drawers – go through every plate – papers could be hidden there,' Kennedy ordered. And so my dirty plates and cutlery and pots and pans were slowly unpacked and checked for secret messages.

The aftermath of these raids was rather more serious than a member of the security police pawing through my dirty dishes. A number of people were detained, including some Wits students. It soon emerged that the raids had been precipitated when police intercepted a car driven by Ahmed Timol and Salim Essop, the medical student I had befriended a few months earlier. When they searched the car, ANC and Communist Party pamphlets were found in the boot, and the occupants detained. The raids on early Sunday morning targeted people who police thought might be linked to Timol and Essop.

Within days, an atmosphere of fear had permeated those communities which police were targeting in their raids. The Indian 'group area' outside Roodepoort was particularly affected, as were Fordsburg and suburbs, such as Braamfontein and Parkhurst, where students lived. Security police would arrive at a home or place of work, often in the early hours of the morning. Announcing their presence with violent knocks and kicks on the door, they would search the premises, turning everything upside down, pulling out clothes, emptying cupboards and drawers, overturning beds and chairs, climbing through ceiling trap-doors, shaking out books and then dropping them on the floor, rifling through papers and leaving them in disarray. The process of instilling fear, of taking control of subjects' lives and stripping away their dignity, was beginning.

The fear of detention was very strong during these raids. Police had the legal authority to detain anyone present under one of the security provisions allowing for interrogation and imprisonment. Those released from detention were often damaged both physically and emotionally. Ex-detainees sometimes showed the symptoms of post-traumatic stress for years after release. They were, however, not the only casualties of this corrosive system. Some members of the judiciary and the medical and legal professions collaborated with the state to hide what was happening to detainees under interrogation, compromising and undermining institutions which should have been protective of those subject to the massive repressive powers granted to the police.

* * *

Ahmed Timol was a young schoolteacher in Roodepoort. Recruited to the Communist Party underground while in London, he returned to South Africa with a mission to increase the visibility of the ANC and the SACP through the distribution of pamphlets and underground publications. He enlisted the assistance of Salim Essop, a medical student at Wits University. They were apprehended by police on the evening of Friday 21 October 1971, when their vehicle was found with pamphlets in the boot. Both were detained under section 6 of the Terrorism Act and held at John Vorster Square, where their interrogations began.

By 27 October, Timol was dead. Security police claimed he had jumped from a tenth-floor window at John Vorster Square. Other evidence indicated that he had been severely tortured, and possibly held upside down by the ankles from a window. He may have been thrown out of the window by security police, dropped deliberately or in error, or may have hurled himself through the window to avoid incriminating others while under torture.

At much the same time, Essop was undergoing similar interrogation and torture. I had made contact with both families after the detentions, and was travelling to Roodepoort most evenings to offer support and exchange information. I remained in close contact with the *Rand Daily Mail* political journalist Tony Holiday. A group of student leaders used to meet Tony regularly at a Braamfontein restaurant and pub, the Saddle Inn, where he was usually willing to stand us to copious quantities of wine and Irish coffee as we discussed the world of politics. In the days following Timol's detention, Tony's already considerable consumption of alcohol increased further.

As soon as I heard that Timol was dead, I used a public telephone to advise Tony of this and ask him to travel with a photographer to the Timol home in Roodepoort. I realised that he had been drinking, but could sense a focus and purpose. What a journalist, I thought at the time; able to sober up on demand to follow a major story.

Some years later, when Tony himself faced Terrorism Act charges for his involvement in underground Communist Party activities, I learnt that he had been part of the same underground cell as Timol. He had been waiting for the security police to detain him, fully expecting Timol to reveal his name under torture. His fellow underground comrade was dead and had not revealed Tony's involvement. Now the journalist had to write the story of this death in detention.

The results of Tony's trip to Roodepoort were immortalised on the front page of the *Rand Daily Mail* that next morning. A lead story reported Timol's death, strongly suggesting that he had been tortured. This was a brave allegation, flirting with the limits of legality. It was accompanied by that most painful of photographs depicting Timol's mother, expressing all the anguish of a parent who had lost a son to security police atrocity.

Soon after, nurses at the Johannesburg General began leaking information that Essop had been admitted to the hospital in a critical condition. Security police became aware that someone among the hospital staff was the source of this, and Essop was moved to the H.F. Verwoerd Hospital in Pretoria. I drove with Mr Essop senior to the hospital in an effort to establish some news of his son's condition. Bravely, Mr Essop climbed up an outside drainpipe to peer through a window, and saw his son lying on a bed, naked except for bandages wrapped around his abdomen.

We rushed back to Johannesburg so that the family could instruct lawyers to bring an urgent interdict restraining security police from torturing or otherwise unlawfully interrogating Salim Essop. Unusually, there was some direct evidence of a detainee's condition, and it was for this reason that the interdict was granted. The presiding judge, Cecil Margo, also suggested that there be a public inquiry into how Essop had sustained his injuries, and that a private doctor chosen by his parents be allowed to examine him. Both proposals were ignored by the authorities.

Back at Wits, there was an angry response to Timol's death, the detention of students, and the torture of Salim Essop. As SRC vice-president, I was invited to address a student meeting at Medical School. Medical students had a punishing schedule of lectures, practicals and hospital rounds. Although they had a reputation for being socially aware and concerned, their time to act on these concerns was limited. However, Essop was one of their own, and a packed venue and rousing response indicated just how outraged these young professionals-in-the-making were at the actions of the state.

The university's vice-chancellor and principal, Professor Bozzoli, joined a picket on Jan Smuts Avenue, protesting against the death of Timol and the torture of Essop. This was unusual in itself, for senior university managers rarely joined student protests. Bozzoli then surprised the protesters further. Climbing up onto a nearby concrete fire hydrant, he took hold of the megaphone, held by a student leader, and addressed the picket line. In a voice shaking with rage, this politically moderate engineer told those present that all 'right-thinking' South Africans now had little doubt that the security police tortured and killed detainees. Even university leadership was being radicalised through police actions.

Father Bernie Wrankmore, an Anglican priest, had started a fast in support of a judicial commission of inquiry into the death in detention of Imam Abdullah Haron, who had died in custody after being tortured the previous year. He began his fast at a Muslim shrine on the slopes of Signal Hill in Cape Town. After 67 days and two attempts to see the Prime Minister, with his health seriously deteriorating, Wrankmore called off his action. Following the death of Timol, he asked all concerned South Africans to fast during the Muslim month of Ramadan in support of the demand for a judicial inquiry into deaths in detention.

Leaders of the Black Sash and the Christian Institute joined Wrankmore, and soon a group of students at Wits began to fast from sunrise to sunset each day, gathering together on the steps of the Central Block to support each other. The fast did not last for long, especially after Wrankmore called off his own participation on medical advice. But it was an indication of how strongly students felt about the torture of detainees at the hands of the security police.

A few days after Timol died, Taffy Adler and I wrote and printed a pamphlet on torture in detention, caught a bus to the city centre at rush hour, and began distributing our message to commuters at the bus terminus. Predictably, we were arrested, taken to Vorster Square and handed over to the same Captain Kennedy who had led the security police raid on my flat earlier that month. After verbally abusing us for over an hour, Kennedy released us with dire warnings about criticising the security police and distributing pamphlets to 'blacks' in town. It was dusk, I was probably a bit shaken by a thoroughly unpleasant hour on the tenth floor of Vorster Square, and I stumbled and fell down the front stairs as I was leaving the police station, cutting my leg.

I stanched the blood with tissues and a handkerchief, and Taffy and I crossed the road to a restaurant, which had a public telephone. We called Helene Perold and Elaine Unterhalter and asked them to fetch us in town, suggesting we meet for a meal at the Chon Hing Restaurant in Chinatown's Alexander Street, uncomfortably situated almost opposite Vorster Square. I continued dabbing at my cut leg while we sat at a table in the basement, waiting for our friends to arrive. Suddenly there was some shouting and scuffling, and Kennedy and another policeman pushed down the narrow stairs to our table. Kennedy pointed to my leg. 'Now don't go telling your friends on the newspapers that we threw you down the stairs,' he warned me. Given the number of detainees who had died in security police custody by 'falling down stairs' or 'slipping on a bar of soap in the shower', Taffy and I failed to see any irony in the situation.

* * *

As the SRC executive member responsible for external relations, I pondered how best to create some protection for detainees, and how to exact some sort of price for security police actions. I thought back to Joan Lestor, and put together an information package on the death of Timol, the torture of Essop and the detention of others. I included a covering message asking her to motivate organisations and individuals within her sphere of interest to take up the issues, and began looking for a way to send this to her without interception.

An SRC colleague, who knew I was trying to find a way to get a message to London, offered the services of a friend who was flying to England. It was naive to accept the offer. However, within the limits of my security consciousness at the time, I had no reason to distrust my SRC colleague, and finding ways to send information out of the country was always difficult. This appeared to be a welcome opportunity.

I handed over the information for delivery, hoping it would spur some action in London. A few weeks later, I was driving to Cape Town with a group of friends to attend the annual December Nusas seminar. We had taken a detour, and found ourselves spending the night in a caravan park just outside Sedgefield, near Knysna. One of our number – Athol Margolis – took a stroll into the village to buy bread, milk and newspapers, but returned at a quicker pacer, shouting 'Mossie' (as he called – and still calls – me), 'you had better look at this urgently'. And there, as the front-page lead of the morning paper, was a report on a press conference held by Prime Minister B.J. Vorster.

Vorster had made his reputation as the strongman of apartheid politics. As Minister of Justice, Police and Prisons, he had overseen the massive expansion of security legislation, including the system of detention without trial for purposes of interrogation. He had, in 1963, stated that Nusas 'was a cancer' in society and that he would deal with it, in his own time. The power and influence of the security police grew enormously on Vorster's watch, and interrogation routinely became associated with assault and torture.

Vorster and his close colleague H.J. van den Bergh – who headed the security police under Vorster before setting up the intelligence agency that became the Bureau of State Security (Boss) – had been held together at the Koffiefontein internment camp during the Second World War, because of their pro-Nazi sympathies.

The government had been stung by the intensity of reaction – both local and international – to the death of Timol and the Salim Essop case. Now Vorster was hitting back, claiming that this was the result of 'agitators' aiming to discredit government. It was all part of a conspiracy to undermine law and order. His evidence for this was the letter and information I had sent to Joan Lestor.

Sitting outside a caravan in Sedgefield, my Nusas colleagues and I discussed what would happen next. It seemed likely that some action against me would follow. Arrest and charges, perhaps a banning order, seemed possible. I wondered how best to respond, particularly from a small village on the coast. Eventually, something of a strategy emerged. It was important not to wait for the state to act, and then react. Far better that I take the fight to Vorster and make the issue even more public than it already was. That might just make it more difficult for the security police to act against me.

From a public phone-box outside the gates of the caravan park, I placed a reverse-charges call to Tony Holiday at the *Rand Daily Mail* and indicated that I wanted to respond to Vorster by means of a statement. The connection was terrible, and Tony and I could barely hear each other. As I began reading my prepared statement in a voice that became increasingly louder, a few 'locals' (big, male, white – and not friendly) began gathering outside the telephone booth. Athol recalls me shouting 'I challenge … the Prime Minister' over and over again, as Tony battled to take notes and make sense of what I was saying. I launched a scathing attack on Vorster, the security police and the system of detention, accusing Vorster of using 'red herrings' to distract from the core issue of security police torture of detainees.

We packed up and left Sedgefield as fast as we could, fearing that the local observers might decide to investigate the furore at the public phone-box further. Whether the tactic of challenging Vorster provided any protection, I will never know. It seems more probable that the Prime Minister was simply using me as a small player in a bigger initiative to deflect criticism from the security police and their practices. Nothing specific occurred as a result of the very public confrontation with Vorster, apart from my learning a little more about the art of secure communications in a repressive environment.

* * *

I drove back from Cape Town together with Jenny Cunningham, who had recently been elected SRC president at Wits, and Steven Friedman, who had succeeded me as chair of Nusas on the Wits campus. We had left considerably later than intended, and decided to stay overnight at a small farm deep in the Karoo, which offered rooms to rent. By the time we arrived seeking accommodation, the Karoo sky had turned dark, and the wind that rustled through the large trees next to the darkened farmhouse created an eerie atmosphere.

Steven and I shared a room. I must have been more anxious over the Vorster run-in than I realised, because I woke from a nightmare in the middle of the night, screaming. Both Jenny and the farmer's wife came out of their rooms to see what was happening. Steve, close colleague that he was at the time, instinctively decided not to embarrass me, and suggested the noise must have come from elsewhere on the farm. Talking to him about the incident early in the morning, I realised that I could not allow Vorster's threats to slow down the momentum against detention which was developing. Personally, I needed to demonstrate – to myself, as much as anyone else – that I had not been overly intimidated by the interception of my message to Joan Lestor and the Anti-Apartheid Movement, or by Vorster's use of this in his propaganda war.

With the end of the year approaching, Steven and I decided to organise an anti-detentions message from religious leaders. Both of us were critical of religious ideology, tending as we did towards socialist agnosticism or atheism. Nonetheless, with the confidence of youth, we used our positions in student government to set up meetings with Orthodox and Reform rabbis, leaders of Catholic, Anglican, Methodist and Presbyterian denominations, Islamic organisations, Beyers Naudé of the Christian Institute and John Rees, general secretary of the South African Council of Churches.

To our surprise, many of those approached were willing to sign a statement condemning detention without trial, expressing concern over increasing allegations of torture of detainees, and calling for the release of detainees. The *Sunday Times* agreed to publish the statement as a New Year's message from religious leaders. As 1971 ended, the conditions of detainees and allegations that the security police were routinely torturing them to extract information were back on the front pages of the newspapers.

4

The student left takes charge

Early in 1972, needing some time for reflection on my first two years at university, I resolved to take a break from student politics. Although subject to challenge from radicals, student institutions were still dominated by a formulaic and symbolic liberalism, with an emphasis on procedure, formal debate, and motions and well-meaning resolutions. There was a tension between those who believed student government should represent the interests of an already privileged student constituency and others who felt that students should be organised and mobilised to challenge apartheid society. I was not certain that the representative institutions of student government necessarily provided the best avenue for these activities, and was increasingly attracted to the unstructured and spontaneous activity which some of the radicals on campus were promoting.

Resigning from my positions as SRC vice-president and Nusas deputy vice-president, I paid some much-needed attention both to my studies and to an on-off relationship that went back to my school years. For the first time since arriving at university, I had some time on my hands.

I continued living in my small Phineas Court flat across the road from the campus. Braamfontein was a vibrant and exciting area during the week, with pubs, restaurants, theatre, a cinema and a thriving community of students. But it died over the weekends, and Sundays were particularly bleak, with an eerie silence permeating the area. Most students who spent time around Braamfontein during the week still lived in their parental homes and tended to return there over the weekends. The usually hectic traffic along Jan Smuts Avenue to and from the city centre tailed off by Saturday afternoon, and the streets emptied as the shops closed. Only the Highway Café stayed open on a Sunday, for newspapers, milk and its notorious toasted sandwiches.

Smells from the Newtown abattoir, west of Braamfontein, always seemed stronger on the weekends. I was startled when, one Sunday morning, I saw a sheep running along Jorissen Street towards the Civic Centre, presumably trying to escape a grisly end. Somehow that's the image of Braamfontein on a Sunday that remains with me: a sheep running on the road, a pungent smell – and a toasted double-decker ham-and-cheese sandwich from the Highway for breakfast.

Two communes where older radical students lived – one in Yeoville, the other in Melville – provided spaces where a younger group joined in discussions over whether the organisations of student government provided a vehicle for or obstacle to the politicisation of students. The anti-institutional mantra of America's counter-culture heroes – Jerry Rubin, Abbie Hoffman – seemed to offer attractive alternatives to the formal processes of student representation. How could one, as a radical, represent students whose interests were embedded in white privilege and elitism? Surely the very institutions of student government were part of the problem and inhibited the 'changes in individual consciousness' that the then-influential Charles Reich believed would result in revolution.[1] Student government was intrinsically authoritarian, hierarchical and part of 'the system' – or so it seemed.

* * *

By March 1972, growing student radicalism was increasingly challenging the strong liberal consensus on campus. A younger group of students who had arrived at university with a background of activism brought welcome numbers and ideas to radical activity. Some had been educated at Woodmead School, a private but progressive institution on the northern fringes of Johannesburg.

Andy Orkin was a central member of this new group. His brother,

Mark, had been SRC president immediately before Ken Costa. The younger Orkin was artistically talented and something of a craftsperson. It was he and a group of his friends who suggested that Nusas should mount a dramatic representation of the Sharpeville massacre on campus to help students and university staff understand the state's violent response to challenge and protest.

Andy acquired a number of white polystyrene boards. At his workshop in his parents' Parkview home, he cut these into the shape of tombstones, and inserted two lengths of sturdy wire into the bottom of each one, to enable simple erection on soft ground. By means of silkscreen printing, the front of each tablet was 'engraved' with black lettering:

R.I.P.
Killed on
March 21 1960
At Sharpeville

Late in the night before Sharpeville Day, Andy arrived at my Phineas Court flat across the road from the campus. The roof of his old green Volkswagen Beetle was stacked high with the tombstones, and it took a number of trips to carry these to my sixth-floor room in the tiny and unreliable lift. All of this had to be done in silence, ensuring that we did not encounter anyone in the parking area outside Phineas Court, in the lift, or along the corridors of this dingy building. Finally, my room was piled to its ceiling with the 'headstones', waiting for removal to the campus in the darkness of early morning. By sunrise, the Wits library lawn had been transformed into a cemetery.

The impact was substantial. Hardly any student or staff member could avoid being confronted by this powerful exhibition representing the consequences of the Sharpeville massacre. It was accompanied by posters, pamphlets setting out the history of Sharpeville, and a meeting on the lawns at lunch-time. A pamphlet issued in the names of Cedric de Beer and Andy Orkin explained why it was important to recall the events at Sharpeville 12 years previously:

Violence in South Africa has become a way of life. Besides the violence of guns and tanks, there is the violence of laws that split families, the violence of the Pass Laws, the violence of starved children in the homelands, the violence of forced removals ...

We are attempting to find a symbol for this institutionalised violence that we have all grown to accept –
So that we may be reminded of it
So that we may recognise it
So that we may reject it
And then remove all traces of it from our daily lives.[2]

The lunch-time gathering on the university's library lawns reflected the transitional nature of student politics. Religious liberalism and the protest music of Bob Dylan, Joan Baez and Pete Seeger were blended with a more radical analysis of the structural and systemic violence which had underpinned the Sharpeville massacre.

Dale White, an Anglican priest from the Wilgespruit Fellowship Centre, told the audience that Sharpeville was a 'rift-valley in the South African conscience'. As a group of mainly white people, 'we must examine how we are implicated in what was done [at Sharpeville]', he continued. In a responsive Sharpeville 'litany for repentance' led by White, those gathered were asked to commit themselves to a non-violent society. God was implored to help whites 'hear the horror and the violence, and understand the rift between the peoples of South Africa'.[3]

At the same time, and coexisting slightly uncomfortably with White's liberal Christian morality, a more radical tone was raised in a pamphlet issued at the gathering, and in a speech linking the violence of Sharpeville and the structure of South African capitalism, including the migrant labour system and control of African workers.[4]

Many of the participants were probably unaware of the subtle distinctions in political emphasis. Reactions to the gathering in general, and the symbolic graveyard in particular, were varied. There was shock, support, interest, avoidance and aggression.

Hecklers challenging the claim that the gathering at Sharpeville had been peaceful were silenced when it was pointed out that this was the conclusion of the official inquiry into the events of 21 March 1960. The most dramatic response came from a lecturer by the name of Tauber (not to be confused with Karl Tober, who subsequently became vice-chancellor at the university). Tauber was infuriated by the symbolism represented by the graveyard and started kicking down the tombstones.

He was confronted by Athol Margolis, one of the emerging young activists on campus, who tried to restrain him. Tauber pulled out a pistol. Athol bravely disarmed the lecturer. He and I then marched Tauber to the vice-chancellor's office in Central Block, and demanded an immediate audience with Bozzoli. To his credit, the vice-chancellor responded swiftly when he realised what had happened and summoned campus security. Tauber was escorted off campus, while Bozzoli retained the pistol as evidence.

Within days, Tauber had been charged in front of a high-level university disciplinary committee consisting of a number of professors from the Law Faculty, and dismissed from his post. For years afterwards, Athol often saw Tauber walking the streets of Braamfontein, where he apparently lived. I am not sure if they ever spoke to each other in these encounters, but I do know that Athol was always wary of any quick hand movements made by the ex-lecturer.

* * *

Nusas's 'Free Education' campaign, launched towards the end of May 1972, was witness to some of the most violent police action ever seen on the predominantly white campuses. Abram Onkgopotse Tiro, a past student president at the Saso-affiliated University of the North (Turfloop), had attacked the system of Bantu Education at a university graduation ceremony. Early in May, he was expelled from the university, and students began a sit-in in Turfloop's main hall in support of Tiro. After suspending the SRC and banning all meetings on campus, the university authorities expelled over eleven hundred students. Within days, there were demonstrations of solidarity and protest at many of the Saso-affiliated campuses, leading to expulsions and police actions against students.

The Nusas campaign aimed to focus attention on the events which had taken place at Turfloop and on other black campuses. In Cape Town, police baton-charged and broke up a meeting of UCT students held on the steps of St George's Cathedral, using extreme violence. Students were even pursued into the cathedral, where some were severely assaulted.

Police reaction to demonstrations on the Wits campus was also characterised by high levels of violence, and involved baton charges onto campus, sadistic assaults and numerous arrests. Jenny Cunningham, who had recently resigned as Wits' first female SRC president, was beaten unconscious by police, arrested, thrown into the back of a police van, and then deposited on the floor of a police cell, semiconscious and concussed.

My participation in these events was initially limited to that of a demonstrator, joining the pickets and marches. However, as the interim SRC president, Graham Craig, had little experience in these situations, I found myself taking something of a leadership role in the clashes with police, trying to reason with their commanding officer, and finally joining the university vice-chancellor in calling on students to withdraw as police – many in plain clothes – invaded the campus, chasing students across the lawns, and beating them with batons. My efforts at drawing back from student politics were not proving as easy as I had hoped.

*　*　*

Early in the year, Prime Minister Vorster had announced the formation of a parliamentary commission of inquiry into Nusas and three other organisations: the Christian Institute, University Christian Movement and Institute of Race Relations. The commission's name changed as successive chairmen were elevated to higher political positions in apartheid's government: from the Kruger Commission

(Jimmy Kruger), to the Schlebusch Commission (Alwyn Schlebusch) and finally the Le Grange Commission (Louis le Grange). All three chairmen subsequently served in apartheid cabinets in the portfolios of justice and police, with Kruger obtaining notoriety for his 'It leaves me cold' response to the death of Steve Biko, whose killers fell under his political control.

Throughout 1972, campus activists worried that the commission would result in action against Nusas and its leaders, and I joined a number of other fairly experienced student leaders in agreeing that we would be available should this take place. Slowly, as the year progressed, I began re-engaging with the structures of student government. I was elected chair of the Arts Faculty Council and, together with close colleagues, began considering how we could strengthen the radical agenda within the institutions of student governance. I applied to be a member of the Wits delegation to a special Nusas congress held in Grahamstown at the end of the year, even though I had not been on the SRC or active in Nusas since my resignations earlier in the year. It was there that the Nusas president, Paul Pretorius, asked whether, in the event of the banning or arrest of existing Nusas leaders, I would again be available to participate in formal leadership. My response came in what Steven Friedman at the time called my 'Niemöller speech' to the congress. If those of us who had left leadership in the past year were untouched by the Schlebusch Commission, then we were duty bound to return in the event of action. Anything else would involve cowardice and collaboration.[5]

Late in February 1973, the Schlebusch Commission recommended the banning of eight Nusas leaders, administrators and advisers. These included the ex-president Neville Curtis, the incumbent president, Paul Pretorius and the Durban political philosopher Rick Turner. Three days later, eight leaders of Saso and the BC movement were also banned, including the founder president, Steve Biko, and his successor, Barney Pityana.

Within weeks, I accepted nomination as a candidate in an SRC by-election, topping that poll by a large majority. Supported by a team of close friends and colleagues – all of us openly identified as political radicals on campus – my easy electoral victory suggested that Wits students were becoming increasingly open to new forms of representation and anti-apartheid opposition.

I had chosen a crucial moment to return to campus politics. Student involvement in labour issues had been growing for some time, and opposition to the whole edifice of 'white power' was deepening. Early in September 1973, I was duly elected SRC president, openly committed to support of Nusas, involvement in worker organisation, and greater student participation in radical opposition politics.

* * *

On the night of 11 September 1973, police opened fire on a group of African mineworkers at the Anglo American-owned Western Deep Levels Mine near Carletonville. At least 11 workers were killed, and a number wounded. Police had been called by mine management when a wage dispute erupted into violence at a compound housing over eight thousand workers, some of whom were threatening to attack mine police and stoning mine property.

African mineworkers at Western Deep, as with almost all South African mining operations, were migrants, housed in single-sex compounds on mine property. Flare-ups of violence between workers, between workers and supervisors, and between workers and police were not unusual in this unnatural environment, where mine management controlled most aspects of working-class life – food, sleep, accommodation, recreation, contact with 'outsiders', and the work process itself.

The shootings seemed to touch a nerve across a wide range of interests. In an unusually muted response, Prime Minister Vorster 'deplored the fact that lives were lost and extended his sympathy to the next of kin'.[6] The Minister of Police noted that mine management had called on the police for assistance because they felt threatened by the actions of workers. 'The police had nothing to do with the wage dispute between the management and employees. The police are there only to keep law and order and do not interfere in wage disputes.'[7]

Western Deep and Anglo American management expressed concern over the deaths. Anglo sent a telegram to the Chief Minister of the KwaZulu bantustan, expressing condolences at the shooting of a 'Zulu' worker. Representatives of Anglo American and Western Deep management, including the manager of Anglo's gold division, attended a wreath-laying ceremony for five migrant workers killed in the incident. In a ceremony held at Maseru airport and attended by thirty thousand Lesotho citizens, King Moshoeshoe II and Lesotho Prime Minister Leabua Jonathan placed wreaths on the coffins of the five Lesotho miners and made contributions to a special fund started for dependants of the victims of the shootings. The chairman of Western Deep Levels conceded that errors might have been made in dealing with the wage demands of mineworkers: 'We may have made a mistake in our wage restructuring ... maybe in the African mind, we have done them an injustice.'[8]

The leader of the United Party, the official opposition in parliament, Sir De Villiers Graaff, called for a full judicial commission of inquiry to establish 'the underlying causes of the disturbance, the activities of the crowd and the action of the police'. This call was supported by Harry Oppenheimer, chair of Anglo American.[9] The United Nations indicated that it wished to send a representative to attend the inquest into the death of the miners, but Vorster responded that his government would not allow entrance to any UN observer.[10]

There had been simmering discontent over wages at the mine for over a month. Geoff Budlender, chair of the Nusas National Council, pointed out that this was not an isolated incident, and would be repeated 'until the Government and industries give attention to the basic underlying issues – full trade union rights for Africans and payment of human wages'.[11] This view was echoed by the trade unionist Lucy Mvubelo, who suggested that communication between employers and mineworkers would be improved through the recognition of trade unions for Africans, and that incidents like the shootings at Western Deep could only be avoided in this way.[12]

Following the shootings, students at a number of universities questioned the relationship between apartheid, employers and their own institutions in maintaining exploitative and oppressive labour relations. A mass meeting at the University of Cape Town called on Harry Oppenheimer to reconsider his position as chancellor of the university unless he used his position in Anglo American to promote trade unionism for Africans and raise wages for mineworkers. Some 600 students at the University of Durban-Westville held a prayer meeting and launched a fund for dependants of the dead miners, while the local Nusas committee at the University of Natal, Durban, started a similar fund. Saso issued a statement condemning the shootings, while students at the University of the North disbanded their SRC because it had not arranged any protest or action in connection with the shootings.[13]

At the University of the Witwatersrand, student involvement in labour had been growing for some time, largely through the Nusas-linked Wages Commission. This had first been formed at the University of Natal, Durban, in March 1971, initially functioning as a subcommittee of the SRC. By July 1971 Nusas had decided to set up Wages Commissions on each of the affiliated campuses. They aimed to undertake research on the wages of workers, make representations for wage increases through the statutory Wage Determination Boards, and expose the way in which local and international companies used apartheid to keep the wages of workers artificially low.[14]

Black Consciousness proponents had suggested that whites should work within their own community to effect change there. Initially, Nusas embraced this approach, and the Wages Commissions focused some of their earliest efforts on remuneration and working conditions at the universities themselves. However, over time some – in Nusas and elsewhere – began to argue that the organisation of worker interests, rather than black identity, provided the best instrument for radical change in society. This shift in approach was reflected in the Wages Commissions' programmes of research, information dissemination and support to factory-based worker initiatives.

By September 1973, the Wits Wages Commission was undertaking research in support of wage increases and pamphleting workers outside factory gates in the early mornings. Its numbers were fairly small, although growing under the leadership of Steven Friedman, who had previously chaired the Nusas local committee and edited *Wits Student*. I had recently become Wits SRC president, and Steven's Wages Commission offices were across the corridor from mine in the Students' Union building. We also shared a house in Orange Grove with a number of other politically active students.

As soon as I heard of the Western Deep shootings early that morning, I went to speak to Steven. Could we, I wondered, link our response to the work of the Wages Commission and the developing anti-capitalist critique which was increasingly central to our anti-apartheid commitment?

After some discussion, we agreed on a plan of action. We would arrange a lunch-time meeting of students to protest against the shootings, and call for a full and independent inquiry into the conflict. However, we would also focus on wages and working and living conditions on the mines, and specifically target Anglo American because of the substantial gap between its quasi-liberal anti-apartheid appearance and the harsh reality of compounds, migrant labour, poverty-level wages and the absence of trade union rights. This would create the context for Steven to present the work of the Wages Commission, and explain how it aimed to improve conditions for workers and facilitate platforms for organisation. He would then invite interested students to sign up as participants in activities such as research, pamphleting at factory gates, and production and distribution of a workers' newspaper. I would then suggest that everyone present should move to Anglo's downtown head office at 44 Main Street, and occupy the building in protest against management actions and in support of an inquiry into the events at Western Deep Levels.

The meeting, held in an overflowing lecture room in the Social Sciences building, proceeded as planned. Alan Fine, one of those who joined the Wages Commission that day, recalled that I undertook what he called the 'anti-capitalist rabble-rousing', while Steven set out the aims and activities of the Wages Commission. Both talks were well received by students, who seemed shocked by the police action as well as by Steve's presentation of working and living conditions on the mines.

The suggestion that some form of direct action should be undertaken at the Anglo head office was received enthusiastically, and students began making their way downtown, using private vehicles, a kombi owned by the SRC, and municipal buses that ran between Braamfontein and the city centre. Eventually, over a hundred had gathered on the pavement outside 44 Main Street. As Anglo personnel hurried to lock the front doors, the student crowd pushed forward, led by the large figure of Craig Williamson. Students moved into the foyer of Anglo's head office. Soon after, uniformed police arrived.

Police tried to move the students from the building. The students resisted. However, the police were not fully committed to the task at hand, possibly because they did not see a sit-in at the headquarters of English-speaking corporate executives as particularly problematic. A young uniformed constable told me that he had no issue with us attacking the bosses, and asked whether we would be willing to pressure police management to increase the salaries of the lower ranks.

Finally, a group of Anglo executives arrived, including Graham Boustred, Dennis Etheredge and Gordon Waddell. The Anglo team tried to divide the crowd, suggesting that they meet separately with a few student leaders, who could then report back to everyone present. We were, however, sufficiently seasoned to dismiss this tactic and insisted that they take questions and comments from the whole group. A heated exchange followed, with questions about union rights, and use of compounds and migrant labour as a way of depressing wages and controlling workers. Anglo was accused of talking the language of moderate liberalism while benefiting from apartheid's systems of labour control. The student group had arrived armed with a petition calling on Anglo to support a full and impartial inquiry into the background and events associated with the shootings, and this was handed over to the executives present.

Some among the student group were involved in literacy training based on the 'conscientisation' model of the Brazilian educator

Paulo Freire. They began engaging the Anglo representatives about access to mineworkers who wanted to attend literacy classes. This was a discussion that continued over the next few weeks, and I met with Anglo's recently appointed social responsibility officer, Alex Boraine, trying to facilitate access to the compounds. Little came of this, although the literacy initiative grew and developed, eventually becoming an important pillar in the strategies of worker education which the Wages Commission brought to the fledgling trade union movement.

* * *

The 1973 conflict at Western Deep Levels mine embodied one of those moments which, in Dan O'Meara's words, 'crystallise the contradictions and conflicts of an entire stage of development and the reactions to it point the way to the future development of a particular social formation'.[15] Reactions to the mine shootings reflected changes in the balance of forces between contending groups in society, and revealed the way in which fault lines would open up in the future. Greater mineworker militancy was emerging in wage disputes. Radicals were applying increased pressure on liberal critics of apartheid, especially those who represented corporate capitalist interests.

Differences over trade unions for African workers were developing within the capitalist fold, with a more liberal wing accepting in principle that unionism was a necessary element in improved industrial relations. Both Harry Oppenheimer and Helen Suzman came out in support of full trade union rights shortly after the mine shootings. But closer to the ground, mine managers at Western Deep were still speaking about 'the native mind'.

The radical responses on the Nusas campuses indicated a growing understanding that capitalism and apartheid were functionally related. Anglo American's Michael O'Dowd had long argued, in a series of influential articles, that capitalist development and apartheid were essentially opposed, and that if capitalism was allowed to develop along free market principles it would inevitably erode the basis of apartheid. This thesis had been accepted by a wide range of liberal critics of apartheid. Now a new generation of left-oriented students, white and black, were beginning to challenge this and identify the functional relationships between the economic system and its political edifice.

Wages Commission activity was boosted by the inflow of talented and committed activists mobilised by the Western Deep events. Students and lecturers from the Nusas campuses who entered worker organisation through the Wages Commissions played central roles in the General Factory Workers Benefit Fund and Trade Union Advisory Co-ordinating Council in Natal; the Western Province Workers Advice Bureau and Workers Advisory Project in the Western Cape; and the Industrial Aid Society in the Transvaal. These constituted the early foundations of an independent trade union movement, which led to the formation of the Federation of South African Trade Unions (Fosatu) in April 1979, and culminated in the launch of the Congress of South African Trade Unions (Cosatu) in December 1985.

* * *

The death of Ahmed Timol in 1971 had drawn me into political activity which extended well beyond the university. My involvement in the Ahmed Timol Memorial Committee, formed in September 1973, played an even more important role in deepening my 'off-campus' politicisation. It was chaired by Mohammed Timol, who had been detained at the same time as his brother Ahmed in 1971. Sheila Weinberg, one of South Africa's youngest political prisoners, who had served an 18-month jail sentence in the mid-1960s, was its secretary. Indres Naidoo, banned after his completion of a ten-year jail sentence for sabotage, played an influential behind-the-scenes role in the committee's work, as did his brothers Prema and Murthi. Jeanette Curtis was a committee member, while Helen Joseph, who was listed and could not legally be a member, was also active.

According to Indres, the committee – which soon changed its

name to the Human Rights Committee – was set up to 'keep the spirit of the ANC alive amongst the people'.[16] Its first act was to plan a rally to commemorate Timol's death in detention two years previously and to call for the release of political prisoners. The open-air rally was scheduled for the Queen's Park grounds in Vrededorp on 21 October 1973. However, three days before it was due to take place, the state imposed a ban on all public meetings where any government principle or policy would be attacked, criticised or discussed, 'or which is held in protest against or in support of or in commemoration of anything'.[17]

Jeanette and Sheila contacted me and asked if there was any way my SRC could assist by providing an indoor venue for the rally. If it was held indoors, at Wits, it might just be deemed a private rather than a public gathering. I convened an emergency meeting of the SRC that Friday, and we considered the issue deep into the night. Legal advice sought was ambiguous. Holding a gathering indoors, on Wits premises, might circumvent the ban – but also might not. It was by no means certain that the university authorities would even allow the Great Hall to be used for these purposes. Some SRC members opposed offering assistance to the Timol Committee on political grounds. Finally, the majority agreed that I could offer to host the meeting at Wits, as long as university management agreed to the use of the Great Hall.

Surprisingly, the Wits administration agreed to this without difficulty, despite a warning from the chief of the security police, Brigadier G.L. Prinsloo, that his men 'would be watching' and would take 'suitable action' if the law was contravened.[18] A member of the police contacted Jen Curtis, warning her that if he thought an offence was being committed at the planned meeting, he would arrest 'every Bantu at the meeting and the organisers'.[19]

The meeting went ahead in a packed Great Hall without incident. Speakers included Helen Joseph and Rokaya Saloojee, whose husband, Suliman (or 'Babla', as he was known), was one of the first to die under security police interrogation. Committee members sat on the stage, each with a placard bearing the name of a detainee who had died in security police custody. Congress veterans were present in large numbers. They included the Reverend Douglas Thompson, an accused in the Treason Trial, who made specific mention of the number of Muslims who had died in detention, and led the gathering in a non-denominational prayer. The Transvaal regional director of Nusas, Jonathan Grossman, as well as a representative from the Nusas-affiliated Johannesburg College of Education, joined me on stage.

I had suggested that Mohammed Timol chair the meeting, both because he led the committee and because the death of his brother was being commemorated. Declining the offer, he asked me to chair, arguing that this would solidify the alliance developing between his committee and Wits students, something he was keen to strengthen. Over the next few months, I worked closely with the Human Rights Committee, producing pamphlets and a bulletin from the SRC offices, and meeting often with Indres Naidoo in Doornfontein. Reggie Vandayar and Shirish Nanabhai, who had been sentenced with Indres and also imprisoned on Robben Island for ten years, were often present. I assumed that they, too, were part of the group working to 'keep the spirit of the ANC alive'.

Cedric de Beer accompanied me to one of these meetings at the Naidoo home one evening, where the indomitable 'Ama' – mother of the three brothers and Shanti Naidoo, who had featured in the trial of the 22 – served us spaghetti for dinner. Cedric and I had been discussing SRC and Nusas politics with the group present, when Indres pointed out that we were not eating. We attacked our plates of spaghetti, only to discover that the meal was very highly spiced. For at least five minutes, we were racked with coughing fits, unable to speak, tears rolling down our cheeks while glasses of water were passed our way. Every time I tried to say something, my throat would constrict, and the coughing would start again. To general laughter, I asked whether the heavily curried spaghetti involved some sort of Indian Congress test to establish whether we were hardened enough to work with HRC members.

* * *

Each December, Nusas held a national seminar to plan for the following year. Executive members, presidents of the affiliated SRCs, chairs of Nusas local committees, and a delegation from each campus attended. Leadership training and political education formed an important part of these events, and there were usually a range of talks and papers delivered. These helped to build a shared understanding of society and develop common strategies on how best to intervene in opposition politics.

By December 1973, Nusas and the student left on the affiliated campuses had defined their core around the radical politics of opposition. A few years previously, there had been intense debate over whether students should be involved in politics. This question had been redefined, and now asked what kind of political activity was most appropriate, rather than whether involvement was acceptable. Strategies were increasingly based on political initiative, rather than responding to state actions through protest politics.

Nusas had weathered storms and faced daunting challenges. The rise of Black Consciousness and separatism posed fundamental questions for a multi-racial organisation committed to liberal principles. In redefining its role, Nusas had moved further away from its liberal base on campus and in the broader community of anti-apartheid opposition. State action had also weakened the organisation. Precarious finances and weak internal administration had combined with these other factors to threaten Nusas's continuing existence.

However, Nusas had emerged revitalised from this potentially terminal situation. Its leadership was more focused in its radicalism and increasingly proactive and strategic in its activities, especially in its growing involvement in worker organisation and education.

Politically, Nusas leaders had realised that strategies of opposition had to be based on more than a broad rejection of apartheid. The nature of the society being fought for influenced the type of activity students should initiate, and this posed questions about long- and short-term goals and the relationship between political means and ends. It was not just *what* was undertaken that was important. The way in which activity was undertaken could not be separated from the longer-term goals of any campaign or project.

The Wits campaign following the shooting of workers at Anglo American's Western Deep Levels aimed to raise awareness about conditions on South Africa's mines. It had also aimed at strengthening the Wages Commission and its work. The success of this initiative reinforced Nusas's growing understanding that campaign action should enhance ongoing project activity, not undermine it by competing for scarce resources. This, together with a focus on proactive campaigning rather than reactive protest, informed and structured discussion at the December 1973 gathering.

* * *

The Wits delegation to the Nusas seminar travelled through the night to reach Cape Town. It was during this trip that, as designated kombi driver, I managed to drive through both Bloemfontein and Kimberley, even though they were on alternative routes. One of the delegates woke up as I went through Bloemfontein, and then again as I entered Kimberley. I had to swear him to secrecy against a backdrop of mutterings about my ability to provide direction.

Failures in physical direction-finding notwithstanding, the new radicalism was beginning to mature, and issues of strategies and tactics, long-term goals and vision, and attitudes to other anti-apartheid groupings were becoming central in the student left's planning. These were the issues foremost in delegates' minds when Nusas's December 1973 seminar convened on a farm near Elgin, outside Cape Town.

The organisers of the seminar programme had decided that delegates would discuss a campaign for 1974 in general terms, and then move on to the identification of a specific theme. The Wits delegation arrived in Elgin committed to a focus on opposition politics, liberation movements and the release of political prisoners.

This had been intensively discussed in Johannesburg over the previous months. However, not all campuses agreed with this approach. Some were concerned that the subject matter was too radical, that more conservative students would not accept it, and that its focus on imprisoned political leaders from banned organisations would bring down the wrath of the state.

With this difference in approach simmering in the background, seminar participants attempted to identify and analyse the general anatomy of a Nusas campaign. Some seminar participants argued that student campaigns involved pointless appeals to a repressive government. It was a waste of valuable and limited resources to expect the ruling classes in general, and the government in particular, to change because of an appeal to morality or some higher notion of justice.

I agreed with this critique of many of the previous Nusas campaigns, especially when they focused on the state's use of repression through bannings and banishment, forced removals and police brutality. Power in South Africa was based on minority rule and protection of the interests of a small, racially exclusive elite. The vast majority of South Africans would never accept the legitimacy of such a system, and the dominant mechanisms of government and control would always involve repression rather than consent. Campaigning on a moral basis for a change in these circumstances was bound to fail.

However, there were other compelling reasons to undertake political campaigns which had little to do with their prospects of success. Political activism among students could have positive consequences, even though they were unlikely to influence government policies and actions. Well-targeted campaigns undertaken on terms set by their initiators, rather than in reaction to state actions, could increase the recruitment of students into longer-term projects, as had occurred after the Western Deep mine shootings. They could assist in the political education of both those participating in and those reached through campaign activity. Organisationally, this type of action could strengthen the identity and unity of Nusas, and create and develop organisational skills among student leadership and activists on the campuses. Political campaigns within South Africa could influence the content of international action against apartheid. This would enable a better alignment between internal and external opposition politics and resistance.

A successful Nusas campaign had to be based on subject matter that was relevant to the political climate. It needed to provoke what the seminar termed 'functional conflict', which might help to change attitudes and allegiances, generate critical thought, and weaken the ideological ties holding groups and individuals to established positions. In addition, short-term campaign demands would need to be blended with a longer-term vision, including ideas of the sort of society being fought for, rather than just what was being opposed. Student campaigns usually involved a 'short period of concentrated activity'. The impact of this would be enhanced if it was preceded by a far longer 'build-up', in which the groundwork for the campaign was laid, information disseminated and a context created in which campaign messages and impact could be more readily absorbed.[20]

* * *

Both the leadership and the constituency of student organisations are, of their nature, in a constant state of flux. Younger members gain experience and move into leadership positions as established leaders complete their studies and leave university. This creates a state of permanent instability and change within student organisation. Although an ordinary pattern in student government, this had an added dimension for Nusas in its political identity and activities. Nusas's activities extended well beyond the remit of the university campus or specific student interests. The nature of its political engagement in a deeply repressive and dangerous society required experienced and stable leadership and an informed and committed constituency. Yet the building of these had to begin anew each year.

Nusas tried to mitigate the effects of this situation through advisory panels made up of older and more experienced advisers. Its leaders consulted widely and regularly with the leadership of organisations such as the Christian Institute, South African Council of Churches, Black Sash and Institute of Race Relations. Progressive academics on the campuses, religious figures, past Nusas leaders and a few individuals who had been involved in political activity in the 1950s and 1960s also formed part of this informal advisory network.

Nusas paid particular attention to leadership training and political education within its own constituency. The bi-annual seminars held in April and December, as well as the annual July national conference, were important vehicles for these ongoing initiatives. In the early 1970s, they often included contributions from political and intellectual activists such as Rick Turner, Keith Gottschalk, Mewa Ramgobin and David Hemson, who joined student leaders in presenting position papers on the wide range of issues facing a student movement fundamentally opposed to the society which had formed it.

I had attended seminars from 1970 onwards where the contribution of left intellectuals was of a consistently higher quality than I experienced in university courses. The central dynamics of society – politics and the structure of the economy, inequality, identity, exploitation of labour and its relationship to race and class, the history of political organisation – were explored and analysed through the prisms of political economy, philosophy, religion and morality.

This reflected one of the most important failings of the English-language universities. Despite a rhetorical commitment to academic freedom and critical inquiry, the content of the courses taught did little to challenge a society based on racism, oppression and inequality. Universities prepared students to take their places as members of an elite which perpetuated a deeply unequal status quo and unquestioningly accepted its position in this hierarchy. Initiatives to counter this, with only a few notable exceptions, developed outside the academic education offered through university courses.

Political education certainly featured on the agenda of the December 1973 seminar. However, there was a stronger focus on strategies and tactics than had been present at previous seminars. The seminar organiser, Mark Wolffe, had structured the programme to allow an exploration of the key issues facing radical students on the Nusas campuses, to locate these within an historical context, and then to chart a strategically sound basis for action into 1974.

Geoff Budlender, previously SRC president at UCT and chair of Nusas's interim management committee set up after the 1973 bannings, had been asked to provide the historical context necessary for strategic planning of Nusas activities.[21] Geoff captured the thinking of the 'pro-campaign' lobby well when he argued that 'the valid post-1970 focus on "action not talk", and the resulting orientation towards projects, has tended to mislead us into viewing "campaigning" action as simply another form of "talk", and thus either irrelevant, or at best relatively unimportant'.

This reflected a new view of campaigning politics, which in the past had largely been restricted to defensive protest action, although there were at least two exceptions to this: the 1956–9 Nusas campaign in defence of university autonomy, and the 1971 campaign against Republic Day celebrations. However, there was a relationship between campaign action and other forms of action. Campaigns provided an important instrument for developing leadership and organisational capacity, educating and politicising students as well as a broader public, and revealing some of the realities underpinning a brutal and repressive society.

Many past Nusas campaigns had serious flaws. While protest action had 'shown up evils', it had 'failed to make explicit the system underlying those evils'. Geoff warned that there were dangers involved in this sort of campaign and protest politics. 'We have not clearly articulated the alternatives facing South Africa, we have not exposed the essential triviality of most "white" politics ... We have provided intelligent and trained people ... [But] many of our best still drop into white consumer society on leaving university.'

Nusas had a growing involvement in facilitating black worker organisation. Now it was proposing a campaign for 1974 which would, of its nature, reach out to the disenfranchised and have major resonance in areas of black politics. 'How', asked Budlender, 'does this tie up with our attitude to Black Consciousness', which had called on white political activists to work within their own communities?

Eddie Webster, a sociology lecturer at the University of Natal, offered some answers to Geoff Budlender's question. His contribution on Black Consciousness and the white left[22] suggested that some type of alliance between these two tendencies would be necessary. Developing thoughtful responses to Black Consciousness would determine the nature and quality of any alliances across the boundaries of race.

When Saso first began to assert its separation and distance from Nusas, some of the more radical student leaders on the white campuses were supportive of these initiatives. The strongest rejections of BC came from within established liberalism, which was horrified by what it saw as abandoning the principle of multi-racialism, the liberal holy grail of anti-apartheid activity.

Soon, however, some liberals began to accept and even embrace BC. While BC was clearly a challenge to 'white' liberalism, it was questionable whether it posed a challenge to the basis of liberal ideology. Both embraced a view of the world in which individuals and their endeavours were central. This manifested itself in a common ideology of self-help, individual morality and endeavour and, often, a Christian-oriented worldview. Both BC and liberalism tended to support market economics, with a limited role envisaged for the state.

In their mutual rejection of class-based organisation and analysis, a materialist conception of history, and Soviet and Eastern Bloc communism, they had much in common. Despite BC's emphasis on group identity, it shared with liberalism a limited grasp of collective interests represented and advanced through the structures of society. This was particularly evident in its lack of success in relating to workers in terms of their class interests, or in developing a critique of capitalism beyond its specific racial complexion.

BC and liberalism parted ways on the question of whether the racial composition of organisations involved a principle or a strategy. As liberals started finding common ground with elements of BC ideology, radical groups influenced by Marxist analysis began questioning the worldview put forward by BC. Nusas leadership largely accepted that racially separate organisations, especially in the student movement, were both necessary and tactically sustainable. Webster quoted the psychologist Chabani Manganyi approvingly to make this point: 'While "colour blindness" may be a sound goal ultimately, we must realise that race is an overwhelming part of life in this historical period. There is no black man in this country who can live "simply as a man". This blackness is an ever-present fact of this racist society whether he recognises it or not.'[23]

Black Consciousness, Eddie suggested, was not primarily aimed at white liberals. Rather, it was an attack on the white power structure and the ideology which underpinned it. Its critique of white liberals was twofold: that they were politically impotent, and that they were hypocritical, especially inasmuch as they had not confronted the essentially racist assumptions that informed their relations and actions. While this position involved criticism of white liberals under apartheid, it did not necessarily entail the rejection of liberalism and liberal ideology.

BC's separatism did, however, involve the rejection of a liberal assimilation model: 'the Black Consciousness position is that integration does not mean assimilation of Blacks into an already established set of norms drawn up and motivated by white society ... The Black Consciousness movement does not accept uncritically white culture as a model to aspire to,' argued Eddie. This was a view shared by white student radicals, who were on their own journey of rejecting the values of the society which had spawned them. Radicals were working to distance themselves not only from the political structures of apartheid and institutionalised racism, but also from the economic, social, cultural and normative institutions and structures of South Africa's ruling class.

Established liberalism assumed that the norms and standards of the English-speaking bourgeoisie were what all 'reasonable' South Africans aspired to, and that it was 'Afrikaners' and 'Afrikaner nationalists' who were the core beneficiaries and supporters of apartheid. If only the majority of society – including blacks and Afrikaners – could gradually be assimilated into their 'civilised' and

'English-oriented' values and systems, then conflict could be averted, and progress assured. 'We need', argued Eddie, 'to turn our critical gaze onto white society to show clearly how its social institutions maintain and perpetuate inequality. We must focus not on the institutions of Afrikanerdom but on those of white English-speaking South Africa – our families, the private schools, the universities, the economic institutions and the churches.' This was not to be an exercise in moralism, involving 'confession' on a road to 'redemption'. As Eddie warned the Nusas leadership, 'The difficulty here lies in developing a balanced response to these "discoveries" as it is all too easy to develop exaggerated feelings of collective guilt.'

For Nusas, understanding and contextualising BC was far more than an analytical exercise. Saso's breakaway from Nusas, and its growing assertiveness as a racially separate student organisation, threatened the *raison d'être* of an organisation that prioritised multi-racialism as a leading principle. Black Consciousness forced white students to confront the meaning of this multi-racial principle, challenging them to define their opposition to apartheid society in more radical ways. Questioning this traditional liberal view also forced a reconsideration of the relationship between principle, strategy and tactics. If organisational multi-racialism was no longer seen as a principled act of resistance to apartheid, then where did multi-racial activity fit into the long-term goal of non-racialism? Was race the only, or even the most important, identity? Where did other social identities, such as class, gender and ethnicity, fit into the spectrum, and how did progressive radicals link their strategies and activities to the interests associated with these identities? What about intellectuals as a social group? How did they link the resources they could mobilise to different interests in society?

These were the sorts of questions being raised by the new Nusas leadership. Eddie Webster outlined three possible responses to BC. Traditional liberals 'responded to the call for separate organisations by re-iterating their basic principles of equality, non-racialism and the protection of civil liberties ... The traditional liberal finds it difficult to recognise the limits of his role in South Africa.'

A second response came from what Eddie described as the 'despairing liberal', who saw in the development of BC the collapse of the non-racial ideal. Despairing liberals accepted that blacks must be the initiators of change, but experienced feelings of guilt because of being white, and 'over-compensate[d] for this by developing an emotional and uncritical support of all BC positions'.

A third response to BC, from within committed radicalism, attempted to understand BC's emphasis on black solidarity and separation as an organisational strategy. However, this also took account of the gaps in BC's understanding of society and how to act on its fault lines. The committed radical, unlike the 'despairing liberal', was not uncritical of BC, pointing 'to the danger of ... the idea that merely being black is an adequate statement of political radicalism, that being black is contributing more to the overthrow of white supremacy than white people could possibly do'.

For Eddie, the writings of Fanon and Nyerere had raised precisely these sorts of issues when they warned that the essential institutions of colonialism might be 'retained in the post-colonial era by a corrupt black bourgeoisie. There is a danger that the stress on blackness obscures and mystifies the problem. Putting it crudely you have not understood the problem until you recognise the fact that exploitation can just as well have a black face as a white face'.

In developing a progressive response to BC, Eddie's 'committed radicals' would retain a commitment to a non-racial future in South Africa, but accept that an emphasis on black solidarity, rather than multi-racialism, might be a strategic imperative. This was especially so in the case of black students and intellectuals and the embryonic black middle and professional classes.

Committed radicals distinguished between non-racialism as a goal for the future and multi-racialism as an organisational imperative and principle. BC had clearly rejected the latter, while the new radicalism and its tendency to socialist analysis increasingly linked non-racialism to both a post-apartheid society and the centrality of class (rather than race) as a basis for the organisation of collective interests.

This focus on class, both as an analytical tool and a basis for organisation, found its expression in the prioritisation of worker rather than black interests which underpinned the Wages Commissions, and in the new forms of worker organisation which were beginning to develop. 'The committed radical sees in the uneven development of capitalism the creation of potential conflicts of interests within the black community and the danger of the emergence of black middle classes who feel their interests are best served by individual careerism,' Eddie suggested to the assembled student leadership.

Geoff Budlender had asked how Nusas's attitude to Black Consciousness squared with its growing involvement in initiatives to organise workers. Eddie suggested that 'committed radicals' were bound by the logic of their analysis to reject the BC proposition that they were inherently 'irrelevant' to change or that they should work exclusively within the white community in efforts to change attitudes. While accepting limitations on their role, he believed this was a result of their class location within society, rather than of racial identity. 'Committed radicals feel they have access to certain skills and a freedom of movement that enables them to play a supportive role,' argued Eddie.

In a stirring conclusion, Eddie echoed one of the core arguments advanced by the banned activist-philosopher Rick Turner. 'The first step to changing reality is to conceive how it could be different. Black Consciousness has mapped out some of the steps needed to change this reality – my task today has been to describe this attempt and the white response to it – our task now is to translate our commitment into meaningful radical action.'

* * *

Nusas leadership had, for much of the previous year, been grappling with whether race could, on its own, explain the evolving dynamics and interests in South African society. The role of progressive whites in new forms of organisation was closely linked to this question, not only in respect of students and universities but also increasingly in the arena of worker organisation.

Karel Tip was about to assume office as secretary-general of Nuswel, the Nusas division which incorporated the Wages Commissions. This also made him vice-president of Nusas. Intellectually and strategically one of the most sophisticated of the new leadership, Tip had been influenced by the teachings of Rick Turner, Michael Nupen and Eddie Webster at the University of Natal, where he was a central figure in establishing the first Wages Commission.

Progressives and radicals in Nusas had started asking both principled and strategic questions about whom they worked with, and for what purposes. Tip faced these issues head-on in his contribution to the Nusas seminar.[24] Black Consciousness notwithstanding, he argued, radical whites had an important supportive role in relation to 'black initiative'. The role of progressive whites, argued Tip, 'is of necessity a secondary and supportive one, enabling and facilitating as far as possible the promotion of black organisation. This amounts to a transfer of resources ... which are at present largely a white monopoly.'

The language used was of its time: 'radical whites', 'black initiative', 'black organisation'. However, the issues Tip raised had been debated and contested in earlier socialist history, notably by Lenin, Lukács and Gramsci, when they grappled with the relationship between intellectuals and working-class organisation. These were the strategic questions which faced the Wages Commissions and the new forms of union organisation and worker support evolving in Durban, Cape Town and Johannesburg. What is the optimal relationship between intellectuals and working-class initiatives? How does apartheid influence that relationship? Where does Black Consciousness as an ideology and organisational initiative fit into this equation? And what about the relationships between non-racialism, multi-racial forms of organisation and intellectual-activists from the (mainly white) petty bourgeoisie?

Tip was careful to distinguish between strategic initiatives implemented by radical white groups and liberal 'action for action's sake'. Radical action was aimed at challenging the fundamentals of existing society, with the goal of a new order based on substantive equality and redistribution. This included a 'reallocation of the constituent elements of the present imbalance of wealth'. Liberalism as a long-term goal, and as a basis for strategic action, presented the danger of modernising the structures of inequality and oppression, seeking to eliminate 'only the harshest edges of oppression and exploitation' while preserving 'the hard core of inequality'.

Nusas's leadership had embraced the idea that students could fulfil a legitimate role in facilitating organisation of black workers. This did not preclude other activities, including campaigning and political education – as long as these did not replicate the liberal programmes and protest politics of the past. Nusas had a responsibility to identify campaigns in which political action would have the maximum radicalising effect on groups such as students who were 'not bound, through vested interest, into the status quo'.

Tip had set out the radical approach to student activism and engagement for the next year. The strategies and goals of liberalism did not pose real alternatives to existing power relations and inequalities. Student political campaigns needed to move beyond liberalism and carefully target those potentially receptive to a radical message. In addition to campaigning and radical political education, students had a role in facilitating the organisation of black workers. This might run counter to some of the tenets of Black Consciousness. However, racial identity as an exclusive basis for strategy and explanation was not adequate unless integrated with a view incorporating class interests.

* * *

Charles Nupen, incoming Nusas president for 1974, summarised the main themes that had emerged at the seminar.[25] Nusas saw no necessary contradiction between being supportive of Black Consciousness in the arena of student politics and at the same time initiating activity in predominantly black constituencies, notably among factory workers.

At the same time, Charles argued that students needed to start defining the sort of society they were fighting for, moving away from vague consensus formulations such as 'equal, democratic and just'. Asking whether socialism or capitalism best captured long-term goals of radicals, Charles called for a more specific conception 'of the type of society we want. With a definite goal we can assess the relevance of our activity and critically examine its direction.'

Student protest and campaigning had often been procedural and formal, involving resolutions calling on government to act in a certain way. Discarding this traditional approach as 'useless', Charles suggested that the formal motion 'constitutes no more than an appeal to the moral sensibilities and ethical standards of a government which has neither'. In similar vein, Nupen advised against overemphasising government attacks on Nusas and its leadership. 'We are subject to legalised violence and legalised repression ... [However], we must regard government intimidation as an occupational hazard which must not be allowed to materially affect our direction.' Liberal outrage against the actions of a repressive state distracted radicals from their programmes. An authoritarian and anti-democratic state should be expected to conduct itself in a repressive manner, and campaigning as if this somehow breached the rules of 'fair play' or the 'rule of law' involved fruitless and misdirected strategies.

* * *

The Nusas seminar had identified the central strategic issues facing the student left as it moved into 1974. These incorporated radical responses to Black Consciousness; white student involvement in worker organisation; the inadequacies of traditional liberal opposition and response; the roles and strategies of political campaigns; and the complex relationships between race and class interests. The Elgin seminar announced a key moment in the development of Nusas and the 'new' student left, and established the basis on which students on the Nusas campuses would challenge apartheid society in the next year.

5

The rediscovery of resistance

The Wits delegation to the December 1973 Nusas seminar arrived back in Johannesburg fired up and motivated. Broad acceptance for a 1974 campaign focusing on the history of opposition to apartheid had been secured. Seminar delegates had also supported a proposal to launch a campaign demanding the release of all political prisoners as a precondition for any negotiations to end apartheid.

The seminar had considered a range of responses to the challenges Black Consciousness posed and how these impacted on Nusas's involvement in projects and campaigns that involved black constituencies. The critique of established liberalism, both in terms of its content and strategies for change, had been deepened and elaborated. Now, with the rest of December ahead, it was time to develop detailed plans.

Shortly after returning to Johannesburg, I drafted a brief reportback on the seminar. This was distributed to the student leadership at Wits, together with Eddie Webster's paper on Black Consciousness and a few marginal notes I penned on the topic. These reflected a tentative grappling with issues of class and identity and the role of intellectuals in popular and working-class struggles.

Along with a number of close political colleagues, I had been influenced by the arguments of Georg Lukács, the Hungarian Marxist, that the working class could only advance from 'false consciousness' to 'class consciousness' with input from revolutionary intellectuals. This complemented Lenin's writings on the role of the vanguard party, Amilcar Cabral's views on class defection and class suicide of petty-bourgeois intellectuals, and Antonio Gramsci's prison writings on the relationship between classes and 'organic intellectuals'.[1]

The house I shared with a group of friends and political activists became a centre for discussions as we confronted socialist debates on class and class alliances, the vanguard role of students and intellectuals willing to identify with the working class, and how these issues related to our plans for the next year. Deep into the night, we discussed ways of linking socialist theory and practice in our political activities. By day, we returned to campus to plan the campaigns we had agreed to at the Nusas seminar.

During discussions at the 1973 seminar, the Wits delegation had argued that the 1974 political campaign should be preceded by a low-key but consistent build-up, aiming to deepen the political education and understanding of students and create a context for more informed participation and activism. This would focus on the history of opposition to apartheid, explaining the context in which leadership of organisations like the ANC, SACP and PAC had resolved to initiate or support sabotage campaigns and armed struggle.

Plans were also made to focus on the history of trade union organisation, from the Industrial and Commercial Union (ICU) to the Council of Non-European Trade Unions (Cnetu) and the Congress-aligned South African Congress of Trade Unions (Sactu). An examination of the National Committee of Liberation and African Resistance Movement and their strategic sabotage campaign in the early 1960s was also proposed. This was seen as particularly relevant to students, because of the links between past Nusas leaders and these groupings.

Some of the groundwork for what became known as the History of Opposition in South Africa campaign had been laid in a series written by Steven Friedman in the 1972 and 1973 editions of *Wits Student*, the weekly student newspaper. Friedman had recorded the history of trade unionism as well as most of the central campaigns of mass action in the 1950s. These included the women's protests against pass laws, the Defiance Campaign and the Congress of the People.

This political history had been well hidden from most students.

Publications that recorded these actions were banned, those who had led the campaigns were jailed or exiled, and the security apparatuses of the state viewed even an interest in those events as an indication of 'subversive' intent. Yet week after week, Friedman produced feature articles on this history of resistance. Readership of the newspaper soared. A print run of six thousand a week meant that almost every full-time student on campus was reading *Wits Student*.

For our History of Opposition in South Africa campaign, at least one event was planned for each week. The series would start with the white opposition political parties, whose leadership would be invited to speak on campus. The SRC would issue pamphlets critically evaluating their policies and practices. Over the weeks and months ahead, smaller seminars would be held on the history of trade unionism, the mass campaigns of the 1950s and the turn to armed struggle. These would be interspersed with occasional mass meeting on topics such as resistance to South Africa's administration of Namibia.

* * *

The security police were quick to respond. Early one January morning in 1974, a large contingent from John Vorster Square, led by Captain Arthur Benoni Cronwright, arrived at the SRC offices. They were armed with a warrant authorising them to search the offices and impound any documents relevant to an investigation into contraventions of the Terrorism, Suppression of Communism, Unlawful Organisations, Riotous Assemblies and Publications Acts. Charges, according to the warrant, were also being contemplated under the Native Administration Act of 1927, which prohibited incitement of hatred between the races.

I occupied a space at the end of the suite of SRC offices, and one of my presidential 'privileges' was that it had two doors. One gave access to the rest of the offices, while the other opened to an external corridor. As soon as my secretary alerted me to the presence of security police in the building, I locked the door between my office and the rest of the rooms occupied by the SRC, opened the external door, and called on students in the corridor to help move documents and files out. I locked filing cabinets, drawers and cupboards in an effort to delay, and if possible frustrate, the security police search.

This cat-and-mouse game continued for some time. Both my office and the filing cabinets remained locked. The security police sent a message to John Vorster Square to summon a locksmith. I handed my set of master keys to an SRC member, asking him to take them round to the front of the office and hide them with my secretary. The police remained unable to open the doors and drawers that interested them.

Finally, one of Cronwright's subordinates worked out that there was a separate corridor with access to my office, and stood outside the door waiting for it to open. As I began another transfer of files and documents, he forced his way in and summoned support from other police. A search began, and the report I had written on the Nusas seminar, together with copies of the Freedom Charter, Eddie Webster's seminar paper on Black Consciousness, and my files on the planning for the 1974 campaign, were added to the growing pile of documents for removal to Vorster Square.

In the days following the raid, there was concern that further police action might follow. I was not certain whether the security police were seriously engaged in building a case against student leadership, or whether the raid was a fishing expedition aimed more to intimidate than prosecute. Either way, the outcome was beyond my control, and there seemed little point in dwelling on police actions. They were to be expected: we could not characterise South Africa as a repressive state and then be surprised when police acted against opposition.

Planning activities for the year ahead continued uninterrupted. The vice-chancellor, Professor Bozzoli, called me in, asked whether I thought security police might act against the student leadership group, and suggested I consider moderating the SRC's political profile. I tried to reassure him, pointing out that nothing the police had confiscated in the raid was of a clandestine or illegal nature, and that I doubted whether material seized could lead to any successful prosecution.

The university had granted me special permission to defer my final examination in the single subject needed to complete my undergraduate degree. I was due to sit for this in mid-January. Bozzoli offered to postpone the exam for another few weeks because he was certain that the raid had disrupted my studying. This was something of an exaggeration, as I had not yet started any preparation for this final academic hurdle. However, I accepted his generous offer without thought. The exam was rescheduled for the end of January. To my dismay, I soon discovered that it now fell on a day I was due to travel to Cape Town for a Nusas meeting. My decision to attend the meeting, and abandon the exam, was an easy one. Its consequences became more complicated when I boarded my flight to find Professor Bozzoli in the seat in front of me, *en route* to a meeting of university principals. To his credit, he made no comment on the fact that I was scheduled to be writing my final exam that day. After a brief exchange of information on our respective reasons for travelling to Cape Town, we settled into an uneasy silence for the rest of the flight.

* * *

A general election for white voters had been called for 1974, and this created the opportunity to examine the policies, practices and interests of the parliamentary opposition parties. Although there was some support for the tiny Progressive Party on the Nusas campuses, white parliamentary politics were severely compromised and none of the opposition parties could claim to represent the aspirations and interests of anything more than a small minority of South Africans.

Gordon Waddell, one of the senior Anglo American executives who had met with students during our occupation of the company's head office in 1973, was running as a Progressive Party candidate in Johannesburg. He asked me if the SRC would support his campaign. At a meeting with him and his campaign manager, Tony Bloom, I explained why I did not believe that the Progressive Party offered a credible alternative for students. This engagement compelled me to think more carefully about how students would respond to the forthcoming election, and I proposed to the Nusas National Council that we issue a communiqué on student participation in the electoral process. This would not advise them how or if to vote, but raise questions about the nature of parliamentary opposition and whites-only elections.

The proposal stirred up considerable controversy among the members of National Council. Some of the presidents of affiliated SRCs had links with the Progressive Party, and Nusas regularly invited Helen Suzman to speak at student gatherings, to assist in liaison with government, and to take up the cases of student leaders denied passports, arrested or detained. Suzman had been an honorary vice-president of Nusas and was unwavering in her defence of human rights. Despite differences in approach, she often supported Nusas in times of sustained attack by the government and its security forces.

At the same time, many in the student leadership were deeply critical of the Progressives' market-driven economic policy, the proposal for a qualified franchise, and the party's relationship to monopoly capital (especially Anglo American). The development of the Wages Commissions, which were challenging wage levels and policies on trade unionism, was throwing relations between Nusas and the Progs into even sharper relief.

After a tense debate at National Council, Nusas issued a carefully worded communiqué expressing 'grave reservations about the electoral and parliamentary process'. It noted that 'Less than one quarter of the population was entitled to cast a vote, that democracy could only begin to function on the basis of a universal franchise and that no white political party could claim to represent the true interest of black South Africans'. Labelling the politics of the major political parties contesting the election as 'white supremacist', Nusas encouraged students 'to decide whether to vote in terms of what they ascertained from questioning candidates and from studying the policies of the parties'.[2]

It was a compromise statement, reflecting efforts to straddle political differences within Nusas. Some representatives on National Council had wanted to call on white students to boycott the election, and attack the Progressive Party's economic policies and links to white capitalism. Others argued that we should draw attention to banned organisations with historical legitimacy in representing the disenfranchised. This would have further challenged political parties claiming the mantle of opposition to apartheid. The eventual statement was relatively mild. Students were being advised to inform themselves, ask questions, think about the issues, and then decide how or if to vote.

The reactions from established liberalism were disproportionate, if predictable. The editor of *The Star* newspaper suggested that Nusas had a 'death wish'. Helen Suzman flew into a fury, and two senior Nusas office-bearers went to see her at home, taking a bouquet of flowers as a peace offering. Suzman – quite rightly in my view – threw them and their flowers out. They had no mandate to see her and apologise, and the issues in dispute involved deep differences in political interests and strategies. Bunches of flowers would not change this.

* * *

The History of Opposition series opened with a focus on the political parties contesting the white general election. The first of these events took the form of a mass meeting in the Wits Great Hall, addressed by a leading United Party MP, Gideon Jacobs, who represented the Hillbrow constituency in Johannesburg.

Prior to the meeting, the SRC issued a pamphlet entitled 'The aims and principles of the United Party'. This was the 'official opposition' in the white parliament which had infuriated student leadership when it participated in the Schlebusch Commission of Inquiry into Nusas and three other organisations. The report of this commission led to the banning of eight Nusas leaders, officials and supporters. While the inquiry was being conducted, Wits students had targeted UP members of the commission, heckling and asking questions at meetings they addressed. A particularly memorable meeting involved the Schlebusch commissioner Etienne Malan, the United Party MP for

Orange Grove. I was part of a group which went to heckle him at a constituency meeting held at the Sandringham High School. Students climbed onto the roof of a school structure to be able to see Malan better and heckle without physical interference from his supporters. When the roof began collapsing, the meeting soon followed its example. The disaster – as far as Malan's re-election campaign was concerned – was compounded when a photographer caught him with his right arm raised to his supporters in what looked suspiciously like a Nazi salute.

Our attitude to the UP was well demonstrated in the image of two pigs which headed the pamphlet we issued on the party's policy. SRC comment was particularly critical of UP economic policy, arguing that it aimed to ensure 'the most efficient working of the capitalist system' and said nothing about an 'equitable redistribution of wealth'. We challenged the UP over its support of a 'free enterprise economy' which 'in no way entails a guarantee against exploitation. This is particularly so in South Africa, where all the wealth and the control of the means of production rests in white hands.' With one eye on the upcoming campaign for the release of all political prisoners, we asked the UP whether the political consultation it proposed in its policy would be with 'leaders of apartheid institutions … or with the true leaders of black South Africa, most of whom are banned or on Robben Island'.[3]

Anticipating drama, students packed the Great Hall. They were not disappointed. A cardboard sheep was lowered from the rafters to hang behind the speakers on stage. It was manipulated like a puppet to nod whenever Jacobs said anything particularly asinine. He could not see what was happening and became increasingly perplexed at the outbursts of laughter and clapping which accompanied some of his comments. This 'guerrilla theatre' had been organised by Aquarius, the cultural wing of Nusas, and expressed fairly accurately the views of the thousand-plus students gathered to hear what apartheid's 'official opposition' had to say.

The next event involved a political party that had recently broken away from the National Party. It had been formed under the leadership of the former Minister of the Interior, Theo Gerdener, and named the Democratic Party. The Great Hall was again packed to capacity. In a background pamphlet, the SRC criticised Gerdener's party for its 'two stream policy' in which coloureds and Indians would be 'assimilated' into the 'white group', while Africans would be granted 'political control of the Homelands, and of areas with a large urban African population'. What, asked the SRC, 'makes white society, with its arrogance, prejudices and exploitative ethic, such an attractive thing to be assimilated into?' The aim of Democratic Party policy, concluded the SRC, was to weaken the 'solid front of black opposition [to apartheid] that is developing'; while Africans would be forced into 'politically independent but totally unviable fragments of land'.[4]

As Minister of the Interior, Gerdener had been responsible for the state department that issued travel documents. During question time, Athol Margolis ambushed him: did his party believe in freedom of movement? Oh yes, responded Gerdener. How then, asked Athol, do you justify withdrawing the passport of our SRC president, Glenn Moss? The audience broke into a combination of laughter, cat-calls and heckling, and Gerdener's tarnished reputation faded even further.

The United and Democratic parties were easy targets. Few students saw them as viable alternatives to National Party rule. Their policies, practices and leadership were identified with a conservatism and paternalistic racism that were deeply unattractive to modern students. The next in the series – the Progressive Party – presented much more of a challenge. Considerably more sophisticated than the UP and DP, the Progs had strong support from many liberal students.

The party sent Gordon Waddell to present their case as a party of opposition. Although it had only one sitting MP, its influence was far more extensive, partly because of its relationship to English mining capital and business. A Scottish and British Lions rugby player, Waddell had married the daughter of Harry and Bridget Oppenheimer, settled in South Africa, and been appointed to a senior management position in Anglo American. He was the Progressive Party's candidate for Johannesburg North, a constituency that was home to numbers of Wits students and their parents.

The SRC's pamphlet on Progressive Party policy set out, in some detail, the student left's critique of liberal economic policy. It acknowledged that the Progs were committed to the formal freedoms and rights: 'the abolition of compulsory segregation; a Bill of Rights to guarantee freedom of speech, worship and assembly; equal access to the courts; and equal protection of the law. They promise equality of opportunity.'

However, continued the SRC's pamphlet,

> To talk of a 'free economic system' and 'equality of opportunity' in a situation where, through historical circumstances, the vast majority of the people are exploited and suppressed, is merely to talk of exploitation under another name. Equality of opportunity only has meaning in redistribution of material resources. Without this, phrases like 'equal access to the courts' and 'equal protection before the law' mean nothing other than that justice is as available to all as bed and breakfast at the Carlton Hotel – you have to be able to pay for it!

And so on to the qualified franchise, the party's Achilles' heel. It was the reason some liberals would not support the Progs after the Liberal Party, with its policy of universal franchise, had been forced to disband. The Progs' policy, argued the SRC, had to be seen within the context of the party's economic policy:

> One only qualifies for the 'A' voters roll if one has a standard eight education or a standard six and the income of a semi-skilled worker. Merit becomes coterminous with opulence. The poor and the exploited, those who suffer most at the hands of the system, may only have a token role in decision making ...
>
> The Progressive Party, perhaps unwittingly, puts forward a programme of subtle psychological totalitarianism, aimed at lining the pockets of big business by streamlining the present system of exploitation. They make no provision to redistribute South Africa's wealth, and in a situation of economic exploitation, the personal

liberties described in Progressive policy are worse than meaningless: they camouflage the true totalitarian essence of their policy.[5]

In the hours before Waddell was due to speak, another pamphlet appeared on campus, issued by 'The good fairies of Braamfontein'. This had been compiled by members of the Wages Commission who had been researching conditions on the mines. Under the heading 'Gordon Waddell – a beacon of humanity', the 'good fairies' pointed out that the average cash wage for a black mineworker was R40 a month, while the minimum wage for a white general mineworker was R350 a month. There were no unions for black workers on the mines. Anglo profits were expected to rise from R58 million to R2150 million in 1974. In the previous year, the gold price rose by 327 per cent, while wages for black mineworkers rose by 26 per cent. 'This', wrote the good fairies, 'is what Mr Waddell stands for. This is what his party stands for. Are you prepared to vote for this?'[6]

The meeting was predictably chaotic. One group of students heckled Waddell, shouted out questions, and aggressively challenged him on Prog policy and Anglo practice. Others applauded his defence of a qualified franchise and free-market capitalism. Educating students to reject the self-serving and racist nonsense offered by the United and Democratic parties was relatively easy. Challenging the more sophisticated Progressive Party, with its championing of liberalism and market capitalism, revealed the fault lines between the radical student leadership and many in the more liberal student body.

A photograph taken at this meeting, and published in *Wits Student*, depicts Waddell addressing the meeting, with a banner erected behind him proclaiming that

> The wages of its [Anglo's] black workers range from R20.60 to R104 a month. The average wage stands at R40 a month.
> Waddell is directly responsible for this state of affairs ...
> On humanitarian grounds he is a criminal.

A recruitment advertisement for Anglo appeared on the same page:

> Do you have those special qualities Anglo American
> is looking for?
> Graduates with drive and initiative can make their careers in the
> Anglo American Corp.[7]

This juxtaposition captured the contradictory position of students at institutions like Wits particularly well.

* * *

Two unusual candidates were nominated in the 1974 general election for whites. Chris Wood had been banned in 1973, one of the Nusas leaders identified for state action in the Schlebusch Commission's interim report. The Alliance for Radical Change (ARC) had nominated him for the Rondebosch constituency in Cape Town, where the United Party leader, Sir De Villiers Graaff, had been returned to parliament unopposed in a number of previous elections. As a banned person, Chris could not address meetings, attend gatherings or be quoted. In the unlikely event of his being elected, he would not be permitted to take his seat in parliament. The campaign run on his behalf was a statement of protest and a way of presenting radical alternatives to the narrow spectrum of white politics.

In Johannesburg, Peter Randall had agreed to run in the Von Brandis constituency as a candidate for social democracy. As with Chris Wood, his aim was not to win the seat, but to present an alternative political vision to white voters. Von Brandis had been a safe United Party seat for years. In challenging the incumbent, Randall also aimed to expose the poverty of the official opposition's policies and practices.

Peter accepted the invitation to speak as part of our focus on opposition, not only as a candidate in the upcoming general election, but also as an educationalist deeply critical of the structure and content of South Africa's education systems. A full lecture theatre heard Randall challenge the capitalist underpinnings of the existing political parties, and put forward an alternative vision of society based on social democratic principles of participation, social welfare, redistribution and production for social benefit rather than profit.

Von Brandis included the Braamfontein area, where I lived. For the only time before 1994, I had reason to vote in a parliamentary election. Access to the polling station at the Johannesburg College of Education involved a journey up a steep hill from my Braamfontein flat. I set off with a friend in my dangerously dilapidated 1965 Simca motor car. The Hoofd Street hill which had to be negotiated proved too much for the aged vehicle, and it stalled halfway up, then refused to restart. Walking the rest of the way, the two of us arrived sweaty and dishevelled, ready to cast our votes in the name of socialist democracy. Imagine our fury when we were denied ballot papers by a polling official, because he claimed our names were not on the voters' roll. After intervention from a party agent, our names were found, and the votes duly cast.

The Randall campaign was never aimed at winning votes, but at presenting political alternatives. To general surprise, including that of the candidate and his electoral agent, Horst Kleinschmidt, Peter received over a thousand votes, more than sufficient to save the deposit he had been required to put up to run as a candidate in the election.

Some students living at university residences, and in Braamfontein next to the university, were eligible to vote in the Von Brandis constituency. Randall's team concluded that many of the votes cast for their candidate came from those areas. If anything close to a thousand Wits students had voted in favour of a social democratic alternative to apartheid, it was likely that many of them had been influenced by the History of Opposition series which the SRC had been running during the first few months of the year.

* * *

By 1974, South Africa's illegal occupation of Namibia had started gaining increased attention on the Nusas campuses, as more and more students called up for compulsory military service were being stationed in the territory.

John Dugard, then a senior law professor at Wits, had recently published an influential book on the politico-legal dispute surrounding South Africa's administration of the country. I had been particularly taken by a statement from the dock delivered by Herman Andimba Toivo ja Toivo, a co-founder of the South West Africa People's Organisation (Swapo), which was reproduced in Dugard's book. Toivo had been part of a group illegally detained under South Africa's Terrorism Act and transported to Pretoria for interrogation and trial. His moving statement captured the core of Swapo's opposition to South African rule in Namibia and his own role in that resistance. Presumably the judge presiding over the trial, Justice Ludorf, was less moved by the statement than I was, for he sentenced Toivo to 20 years' imprisonment, and 19 of the other accused to life imprisonment.[8]

Dugard regularly made himself available to address students on human rights issues in general, and the Namibian conflict in particular. He had both spoken and written about the International Court of Justice's 1971 ruling that South Africa's occupation of Namibia was illegal. Interest on campus in the Namibian struggle, and opposition to South African rule, was growing. It was logical to extend the focus on opposition, and the campaign to release political prisoners, to include Namibia.

Clemens Kapuuo, an Herero leader from Namibia, was invited to address students on the Namibian conflict. He was a prominent opponent of South Africa's efforts to impose bantustan-type policies in Namibia. Elected as a chief by the Herero people, he was not recognised by the South African authorities. Kapuuo represented the Herero group on the National Convention, a co-ordinating structure which included internal representatives of Swapo and the South West Africa National Union (Swanu). However, relations between Kapuuo's National Unity Democratic Organisation (Nudo), on the one hand, and Swapo and Swanu, on the other, were uneasy. Nudo did not support military struggle, campaigning rather for internationalisation of the dispute through petitions and representations to the United Nations.

I anticipated some reaction from right-wingers on campus,

especially those who had served in the Defence Force in Namibia. Even using that name for the country, rather than 'South West Africa', was seen as provocative, as it aligned us with those opposed to South Africa's presence in the territory. The ignorance of many students was well captured in an incident that occurred while I was putting up posters advertising Kapuuo's speech. A crowd had gathered, and some of the students were becoming abusive. I was explaining the SRC's support for the use of the name 'Namibia', when one of the students asked, bewildered, 'Where is this Nambia [sic] place anyway, and what has it got to do with South Africa?'

The SRC's background pamphlet for the Kapuuo meeting focused on the history of Herero opposition to subjugation. This included the 1904 revolt against German administration and the subsequent genocide of the Herero; resistance to the confiscation of Herero land and its allocation to settler farmers; regular petitions to the United Nations requesting the removal of the South African presence; and Kapuuo's opposition to setting up an apartheid-style tribal authority to replace the elected chieftaincy.

Hosting a black dignitary was by no means easy. Black guests could not be put up at any of Johannesburg's ordinary hotels, with only the 'international' hotel at Jan Smuts airport admitting people of colour as guests, at exorbitant rates. Jack Unterhalter, a senior counsel at the Johannesburg Bar, and his wife, Beryl, agreed to accommodate Kapuuo at their home during the visit to Johannesburg. I wanted to take them out for dinner in appreciation, but apartheid laws did not allow black and white to be served in the same restaurant. Only the 'international restaurant' at Jan Smuts airport allowed for this, and we had to take our guest and his hosts there before we were permitted to sit at a table together over a meal.

Kapuuo's presence raised campus awareness of South Africa's illegal administration of Namibia, and it was partly as a result of this that we invited a Namibian leader to address our subsequent campaign on political prisoners, and focused on Toivo in publications to accompany it.

* * *

Over the next two months, the SRC organised meetings and seminars every week. Guest speakers introduced students to a history they did not know, through lectures and discussion on political opposition and resistance to segregation and apartheid. Tom Lodge led a seminar on Sharpeville, the PAC and Poqo; Philip Bonner gave a series of talks on the history of trade unionism, as well as ANC campaigns in the 1950s and the decision to initiate armed struggle; Alf Stadler spoke on land invasions and squatter movements as a form of resistance to apartheid's urban policies. Michael Nupen lectured on the role of different ideologies, including Marxism and liberalism, in South African political opposition. A former editor of *The Star* newspaper, René de Villiers, introduced students to the place of the Liberal Party in resistance politics of the 1960s. John Dugard delivered a lunch-time lecture on why South Africa's presence in Namibia was a contravention of international law.

Each week brought new knowledge and a deeper political focus for those attending these meetings. More and more students were being exposed to a political education that was largely absent from their university courses, from the newspapers and magazines they read, or the radio news and commentaries which were a feature of every white South African home.

6
Release all political prisoners

Delegates to Nusas's December 1973 national seminar had identified two campaign areas for 1974: the history of opposition to apartheid, and a call for the release of all political prisoners as a precondition for negotiating an end to apartheid.

These two focus areas were part of an integrated strategy. Understanding the changing nature of resistance formed a necessary background to the imprisonment of credible political leaders who would have to represent the majority of South Africans in any negotiations process or national convention.

The situation of political prisoners had been raised by Mewa Ramgobin during 1971. A former SRC president at the University of Natal, Ramgobin had been banned in 1965. When this restriction order expired in 1970, he immediately threw himself back into political activism.

As part of its celebration of ten years of a Republic, the government had announced that it would be granting clemency to selected categories of common-law prisoners. Ramgobin formed a Committee for Clemency, which aimed to use the anniversary of South Africa's declaration as a Republic to appeal for clemency for political prisoners. Committee members included Rick Turner, Archbishop Denis Hurley and Sonny Leon.[1]

Although the campaign focused attention on political prisoners, its 'plea for clemency' did not address the role of imprisoned leadership in South Africa's future, and reflected the exceptionally narrow boundaries within which opposition politics functioned at the time. However, even the moderation of this plea did not protect Mewa from state action, and he was issued with a new banning order late in 1971.

* * *

The Nusas campaign to release all political prisoners, which was launched during May 1974, differed notably from previous Nusas actions. It was not driven by the politics of protest, in which students reacted to state attacks on civil liberties, human rights or the universities. Rather, its focus on imprisoned leaders was designed to broaden debate about political alternatives to apartheid.

Campaigning for the participation of imprisoned leaders in a political process raised questions about the programmes and policies of the organisations they had led. The Freedom Charter, as the most developed statement of the sort of society the liberation movements envisaged, was central to any discussion of the future, and ways had to be found to place it in the public domain.

The campaign planned to test legal limits and boundaries. Since the early 1960s, it had become increasingly dangerous to show an interest in the liberation movements, their policies, programmes, actions and leaders. Focusing on these organisations and their leadership would test the parameters of above-ground opposition and establish the degree to which public political campaigns could be undertaken without repressive consequences.

The aims of the campaign were clear, but how best to implement them? Who could speak at the series of mass meetings scheduled for the last week of May 1974? Identification of appropriate speakers was no easy process. Many of those who would be prepared to participate were themselves banned or listed, and could either not speak at public gatherings or not be quoted in any publication. Yet we needed speakers with a sufficiently high public profile to attract students to meetings, and for their messages to be taken seriously by the media.

We faced another dilemma. A number of people associated with state-created institutions, such as bantustan and tribal authorities and the Urban Bantu and coloured and Indian councils, had spoken out in support of the release of political prisoners. They included Buthelezi and Sonny Leon, who had led the Labour Party in the Coloured Persons' Representative Council. These leaders had credibility among some sections of the disenfranchised, but were rejected by others because of their involvement in institutions created to advance apartheid policy.

On a trip to Natal in 1973, Congress supporters advised me that the ANC-in-exile was discussing strategic alliances with potentially sympathetic bantustan leaders, especially KwaZulu's Buthelezi, who had been an ANC member in the 1950s. He had called for the release of political prisoners and seemed sympathetic to the unbanning of prohibited organisations so that they could participate in a political process. At the same time, he was now the head of a 'homeland' government administration, even though he had made it clear that he would not accept the sort of nominal 'independence' which was subsequently imposed on Transkei, Ciskei, Venda and Bophuthatswana.

I began a complicated dance with Buthelezi and his office, after I extended an invitation to him to open our campaign. Initially, he was enthusiastic. However, over the next few weeks, officials from his office began calling me, and asking questions about the campaign and the role envisaged for Buthelezi. Communication was not easy. There were no faxes or cellphones, and the telephone lines to the area where Buthelezi had his offices were of poor quality. Finally, someone in his office gave me his home number and suggested I call him there one night. There was no direct dialling to Nongoma, where he lived, so I had to book a long-distance trunk call through the exchange. After a less-than-satisfactory conversation, punctuated by interruptions as a result of primitive technology and the security agencies listening in on the call, Buthelezi indicated that he was no longer available on the date we had previously agreed to.

A cabinet minister in the Lebowa homeland administration, Collins Ramusi, had been building a reputation as an outspoken individual sympathetic to the national liberation movements. He had recently called for the release of political prisoners and the unbanning of the ANC and PAC, and I tried to make contact with him at his offices in Seshego. Again, communication proved difficult. Finally I received a message that he could meet me at his Lebowa office, deep in the Northern Transvaal.

Early one morning, I set off on the long drive to Seshego in the SRC's kombi, accompanied by my close colleague Cedric de Beer and another SRC member, Derek Brune. The 'capital' of the Lebowa bantustan was less than impressive. Mini-gorges carrying waste water ran down the sides of the gravel roads, and our vehicle left a trail of dust in its wake as we roamed the area, looking for the 'government' offices. The one tarred road was deeply pot-holed and had to be negotiated at walking pace.

Finally, we came to a set of prefabricated buildings clustered together behind a sagging wire fence. This was the centre of government for the 'self-governing' territory of Lebowa. Paths overgrown with weeds meandered between the cabin-like buildings. Nobody challenged us as we wandered around, occasionally asking passersby where we might find the offices of Collins Ramusi. Eventually we were directed to a low rectangular building raised above the ground on bricks. We walked up the shaky wooden stairs, knocked on the door and entered. Seated behind a desk was Collins Ramusi, and he invited us to sit down on the canvas camp chairs in front of his desk.

I set out the background to the political prisoners campaign and asked him if he would open it on the Wits campus. Ramusi seemed to be uncomfortable, almost embarrassed. Then he explained that the internal politics of the Lebowa administration made it difficult for him to accept such an invitation. However, he was certain that his 'leader', Chief Minister Cedric Phatudi, would be honoured to open our campaign.

Ramusi lifted the old telephone on his desk and dialled a single number. Then he put it down. 'The lines are still not working,' he explained. He ushered us out of his office to a brick structure nearby and into a reception area. Knocking on the door behind the vacant reception desk, he opened it and led us into Phatudi's rather more opulent office, with its carpets, large desk and upholstered chairs.

Phatudi had clearly been briefed on the purpose of our visit and, after a few pleasantries, and without being asked, accepted the 'invitation' to speak on the Wits campus on behalf of his 'government'. We had been railroaded into having our campaign kicked off by a low-profile bantustan leader of little credibility.

The remaining speakers fell into place with less difficulty. Helen Joseph was no longer under draconian banning and house arrest orders, but was still listed under the Suppression of Communism Act and therefore could not be quoted. She had been a Treason trialist, and a close confidante of ANC leaders such as Mandela and Govan Mbeki. Detained during the 1960 state of emergency, Helen had been one of the leaders of the 1956 women's march, which had seen twenty thousand people gather at Pretoria's Union Buildings in protest against the planned extension of pass laws to African women.

Banned in 1957, she was the first South African to be placed under house arrest in 1962 and remained under severe restrictions until 1971, when most of the conditions were lifted after she was diagnosed with cancer. Helen immediately threw herself back into oppositional activism, became a close friend of Nusas and the student movement, and was an important link to the elders of the Congress Alliance still in South Africa. She had been elected honorary president of Nusas but, as a listed person, was unable to accept this nomination: Nusas resolved to leave the post vacant and declared her 'honorary un-president'.

A couple of years earlier, in the course of a public meeting at Wits, Helen had rescued me from a difficult situation. It was 1972, and Lilian Ngoyi, past president of the ANC Women's League and one of the leaders of the 1956 women's march, had been unbanned. Through Helen, I approached Lilian to break her years of enforced silence and speak to students. Helen and Lilian, as banned people, had not been permitted to communicate for over a decade, under threat of imprisonment. Helen had a treasured scarf belonging to Lilian, which she often wore as a symbol of their extremely close friendship and shared history.

After extensive publicity and an explanation of Lilian's central place in the struggle against apartheid, we had a hall full of excited and expectant students. For many, this would be the first time they would hear one of the iconic Congress Alliance leaders of the 1950s speak. This was a person who had stood shoulder to shoulder with the giants of Robben Island, the men of the Rivonia trial, the leaders of the MK and communist underground – Mandela, Sisulu, Mbeki, Fischer and many others.

Briefing MaNgoyi before the meeting, I asked how her long she would speak for: 45 minutes, I heard. Perfect for a lunch-time meeting. The Great Hall was hushed as she stepped up to the microphone. But after a short and uncertain talk, she sat down, and I realised with horror that she had said she would speak for four to five minutes, not 45 – understandable for someone who had not been permitted to speak in public for over a decade. I wondered how to rescue the situation, and my eyes fell on Helen Joseph sitting in the audience. 'We are privileged to have one of Lilian's closest comrades with us today,' I improvised. 'I see she is wearing Lilian's scarf, the symbol of their enduring friendship over years of enforced isolation from each other. I wonder if I could ask Helen Joseph to tell us something about her life and times with Lilian in the struggle.'

Helen captured and captivated the audience for the next 40 minutes, telling the stories of their time in the Treason Trial, of the Congress of the People and the 1956 women's march, their friendship with Mandela and other ANC leaders, of meetings and arrest and jail.

In the political prisoners campaign of 1974, Helen was scheduled to share a platform with Aelred Stubbs, an Anglican monk. He had been principal of the Federal Seminary near Alice, where a number of early BC leaders had been among his students. In the early 1970s Stubbs had become a close friend, mentor and confidant of Steve Biko.

Some of the other speakers for the week had been invited by Nusas's national leadership and were due to address campaign meetings at both UCT and Wits. Gerson Veii was a founder member of the South West Africa National Union (Swanu), who had served five years on Robben Island at a time when Swanu was organising military opposition to South Africa's administration of Namibia. Veii was Swanu's representative on the internal National Convention, which had demanded the immediate withdrawal of South Africa from the territory. His presence as a speaker strengthened the focus on Namibia initiated when Clemens Kapuuo – also a member of the National Convention – spoke during the History of Opposition lead-up to the campaign.

Sonny Leon, chair of the Labour Party, was also due to speak. Although compromised in the eyes of some because of his party's presence in an apartheid institution, he had moved closer to a younger group of Black Consciousness adherents and had been a prominent supporter of Mewa Ramgobin's campaign for clemency in 1971. Leon was becoming more and more outspoken about the need to release political prisoners and in his criticism of apartheid as an institutional system. Nonetheless, there was some ambiguity about his presence as a politician associated with 'coloured' rather than national politics, and his leadership of a party which participated in an apartheid-created council.

* * *

In the days leading up to the campaign, the *Rand Daily Mail* published a number of reports on Nusas's planned activities. Tony Holiday wrote that 'much activity this week will centre on political prisoners serving sentences on Robben Island and on people restricted by banning and house arrest orders'. The campaign, he continued, 'rests on the argument that all talk of a national dialogue on South Africa's future is meaningless while men like Nelson Mandela, Walter Sisulu and Robert Sobukwe are prevented from participating in it. These people, say the campaigners, are still regarded as leaders by the country's Black majority.'[2]

The next day, the newspaper reported that Nusas had received substantial international support for the campaign. The exiled cultural activist Breyten Breyenbach and the human rights lawyer Joel Carlson contacted Nusas leaders to express support. Endorsements arrived from student organisations in Mozambique, the United Kingdom, Australia and the United States. The World Union of Jewish Students sent a strong message of support for the campaign, as did the World Confederation of Labour.[3]

Campaign implementation began on Sunday 26 May, when a group of students spent the afternoon putting up hundreds of 'Release all political prisoners' posters and stickers on the campus, and erected a large banner making the same call. By early next morning, most of these had been pulled down, presumably by members of the student right and their associates from John Vorster Square.

I had arrived on campus early on Monday morning, intending to hand out pamphlets promoting the campaign. Instead, we began re-erecting the banner and again putting up posters and the large red stickers with the 'Release all political prisoners' message. By mid-morning, the campus was again covered in campaign media, and we began distributing the first of a series of pamphlets prepared for the week.

The call to release political prisoners, we told students, had been supported by people like Gatsha Buthelezi and Cedric Phatudi, Collins Ramusi and Sonny Leon.

> The international community, including the United Nations, is almost unanimous in its call for the release of all South African political prisoners. Both the SRC and NUSAS have received numerous messages of support from international organisations who have noted the campaign, and at a time when authorities in South Africa are becoming increasingly rigid in their repression, international solidarity is of some comfort ...
>
> It is not ... on the basis of clemency that we call for their release:
> - It is because white South Africa, by its repression, exploitation and racism, forced these people to defy laws;
> - It is because many prisoners were convicted on the basis of evidence of witnesses who had been held in solitary confinement for months

by Security Police, and whose evidence must therefore be suspect;
- It is because the present political prisoners worked peacefully for years, but were frustrated and brutally repressed by whites at every turn ...
- It is because the release of political prisoners would be the first act which would prove that whites are really concerned to find a real solution to racist exploitation, based on negotiation with the true leaders of the oppressed.[4]

Reference to support from prominent people who worked within 'the system' again reflected the ambiguity in our choice of speakers and supporters. Phatudi and Leon were moderates, compromised politically in the eyes of some on the left. Yet it was difficult to find a sufficient number of progressive public voices to champion the call, because so many were silenced by banning and listings, imprisonment, banishment and exile, and because of the well-founded fear that participation in such a campaign might have serious consequences. Security police had raided the Wits SRC offices in search of evidence that the campaign plans contravened a range of laws. They often intimidated and harassed opponents of apartheid in other ways. Late-night phone calls and threats, damage to property, interception of mail, withdrawal of passports, and pressure on employers to rid themselves of 'troublesome' individuals had become common occurrences. Speaking out in support of a call to release Mandela, Sisulu, Mbeki, Fischer, Toivo and all other political prisoners so that they could participate in political processes was undoubtedly dangerous and required courage.

* * *

The campaign publicity had done its job, and by lunch-time the Great Hall was packed beyond capacity, with over 1300 students in the aisles and standing areas and flowing out of the hall's back and side doors. Then our induced 'choice' of an opening speaker revealed itself for what it was – a mistake. Phatudi refused to extend his call to the release of *all* political prisoners, distinguishing between 'communistically oriented' and 'democratically oriented' prisoners. Only the second grouping should be released, he asserted.

Campaign '74 seemed to be deflating before our eyes. The audience had been stunned into near-silence, and Phatudi's speech was met with lukewarm and polite applause. Most students left the hall immediately the speech ended and missed the awesome sight of Helen Joseph leaping onto the stage and asking whether he seriously meant that Govan Mbeki, a lifelong communist, should not be released. 'Do you mean Govan should not come out?' she shouted, as she repeatedly poked his chest with her outstretched finger.

The remaining students moved out to the Jan Smuts Avenue border between campus and Braamfontein, and staged a picket calling for the release of all prisoners. 'But the pall hanging over campus after Phatudi's speech was heavy, and the picket broke up after an hour.'[5]

That night, I met with a number of other student leaders and campaign organisers to discuss how we could repair the damage done by our opening event. We decided to move Tuesday's lunchtime meeting to the open air piazza in front of the Great Hall. This more informal space was likely to attract greater numbers of students because of its easy access and location right in the middle of campus. Almost every student and staff member would pass close to the area at some stage during lunch-time.

Aelred Stubbs from the Community of the Resurrection had been asked to speak about 'the country of the banned'. Although not in formal jails, those banned, banished and house-arrested were also political prisoners and numbered among their ranks leaders of the Congress Alliance, Liberal Party, Pan Africanist Congress and Unity Movement. On the day of Stubbs's speech, the Institute of Race Relations revealed that 1240 people had been banned or placed under house arrest since the first actions under the Suppression of Communism Act in 1951.[6] The student movement itself had lost 16 key personnel to banning in 1973, including Saso and Nusas past and serving presidents Steve Biko, Barney Pityana, Neville Curtis and Paul Pretorius.

Stubbs raised a cheer when he announced that Manas Buthelezi, the Natal regional director of the Christian Institute, had just been released from his banning order. Stubbs expressed the hope that Sobukwe would be released the following day, and Mandela the day after that.

In preparation for the campaign, I had asked a number of banned people whether I could announce that they were fasting in support of the campaign. This was difficult ground. If they communicated that they supported the campaign, they risked arrest and imprisonment for contravening their banning orders. If I repeated anything they had said to me, I faced the same dangers for quoting a banned person. I concluded that a simple announcement that certain people were fasting in support of the campaign might pass without legal consequence. And so, at this gathering, I reminded the audience that Helen Joseph, the next speaker, had been banned and house-arrested for many years, and was still listed. Then I announced that Indres Naidoo, recently released from Robben Island after serving a ten-year sentence for sabotage, and then banned and house-arrested, was fasting in support of the campaign. So was Steven Hayes, a priest who had been deported from Namibia before being banned to Pietermaritzburg.[7]

In her speech, Helen challenged Phatudi's distinction between releasing 'democratic' and 'communist' political prisoners. She referred to the Rivonia trial, where eight of the accused were 'convicted under the Sabotage Act, yet not one was convicted as a communist. But Govan Mbeki declared himself [to be a communist]. So where does that get you? Release Mandela and Sisulu, but leave Govan in jail for life? Or release Denis Goldberg, but leave Bram Fischer in jail for life?' What, she asked, about the use of violent methods of struggle? These were only adopted, she explained, 'after long, frustrating, disappointing years of non-violent struggle ... Was it any wonder that finally despair prevailed and non-violence was abandoned as useless?'[8]

Just before the meeting began, Helen told me that she had received a handwritten message of support from Robben Island and intended reading it out. Imprisoned leaders of the national liberation movement had learnt of the campaign, and through this message were expressing strong support for the student initiative.

This was a remarkable moment in the campaign. Somehow, through routes unknown, prisoners on Robben Island had sent a message of support for our campaign. When Helen read the message, she was conveying the words of Mandela, Sisulu, Kathrada and Mbeki. Phatudi had attempted to drive a wedge between 'democratically oriented' prisoners and 'declared communists'. Standing on the steps of the Great Hall, looking out over a piazza packed with students, Helen Joseph read out the words from communist, nationalist and non-racialist leaders who had not been heard for over a decade. She had limited the damage caused by Phatudi the day before, and brought students a message of solidarity and unity from the prisoners of Robben Island.

I watched Helen crumple up the sheet bearing the message and carefully place it in her pocket, presumably for later disposal. Reading it out had exposed her to possible prosecution for furthering the aims of the ANC and contravening the Prisons Act, and she was wisely destroying the physical evidence. There were no reports on the message from Robben Island, because quoting Helen, a listed person, was an offence which could lead to arrest, prosecution and imprisonment. The handwritten message on that crumpled sheet of paper was lost forever. But its contents surely continued to reverberate in the minds of those who heard it.

* * *

Groups of students fanned out from the meeting into the streets of Johannesburg, to distribute pamphlets printed in English, Zulu and Sotho. 'Students in Johannesburg and Cape Town have called for the release of political prisoners,' began the pamphlet.

> They have done so because many of them believe that men like Mandela are the true leaders of black people in South Africa.

If black men and women are to work for a new South Africa, where their children do not have to carry passes, and will be able to earn a living wage, then the leaders must be released ...

IF PASS RAIDS ARE TO END;
IF MEN ARE TO BE ABLE TO LIVE WITH THEIR WIVES AND CHILDREN;
IF COMFORT IS TO REPLACE POVERTY,

If these are to be so
THEN MANDELA, SISULU, MBEKI AND MANY OTHER PEOPLE WHO ARE IN JAIL BECAUSE OF THEIR FIGHT AGAINST APARTHEID MUST BE RELEASED.[9]

Pamphleting students were subject to considerable police attention. Uniformed police were joined by members of the security police, CID and the dog squad in efforts to confiscate pamphlets, search vehicles, impound film being taken of the action, and record the names and addresses of those handing out material. Black workers on the streets at the time, and especially those near the railway station in central Johannesburg, reacted with enthusiasm to the pamphlet's message.[10]

Prior to the campaign week, I had applied to the City Council for permission to hold a demonstration in support of the release of all political prisoners. This was the first phase of the legal requirement, in which permission had to be sought from the local authority and thereafter from the city's chief magistrate under the provisions of the Riotous Assemblies Act.

Late the previous week, the City Council had granted the required permission. However, on the afternoon before the day the march was due to take place, a letter arrived from the office of the chief magistrate, advising the SRC that 'permission for the holding of a street procession' had not been granted. Tony Holiday called me soon after, asking for a statement on this refusal to grant permission for a march. I remember him advising me to be very careful, because neither he as a journalist nor I as a student leader wanted to be accused of inciting students to break the law. 'The refusal of permission is, of course, in terms of the law,' I commented. 'This is just another example of unjust laws in South Africa.'

> The sooner students realise that in South Africa they are neither operating within a democracy nor a legal system based on justice, the sooner we will be able to change that system.
>
> As the people whose release we are calling for broke unjust laws in their attempts to create a just society, so students must realise that right and the law do not always coincide. The use of this Act is a clear example of this.[11]

* * *

During Gerson Veii's speech on the crowded piazza, I noticed a number of security police moving among the crowd, including two I recognised from the January raid on the SRC offices. I drew student attention to the presence of captains Cronwright and Van Niekerk, noted that they were monitoring the meeting, and invited them to step out from behind the trees they were using for cover. The security police were clearly agitated by this. They placed great reliance on being anonymous and able to infiltrate meetings. This was particularly absurd in the case of Cronwright, who sported a small Hitler-type moustache, and also for the enormous Van Niekerk (known by the name 'Tiny'), who looked like a caricature of a brutal police officer.

After identifying some of the other security police present, I told students that permission to stage a public demonstration in the city centre had been refused. The response was angry, and already groups of students were chanting 'March, march', similar to the call of those who had undertaken illegal defiance in 1970 over the continued detention of 'the 22'.

Many from the crowd moved off to Jan Smuts Avenue, and mounted the biggest demonstration of the campaign yet, lining the boundary between university property and Braamfontein. Soon a group broke away and began marching down Jan Smuts Avenue under a 'Release all political prisoners' banner.

I was in a difficult situation. As a student leader who had, in effect, advised students that unjust laws might have to be broken, I felt politically responsible for an illegal demonstration which could easily lead to violence and arrests. At the same time, I would be an obvious target if police decided to use extreme force to break up the march or even open fire on students. If charges were to follow, I was vulnerable to being singled out for special attention by police and prosecutors. All this was running through my mind as I joined the front line of the marchers. If I had any responsibility for what was happening, then I had to be part of the demonstration. We turned off Jan Smuts Avenue into Jorissen Street, and started moving towards the Civic Centre. Traffic was brought to a standstill as we marched along the middle of the road.

After a few minutes, one section of the march broke away and set off in another direction. Suddenly the main group seemed very small and vulnerable to attack from police or the white right-wingers gathering on the streets of Braamfontein. We turned round and marched back to rejoin the picket line.

A large contingent of police arrived at the picket, occupying the traffic island in the middle of Jan Smuts Avenue. As police gathered, so more students joined the demonstration. Suddenly a police offer called out something through a megaphone. 'Uniformed police then rushed on to the campus, seized students and dragged them to the waiting vans. In some cases several police were used to arrest a single student.'[12] Students who had retreated onto campus re-formed the picket line and, despite various skirmishes with police, the demonstration continued late into the afternoon, finally dispersing without any more arrests.

Meanwhile, another group had broken away from the picket line and moved towards town to hand out pamphlets calling for the release of prisoners. As they reached the city centre, an excited crowd of mainly black workers gathered around to read the pamphlets. Soon police arrived under the command of Colonel Theuns Swanepoel.

'Rooi Rus' had been chief interrogator for the security police and now headed the police's Flying Squad. There were 'ugly scenes at a pamphleting point in Noord Street (a transport hub for workers) where police used dogs to disperse Africans being handed pamphlets by students'.[13] Police also confiscated pamphlets, searched vehicles, took down names and addresses of students, and detained some for questioning.

* * *

Lunch-time the next day saw over a thousand students gathered on the piazza to hear Sonny Leon add his voice to the call for the release of political prisoners. As his talk progressed, I became aware of the steady arrival of more and more security police. We intended to undertake a mass pamphlet campaign after the meeting, aiming to distribute ten thousand pamphlets at different locations before police were able to intervene and stop the action. Boxes of pamphlets for distribution were stored behind the pillars on the steps of the Central Block building, awaiting collection by group leaders.

As Sonny Leon's talk ended, Captain Cronwright moved up to the microphone and served a search warrant on Cedric de Beer, who was chairing the meeting. It authorised confiscation of the pamphlets and the searching of SRC offices. Students were incensed, and some of them believed that Cronwright had warrants to arrest student leaders. A fracas developed, with security police being pushed away from the boxes of pamphlets they were trying to confiscate. Cronwright later claimed that the crowd had been incited to attack him, and that he had been seriously injured when he was pushed down the stairs of the Central Block. The massive Van Niekerk alleged that Alan Fine – half his size – had assaulted him.

A group of students decided that the security police were not going to be allowed admission to the Students' Union, which housed SRC and Nusas offices. They rushed down to the Union, barricaded doors and windows, and prepared to defend the building. The police were probably wise to withdraw. They were outnumbered by a large contingent of extremely angry and militant students who had taken control of the high-pressure fire hoses at the top of the stairs to our offices, and were prepared to use them on any police climbing the staircase.

After the police withdrew, an excited student group moved back to Jan Smuts Avenue to picket. By this time, tempers were running high. When a group of vehicles tried to side-swipe a group of picketers, they were met with kicks and punches to their bodywork. The vehicles circled Braamfontein and returned. This time their occupants had eggs, which they threw at the picket line – but from a safer distance.

Late that afternoon, the picket line was disbanded. Students were invited to close the campaign at an evening event which included a viewing of *The Confession*, a popular political thriller dealing with interrogation and show trials under repressive regimes.

* * *

The weekly student newspaper had become an important medium for political education on campus, and had grown over the years from a relatively small-circulation publication to one which reached most full-time students on campus. News about campus political activities, and a focus on South Africa's political past, were by now regular features, as was critical comment on the national government. One editor, Mark Douglas-Home, had been deported. Another, Derek Louw, had been charged in court and suspended from university together with Franco Frescura, a satirical cartoonist. The editor for 1974, Tim James, was a member of the Wits delegation to the Nusas seminar which had conceived plans for the campaign on opposition and political prisoners. He was fully committed to supporting the campaign and its aims through his newspaper.

Tim and I shared a student house with a number of permanent and occasional residents involved in the campaign, including Cedric de Beer, Jonathan Grossman and Steven Friedman. We planned to publish two special editions of *Wits Student*, dealing exclusively with the political prisoners campaign. I prepared a number of the articles, often using publications that had reached us through the United Nations Special Committee on Apartheid, which was an invaluable source of information at a time when censorship made the sourcing of opposition-oriented material difficult.

The SRC had set up its own printing works in the basement of the Students' Union, largely to be able to have control of the content and timing of what we published without interference from university authorities or state institutions. We had bought an old full-colour litho machine and plate-maker, and employed a skilled litho printer. Simon Behrens was willing to work at unusual hours of the night to ensure that publications could be printed in relative secrecy, and then distributed early next morning to avoid raids, confiscation and banning. An internal design and typesetting unit allowed us to produce publications of reasonably professional quality without recourse to commercial services, which were often subject to security police intimidation.

The first special edition was printed on the night of Monday 27 May and distributed as students arrived on campus the next morning. In a message to students, the Nusas president, Charles Nupen, confronted the issue of political violence and illegality:

> We are aware that many of those imprisoned were found guilty of committing acts ... of violence. We are equally aware that these acts were a culmination of a long history of attempts ... at peaceful negotiation and passive defiance ... When these attempts met with repression, when leaders were banned, and when finally their organisations were banned, they saw violence and clandestine organisation as their only viable option for realising ... a just and democratic order ...
>
> The release of over four hundred South Africans, banned, banished, detained or imprisoned for active opposition to apartheid and white domination, will constitute the first step towards a new political dispensation. Many of these people are regarded as true leaders in South Africa and have a rightful claim to participate in this negotiation.[14]

A second special edition of the paper was published two days later. This included the full text of the Freedom Charter, which occupied a page of the newspaper under the headline 'Freedom: Release all political prisoners'.

Both editions paid particular attention to prisoners and restricted people who were widely acknowledged as leaders of the struggle against apartheid and for democracy: Mandela, Sisulu, Mbeki, Fischer. I had wanted to do a profile on the PAC's Sobukwe, and had asked him whether I could announce that he was fasting in support of the call to release political prisoners. However, his close friend and *Rand Daily Mail* journalist, Benjamin Pogrund, had contacted me and told me that Sobukwe was not well, and that efforts were under way to have his banning and restriction to the Kimberley area lifted or eased because of his health. Pogrund asked me not to interfere in these delicate discussions. It was for this reason that Sobukwe was not given prominence in the special editions.

The theme of opposition to South Africa's administration of Namibia was retained, with the Swapo co-founder Herman Toivo ja Toivo's statement from the dock being published in full. This speech was as important in the struggle for Namibian independence as Mandela's more celebrated statement from the dock in the Rivonia trial. It laid bare the fundamental lack of credibility and integrity of the South African legal system, corrupted as it had become as an instrument for political control and repression. 'My Lord,' began Toivo, at the conclusion of his trial in Pretoria under South Africa's Terrorism Act,

> We find ourselves here in a foreign country, convicted under laws made by people whom we have always considered as foreigners. We find ourselves tried by a Judge who is not our countryman and who has not shared our background ...
>
> We are Namibians and not South Africans. We do not now, and will not in the future recognise your right to govern us, to make laws for us in which we had no say: to treat our country as if it were your property and as if you were our masters ...

> The South African government has again shown its strength by detaining us for as long as it pleased: keeping some of us in solitary confinement for 300 to 400 days and bringing us to its Capital to try us. It has shown its strength by passing an Act especially for us and having made it retrospective. It has even chosen an ugly name to call us by: one's own are called patriots or at least rebels: your opponents are called Terrorists ...

Toivo was particular incensed that the presiding judge had labelled him a coward:

> My Lord, you found it necessary to brand me as a coward. During the Second World War, when it became evident that both my country and your country were threatened by the dark clouds of Nazism, I risked my life to defend both of them ...
>
> But some of your countrymen when called to battle to defend civilization resorted to sabotage against their own fatherland. I volunteered to face German bullets ... Today ... [the saboteurs] are our masters ... and I am called a coward ... I am proud that my countrymen have taken up arms for their people.[15]

Toivo was sentenced to 20 years and imprisoned on Robben Island.

* * *

Trials and other legal proceedings were a fertile source of material for the special editions. During a Pietermaritzburg trial of Apdusa and Unity Movement activists held in 1972, details of a security police interrogation camp in the forests of Pondoland had been revealed. I had blundered into this camp by coincidence while on a trip through the Transkei towards the end of 1971. My travelling companions and I had passed through Lusikisiki and had been horrified when we drove past the local coffin-maker's workshop. It was not just the number of newly made cheap pine coffins that upset us. It was their size. The majority were very small, made for the bodies of children.

A more graphic demonstration of infant and child mortality rates in South Africa's bantustans was hard to contemplate.

Shortly after we left Lusikisiki, we decided to take a break from driving to gather our thoughts and composure after seeing the rows and rows of tiny coffins. Turning off the road towards a forest, we followed a dirt track, only to be stopped by a number of armed police in uniform. Their aggression piqued our curiosity. Although we could not proceed along the track, we did get out of the kombi during the shouting match with the police and made every effort to see what they were guarding. A little further on, in a clearing in the forest, lay a small tent settlement. This was where 'Rooi Rus' Swanepoel and his interrogation team were holding the Apdusa and Unity Movement detainees and subjecting them to ongoing torture. At least one of the group, Mthayeni Cuthsela, died in that camp while under interrogation.

More material for the *Wits Student* special editions was drawn from the inquests into the deaths in detention of Solwandle 'Looksmart' Ngudle and James Lenkoe. Details of the torture of detainees had been revealed during these proceedings, while the antics of magistrates and prosecutors in suppressing information demonstrated the growing judicial collaboration in covering up this brutal system.

A full-page feature on the Rivonia trial included extracts from Mandela's 'I am prepared to die' statement from the dock, and asserted that the accused 'represent the highest in morality and ethics'. Profiles of Bram Fischer and Govan Mbeki allowed us to tell students that communists and whites had been centrally involved in political struggles against apartheid and in the decision to introduce armed struggle under MK.

By using information gleaned from trials, we were able to narrate a political history which had been suppressed through bannings, censorship and criminalisation of political support for the ideas of unlawful organisations. This history was not taught at schools or in universities, and books which recorded it were usually banned. For a generation of university students, this was the first time they had been exposed to the history of opposition and resistance, to the organisations and people who had led 'the struggle', and to those who were now imprisoned on Robben Island and in Pretoria. For many, it was the first time they had read the Freedom Charter.

* * *

The campaign for the release of all political prisoners had tested the boundaries of above-ground public politics under apartheid. Documents often considered prohibited, such as the Freedom Charter, had been published. The views, aims and actions of imprisoned political leaders and the organisations they represented had been placed at the centre of South African politics, at least for a week. Security police abuse of detainees under interrogation was repeatedly emphasised, and the corrosion and corruption of the legal system in the prosecution of political trials were laid bare.

The campaign challenged a number of views which had substantial sway within the broad anti-apartheid opposition. The call for the release of prisoners was not based on appeals for clemency or mercy, but because those prisoners and the organisations they led were an essential part of any initiative to dismantle the apartheid system. This included political leaders of different ideological persuasion: communists, Africanists, nationalists, non-racialists, liberals, Trotskyists. No legitimate and credible political leaders could be excluded or discounted on the basis of their ideological orientation or affiliation.

Many liberals eschewed any resort to 'violence' in political struggle. The campaign had challenged this, explaining the circumstances in which campaigns of sabotage and armed struggle had been endorsed by many of those serving sentences on Robben Island and in Pretoria. Involvement in acts of violent or armed resistance had to be understood, not judged or condemned.

Through the campaign, students and their organisations asserted that they had a role and place in national and radical politics. This need not be limited to the campuses or in defence of university 'autonomy'. The campaign had taken the initiative, setting the terrain on which student activism would be expressed, rather than reacting to state incursions into university independence.

Saso had advised white students to work in their own communities. To some extent, the campaign was directed towards students on the Nusas campuses. However, its impact and audience were far wider – through the national newspapers, through the pamphleting of black urban workers in the city, through picketing and marches on the streets of Johannesburg. A new breed of radical white students had responded to the challenge of Black Consciousness and redefined their political role in assertive and innovative ways that neither challenged BC nor uncritically accepted its injunctions.

Students had shown militancy and physical courage when they confronted security police, prevented them for entering the Students' Union building to effect a search warrant, and finally drove them off campus.

The campaign had also placed the question of South Africa's occupation and administration of Namibia firmly on the student agenda, and drawn attention to the movements and organisations which had committed themselves to a South African withdrawal and Namibian independence. As more and more military conscripts were called up to war in the north of Namibia and then across the border in Angola, South Africa's military presence in the region became a central issue in radical student politics.

The most obvious failures in the campaign involved the choice of speakers at meetings. In an editorial in one of the special campaign issues of *Wits Student*, Tim James criticised the SRC and, by implication, my leadership:

> It was unfortunate that the SRC chose Cedric Phatudi as the opening speaker in the Nusas campaign. It should not have been expected that a government stooge ... would not have spoken in favour of the policy of separate development ...
>
> The SRC should have immediately denounced Phatudi's speech, preferably in front of him and the assembled press ...
>
> We demand the release of *all* political prisoners ... They are the

people's leaders, and the people need them. All of them. Fischer and Mbeki the communists, as much as Mandela and Sisulu.[16]

As Tim and I were staying in a student house at the time, his harsh – but legitimate – criticism of my conduct in not immediately remonstrating with Phatudi made shared evening meals fairly tense for a few days.

A day-by-day report on the campaign week, published in the following week's student newspaper, analysed reactions to Phatudi's speech in greater depth. His speech was a 'typical example of Wits' sense of inverted racism', argued a student reporter: 'If a white man ... had delivered the selfsame speech, he would have been hissed, booed and jeered off the stage. But because Phatudi is Black everyone listened and applauded very politely even if he is obviously a government stooge ... spouting Nationalistic propaganda.'[17]

Neither Gerson Veii nor Sonny Leon had been particularly inspiring choices either. Veii was a poor communicator, at least in English, which was his second language, and a speaker from Swapo rather than Veii's Swanu would have tied in better with the campaign theme and focus. Leon, despite his increasingly outspoken calls for all prisoners to be released, had a history of compromise through participation in the Coloured Persons' Representative Council. The profile of public speakers should have been more carefully aligned to the aims and messages of public political activity.

Another valid criticism of the campaign, which was not levelled at the time but should have been, involved the total absence of women prisoners from the focus. At the time, two women political prisoners were serving jail terms: Dorothy Nyembe and Amina Desai. Nyembe was a leader of considerable importance, especially in Natal, where she had been active in the ANC and MK for decades. In 1969 she had been sentenced to 15 years under the Terrorism Act, having been found guilty of involvement in MK activity. Many important women leaders, such as Albertina Sisulu and Winnie Mandela, were under restriction, and it is startling that we gave them no prominence. A more developed understanding of gender issues in political struggle would have led to a focus on the role of women's leadership in opposing apartheid.

Students supported the campaign in surprisingly large numbers. They came, after all, from deep within an enclave of white privilege, and their immediate material interests and upward mobility were well served by the existing class and racial structures of society. Yet thousands participated actively and responded positively to the messages of the campaign. As Tim James wrote in his final editorial on the campaign, 'It is perhaps surprising that a Nusas campaign of this nature – probably the most radical Nusas has conducted – met with the reception it did. There were a few poster pull-downers ... but there was a solid core of students at all the meetings and pickets, and it was heartening to see the Special Branch prevented from raiding the Students' Union.'[18]

Substantial numbers of students, born in the 1950s, influenced in the 1960s by the anti-authoritarianism of the counter-culture, and now at university in the 1970s, had shown they were available for principled and progressive politics, given the right issues, organisation and opportunity.

* * *

Reaction from the state and its surrogates was to be expected. In the weeks following the campaign, the *Citizen* newspaper published an attack on me, claiming that I had orchestrated the political prisoners campaign together with 'communists' in London. The writer was a well-known right-wing columnist, Aida Parker. Rumour had it that she was romantically involved with a senior security policeman from John Vorster Square who gave her access to information from intelligence files.

An Afrikaans-language newspaper attacked me for my lack of understanding of democracy. This was difficult to comprehend, wrote a columnist, because they believed I had been brought up in the household of a well-known United Party member who had been mayor of Johannesburg. The absurdity of suggesting that the ineffective, compromised and deeply conservative United Party could understand democracy was equalled only by the writer's error about my ancestry: Sam Moss, the UP leader referred to, was no relation of mine.

Then an editorial and 'exposé' appeared in the National Party-supporting Afrikaans-language daily *Die Transvaler*, setting out in considerable detail the way in which 'eight communists in London' had conspired with Nusas to run the campaign to release all political prisoners. This was followed by a set of anonymous pamphlets distributed on campus. I had apparently 'masterminded' the campaign with 'South African communists in London'; led a 'shameless storming' of Anglo American's head office after the Carletonville mine shootings; and told a Stellenbosch SRC delegation that I was 'dedicated to revolution'. The pamphlet was silent on why I would have made such a dangerous statement to a delegation which included the sons of Prime Minister Vorster and one of his cabinet ministers, Chris Heunis.

Over the next few months, my motorcycle was vandalised and sugar poured into its petrol tank. Around the same time, two 'thugs' arrived at my flat one evening apparently with the intention of beating me up. They found Cedric de Beer there cooking a meal with his girlfriend, with whom I shared the flat. Deeply frustrated, they attacked Cedric before he managed to push them from the kitchen and lock the door.

From the time of the security police raid on the SRC's offices in January 1974, it seemed possible that state action of some sort would follow the political prisoners campaign. These latest developments suggested a 'softening up' process in preparation for an attack on Nusas and the campaign organisers.

7

Students, intellectuals and worker organisation

The first student Wages Commission had been set up at the University of Natal in March 1971, during the period of intellectual and cultural ferment which Tony Morphet famously named the 'Durban moment'.[1] Major influences in this 'moment' included Rick Turner and his work on participatory democracy, published as *The Eye of the Needle*, and Steve Biko, who was 'in the process of formulating not only the intellectual core, but the political discourse and practical programmes of Black Consciousness'. At the same time, Dunbar Moodie was 'busy with a major reinterpretation of Afrikaner power', and Mike Kirkwood was producing 'the first terms for a thoroughgoing reinterpretation of South African English literature'.[2]

However, as Morphet noted, 'To mention only these inevitably misses the atmosphere of intellectual ferment and the countless details signalling a structural shift in the received intellectual patterns of the social world. Moreover, the things ... mentioned [above] refer only to an intellectual élite – both white and black – and what was going on beyond the limits of the élite was still more surprising.'[3] The influence of the 'Durban moment' spread like a wildfire in and around the city. Intellectually and politically, in the fields of culture and art, in literature, poetry and lifestyle, there was a flowering of fresh ideas and practices. These found strongest expression through the universities and through individuals living, teaching and studying there.

The ideas and organisational initiatives of Black Consciousness, especially through the South African Students' Organisation (Saso), constituted one of the strongest influences in the 'moment'. Steve Biko, Saso's first president, was studying at the University of Natal's black medical school and living at its Alan Taylor Residence. Emerging BC leaders like Saths Cooper and Strini Moodley had been students at the University of Durban-Westville.

University of Natal academics such as Turner, Michael Nupen, Eddie Webster, Mike Kirkwood, Dunbar Moodie, Tony Morphet and Raphael de Kadt were challenging students to think in new and more critical ways. Some were introducing the ideas of Western Marxism. Standing in stark contrast to the 'democratic centralism' and rigid ahistorical Marxism of the Soviet Union and the countries and political parties it supported, the 'new left' influenced the ways a generation of students sought to act in and on the world. At the same time, the 'counter-culture' with its strongly anti-authoritarian and pro-freedom lifestyle was dislodging relatively privileged white students from the conservative and materialistic values that had dominated their parents' generation.

This was the cauldron in which discussions over a role for white students in worker organisation bubbled up.

* * *

The formation of the Wages Commissions on the Nusas campuses has often been misunderstood. In some cases, this is the result of political agendas that dictate the rewriting of history. In others, it appears to be based on ignorance and the repetition of inaccurate assertions as a mode of proof.

Interviewed 20 years after he first became involved in the worker education programmes of the Johannesburg-based Industrial Aid Society (IAS), Sipho Kubheka characterised students from the Wages Commission as 'feeling very bitter and rejected by the black students who pulled out of Nusas and formed Saso. So they became involved in the labour scene.'[4] This view was repeated by Jabulani Sithole and Sifiso Ndlovu in their contribution on the revival of the labour

Wits students marching to John Vorster Square to protest against the detention of 'the 22', May 1970. (Wits archives, Ph/77-17b)

Rick Turner. (Courtesy of Foszia Turner-Stylianou)

Neville Curtis (right) with Ernest Mojalefa Ralekheto, a Nusas vice-president, in 1970. (Museum Africa, PH2014-60)

*Steve Biko at a student conference, 1971. (John Reader/*Life *magazine)*

School children salute the Republic of South Africa on its tenth anniversary at the Rand Stadium, Johannesburg, May 1971. *(*Wits Student, Wits *archives)*

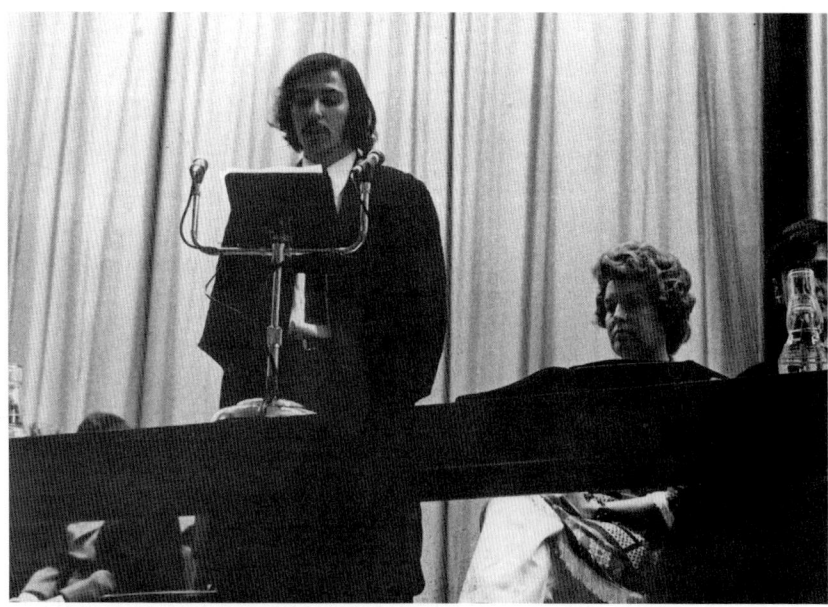

Joan Lestor, Richard Feetham Academic Freedom lecturer, is thanked by Glenn Moss, Wits University, August 1971. *(Glenn Moss collection)*

Wits students heil *the Republic at the Rand Stadium, May 1971. (Museum Africa, PH2014-25)*

The Timol family mourns the death of a son and brother. (Museum Africa, PH2014-7)

Wits students heil *the Republic at the Rand Stadium, May 1971. (Museum Africa, PH2014-25)*

The Timol family mourns the death of a son and brother. (Museum Africa, PH2014-7)

Yusuf Timol on hearing of his son's death. (Museum Africa, PH2014-17 8b)

Wits students protest the death of Ahmed Timol while in detention. (Wits Historical Papers, AD1718-A6-44)

The 'cemetery' commemorating the Sharpeville massacre, Wits University library lawns, 1972. (Wits archives, Ph/Y72N-70a)

Police prepare to invade Wits campus, June 1972. (Wits Historical papers, AD1918-A6-69)

Glenn Moss addressing an Ahmed Timol memorial meeting, Wits Great Hall, 1973, with Helen Joseph third from the left. (Glenn Moss collection)

Students sit in at the Anglo American offices in downtown Johannesburg after protesting miners were shot at Western Deep Levels, 1973. (Wits Historical Papers, AD1918-A6-43)

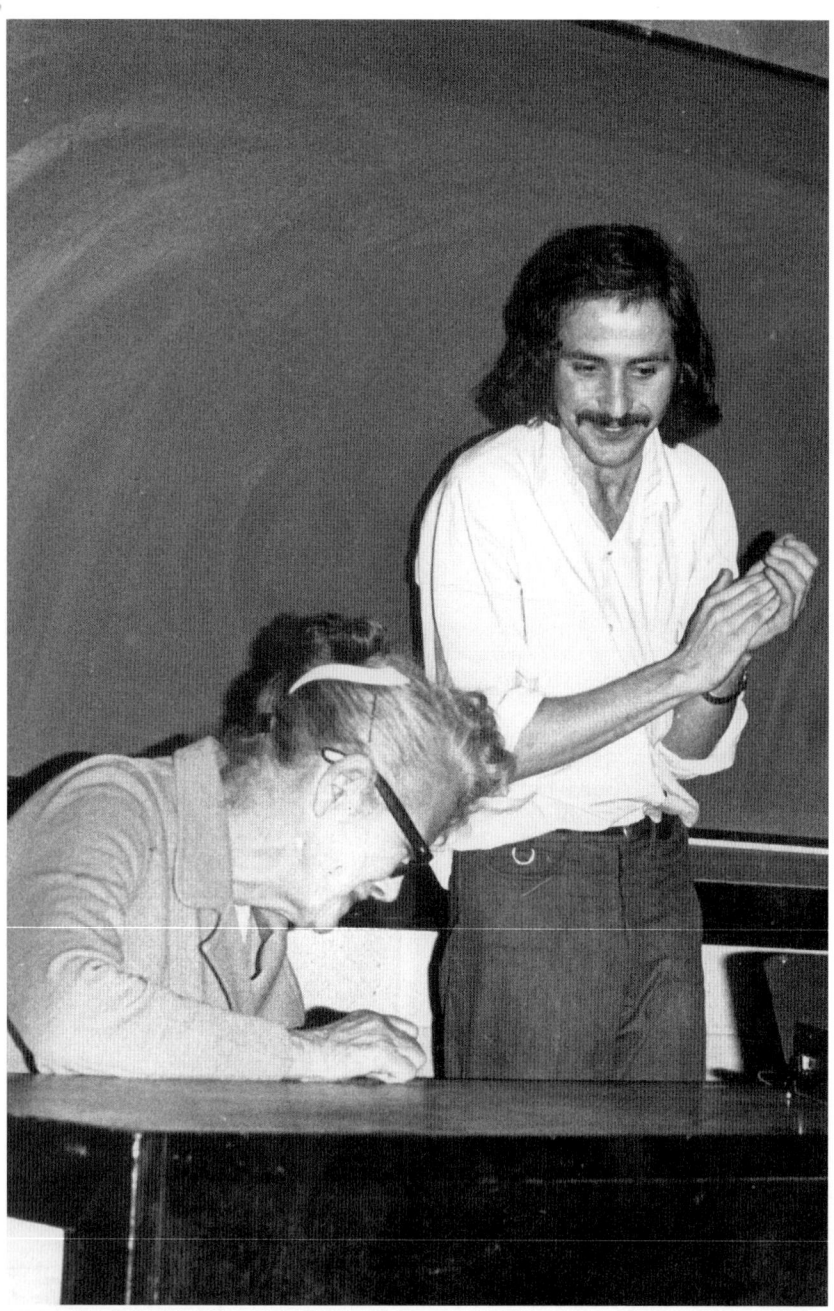

Helen Joseph and Glenn Moss at a meeting at Wits, 1973. (Glenn Moss collection)

Helen Joseph addresses a mass meeting at Wits during the campaign to release all political prisoners, May 1974. (Wits Historical Papers, AD1918-A6-12)

Peter Randall campaigning as a Social Democrat candidate for the general elections, 1974. (Museum Africa, PH2014-68)

Jeanette Curtis. (Courtesy of Fritz Schoon)

A demonstration calling for the release of political prisoners, Wits, 1974. (Wits Historical Papers, AD1918-A6-13)

Nusas Wages Commission members protest against slave wages paid to workers in the 'border' areas, Babelegi, 1973. (Jonathan Katzenellenbogen/ independent contributors/Africa Media Online, APN162164)

An SRC of spies: the 1972/73 Wits SRC included Paul Sarbutt (of Boss, back row, left); Craig Williamson (of the security police, back row, fourth from right); Arthur McGiven (of Boss, front row, second from left); and Derek Brune (of the security police, front row, third from right). The author is third from left in the back row. (Wits archives, Ph/78-618)

Glenn Moss, Karel Tip and Cedric de Beer during the Nusas trial, 1976. (Museum Africa, PH2013-235)

Brother Darryl (front) and father Solly (rear) collect the author on his release from jail in Pretoria, November 1975. (Museum Africa, PH2014-156)

Nelson Mandela with the Nusas trialists: (from left) Eddie Webster, Charles Nupen, Karel Tip, Glenn Moss and Cedric de Beer, December 1996. (Moss family collection)

Nelson Mandela accepts drawings from Michael (5) and Anthony (3) Moss, December 1996, while the author looks on. (Moss family collection)

movement, published as part of the monumental *Road to Democracy in South Africa*. 'The decision [to form the Wages Commissions] was primarily in response to Nusas's rejection by black students who broke away to form Saso in 1969, and the realisation that they were being marginalised from mainstream resistance politics.'[5]

Sithole and Ndlovu reiterated this view in their comments on the involvement of the Wits Wages Commission in the formation of the IAS: 'Many of these students and academics [involved in the IAS] were still smarting from their rejection by the black students who had pulled out of Nusas to form Saso; they campaigned on an anti-nationalist ticket and emerged as the dominant political force in the IAS.'[6]

Martin Legassick has also argued that white students turned towards black labour because of the impact of Black Consciousness. 'Rebuffed by Saso, and smarting under criticism from black students, a small minority of white radical students worked to make a turn towards the black masses', although he seems to contradict this by also referring to the 'warm mutual respect and regard between black and white student leaders'.[7] Legassick concluded that Wages Commissions were formed as a result of radical white students' rejection of Biko's proposal that they should work to change attitudes in the white community. 'Since radical white students regarded with contempt and as a waste of time the idea of trying to engage with racist whites in door-to-door campaigns or in other forms of activity, they turned to the black working class as an alternative.'[8]

These explanations for the formation of the Wages Commissions misunderstand what was occurring among the emerging radical left. They also misinterpret the influence of Black Consciousness in these developments. The Saso breakaway from Nusas was one factor in challenging established liberalism, for which multi-racial forms of organisation were a *sine qua non* of opposition to apartheid. However, as Rick Turner argued on a number of occasions, the formation of Saso – and its championing of Black Consciousness – was not at core an attack on white students or even liberalism. Rather, it was a strong rejection of a white supremacist political system (what point 1 of the Saso manifesto referred to as 'white racist society'). Rejection of whites as individuals and of white liberalism was, to quote Turner, 'of relatively minor importance [and has] ... been given disproportionate significance'.[9]

Saso's break from Nusas, as well as the development of the ideology of Black Consciousness, was one important challenge to whites opposing apartheid to find more progressive and effective strategies of opposition. This was a factor among others that resulted in a radical critique of the multi-racial liberalism that had dominated opposition politics after Rivonia, and in an assessment of the place of race and its relation to class in apartheid society.

In this search, emerging student radicals on the Nusas-affiliated campuses explored different forms of Marxist and socialist critiques of capitalism as they sought to understand the functional relationship between South Africa's economy and its apartheid edifice. It was in this sense that Saso's breakaway from Nusas created one of the conditions for the development of a new radicalism among white students. Another involved the undoubted importance of Western Marxism and the new left, and its assertion of the primacy of working-class organisation and interests over other identities, such as race.

It was this mingling of influences that found organised expression in the Wages Commissions, rather than any emotional reaction to, or sense of rejection by, the ideology of Black Consciousness. The involvement of the Wits Wages Commission in the formation of the IAS had little to do with white students or university intellectuals 'smarting' from the reality of racially separate organisations. Rather, the Wages Commissions reflected an understanding that it was the African working class (not 'blacks in general') which had the strongest interest in challenging capitalist economic relations and the apartheid policies and structures that underpinned them.

Sithole and Ndlovu were also misinformed when they suggested that Wages Commission participants in the IAS 'campaigned' on an 'anti-nationalist' ticket. Asserting that there were different class interests among the racially oppressed did not deny the importance of racial solidarity or nationalism in the anti-apartheid struggle. Rather, it introduced a more nuanced approach to understanding society, and hence to the formulation of appropriate strategies and tactics in confronting both political oppression and economic exploitation. Most of the students involved in the IAS strongly rejected what they saw as the apolitical 'economism' and 'reformism' of the Durban-based Trade Union Advisory Co-ordinating Council (Tuacc), as well as its 'workerism', which opposed alliances of classes in political struggle. Under the leadership of Steven Friedman, they tended to be broadly supportive of the politics of the national liberation movements. Initially, most were aligned with the IAS founder members Jen Curtis, Pindile Mfeti and Miriam Sithole, all of whom had allegiances to Sactu and, in some cases, to the ANC and MK.

Although they write on these matters from a different perspective, David Hemson, Martin Legassick and Nicole Ulrich fall into the same trap as Sithole and Ndlovu when they assert that 'Unlike the cordiality that characterised relations between students and Sactu activists at WPWAB [the Cape Town-based Western Province Workers Advice Bureau] and Tuacc, relations at the IAS between the students and Sactu members became strained from the beginning'.[10] This misconstrues the nature of the alliances formed and dissolved in early IAS history. The differences that emerged were not between 'students' and 'Sactu members'. Rather, they formed between those who supported the Tuacc position on industrial unionism and organising strategies and those who sought a set of different strategies for unionism in the Transvaal that blended elements of the general unionism being promoted in Cape Town and the narrow industrial unionism of Tuacc.

These strategic and tactical differences cut across Sactu (and ANC) supporters, students, academics, organisers, educators and others who made up the IAS at the time. The issues in dispute were far more complex than simple differences between students and supporters of Sactu (where there was, in any event, an overlap).

* * *

Any involvement of white students in issues affecting black workers had to confront a huge array of obstacles. There were the immediate hurdles of race, class and language. Nusas had initially accepted the logic of BC that whites should not organise or act across racial divides, at least in student affairs. Yet this was being challenged through involvement in black worker initiatives, where white students had to face the enormous chasm between African workers and white intellectuals-in-the-making.

In addition, the institutions of labour were largely alien to students, who knew little of the convoluted and technical procedures involved in the Wage Boards and the Industrial Councils, which set minimum conditions of service for most economic sectors. They also had little experience of the works and liaison committees, which provided for some very limited and compromised forms of worker representation within the workplace.

Even progressive-minded students tended to be ill informed about the bread-and-butter issues confronting employed workers: wages, deductions, hours of work, contracts of employment, migrancy and urban residential rights. The most active students had generally been involved in anti-apartheid political activity. They had defended their universities from government attacks, protested against repressive legislation, and reacted to attacks on civil liberties. It was not immediately clear where unequal relations between classes fitted into this worldview. Apartheid had been the target for activist students, not capitalist economic relations.

A report on the establishment of the Wages Commissions, presented to the July 1971 Nusas congress, opened with an unattributed quote which attempted to explain why students should be interested in wage levels, even if they knew little about the mechanisms that established them.

> Students may feel that wages ... are peripheral to student concern, but in a capitalist society, wages are the key to food, shelter, health, education, clothes, transport and recreation. Wages are a variable in our society controlled by strict institutional procedures which have

effectively excluded workers from putting the case for a living wage. The function of students is to redress the imbalance by using the facilities provided by a university: information gathering, correlation and dissemination and undertaking social action to make people aware of the situation of poverty wages.[11]

There, in a nutshell, was the motivation for students to be involved with worker issues. Low wages in a capitalist society like South Africa prevented workers and their families from acquiring the essentials of life. This was a consequence of capitalist relations, not just apartheid or racism. The majority of workers did not have access to the institutional mechanisms where wages were set. Students could assist workers in gaining access to these institutions and create a more amenable environment for increasing wages, through using the resources and facilities of the universities where they studied.

Those guiding this fledgling initiative were increasingly able to demonstrate the functional links between capitalist development and apartheid, between class and race, low wages and the migrant and contract labour systems. Opposition to apartheid necessarily involved an attack on the low-wage ultra-exploitation which apartheid facilitated and which benefited the owners of capital so handsomely. This was the relationship between working for the Wages Commissions and opposing apartheid.

* * *

The core group that formed the first Wages Commission in Durban included David Hemson, Halton Cheadle, David Davis, Karel Tip and Charles Nupen, who were students, and the political science lecturer Rick Turner.

A proposal to extend Wages Commissions to the other Nusas-affiliated campus was adopted at the 1971 Nusas national congress, following a motion put forward by Jeanette Curtis and Paula Ensor. Initial activity would involve research into the wages of workers at the universities themselves, with the aim of pressuring university administrations into improving these. This would be followed by research and investigation needed to support representations to the Wage Boards for increased minimum wages. A third sphere of intended activity involved research into the manner in which both overseas and local companies were using apartheid to exploit black labour.

Nuswel, the division of Nusas mandated by congress to set up commissions on the campuses, recommended that each unit build up information centres of publications, research papers, newspaper clippings and lists of other resources as part of ongoing research into wage levels. These centres would gather and distribute information on wages and social conditions; develop research policies and directions; compile data on worker organisations; arrange to have questions raised in parliament; liaise with the local Department of Labour; and undertake research into rising costs of food and transport for workers.

A model analysis of the sort of information required in presentation of evidence to Wage Board sittings was included in the report. For each industry, it was envisaged that data would be needed on the categories of work, existing wage determinations, characteristics and profits in the industry, an analysis of the labour force by province, race and skill, as well as wage levels for both unskilled and skilled work. Wages would then have to be compared against living costs, including costs of food, rent and transport. This would form the basis for wage demands presented to the relevant Wage Board.[12]

Nuswel advised students setting up Wages Commissions to focus initially on employment practices and wage levels at their own universities, and thereafter expand this to assisting workers in making representations at Wage Board hearings and Industrial Council negotiations. It also recommended research, information gathering and communication strategies on domestic, agricultural and municipal workers, especially in regard to wage levels, rising costs of food and transport, and ways of estimating a poverty datum line and a minimum effective level for wages.

These were the areas on which the Wages Commission at Wits

concentrated from its inception in the second half of 1971. The next year, the commission shifted focus to employment in the 'border areas' defined by the government's industrial decentralisation policy. This granted a range of incentives for employers to relocate production to areas bordering the bantustans, including cash grants, loans to acquire land, tax concessions and rebates on transport costs. In addition, employers could be granted exemption from minimum wage determinations made by the Wage Boards and Industrial Councils.

By the end of 1972, a number of exemptions from minimum wage provisions had been granted for industry in these border areas, or 'growth points', as they were also known. As a result, minimum wages paid to African workers in these areas fell below the already pitiful levels in force in the urban areas. Research undertaken during 1973 suggested that the poverty datum line – the lowest possible wage for survival in the short term – in an area like Pretoria was R85 a month. A better measure was provided by the minimum subsistence level, which included some provision for health care and education; it was calculated at R113 a month.[13] But in the border area growth points, the *Financial Mail* reckoned in May 1973 that monthly wages ranged between R26 and R40 a month. In Babelegi, 50 kilometres north of Pretoria, average monthly wages were estimated to be R28.[14] This area, on the edge of the Tswana bantustan, was home to Kool Look Wigs, an enterprise owned by the brothers Sol and Abe Krok of Twins Pharmaceuticals.

The Krok twins were controversial entrepreneurs. They made a fortune through skin-lightening creams sold mainly to African consumers, which contained bleaching chemicals with long-term health consequences. The brothers embraced a strong Jewish identity, and politically progressive members of the Jewish community found their payment of sub-poverty wages and their marketing of products like skin lighteners and wigs to vulnerable and ill-informed black consumers morally disgraceful, and one of the worst forms of rampant exploitation of apartheid conditions. Investigations into Kool Look Wigs confirmed the Krok twins as leading beneficiaries of ultra-exploitation through judicious use of apartheid policy.

The Wits Wages Commission launched a public campaign to expose wage levels in the border areas, and were particularly damning of the Kroks' Kool Look Wigs. This built on Adam Raphael's highly effective *Guardian* series on the wages paid by British companies invested in South Africa. The result of these cumulative pressures led to fairly immediate increases in wages paid by some British firms and, over time, some improvements in wages paid in the border areas.[15]

* * *

The Wits Wages Commission had recruited a number of energetic and motivated young students following the September 1973 shooting of mineworkers at Anglo American's Western Deep Levels mine, near Carletonville. Intense anger among students over wages and working conditions proved an important catalyst for the expansion of Wages Commission activity.

New initiatives were undertaken in support of the Industrial Aid Society (IAS), formed in Johannesburg towards the end of 1973. Initially, this involved producing a worker newspaper and distributing it, along with pamphlets, at factory gates in the early mornings. The publications provided details about IAS services, especially the complaints and advice bureau, and explained to workers how they could make contact with IAS organisers.

These activities were co-ordinated with IAS organising priorities. Both the factories targeted and the messages communicated to workers were decided on jointly by IAS and Wages Commission representatives. Eventually, some of the more experienced Wages Commission members joined IAS committees initiating worker education and literacy programmes, staffing the complaints and advice service run from the offices, and assisting in transporting workers to and from meetings.

The IAS pioneers included Jeanette Curtis, who had assumed national responsibility for the Wages Commissions when she served as Nuswel secretary-general in the Nusas head office during 1972; Steven Friedman, head of the Wits Wages Commission; Pindile Mfeti, a nephew of Govan Mbeki and cousin of Thabo Mbeki, who was working with Jeanette at the Institute of Race Relations; and Miriam Sithole, who had worked with Sactu in the early 1960s.

Similar initiatives aimed at providing services to workers had already been set up in Durban (the General Factory Workers Benefit Fund) and Cape Town (Western Province Workers Advice Bureau and Workers Advisory Project). There were differences in the strategic approaches and underlying politics between the Cape Town and Durban groups. These revolved around the relative merits and demerits of general and industrial unionism, and the role of trade unions in political opposition to apartheid. The differences in approach between the centres also manifested themselves in attitudes to Sactu, the Communist Party, the ANC and MK.

In setting up the IAS, Jeanette and Pindile had solicited the support of a group historically associated with Sactu in the Transvaal, as well as individuals who had histories in the ANC and SACP. When I first became involved in IAS activity late in 1974, it was apparent that individuals supportive of Sactu had some influence within the fledgling organisation. Discreet assistance was being provided by the SACP and Sactu veteran Eli Weinberg, who had been imprisoned for underground Communist Party activities and was banned and house-arrested at the time.

When Jeanette and Steven began setting up the IAS, I was SRC president at Wits. They kept me informed of these developments, partly because of the Wages Commission's relationship to Nusas, and also because I was able to channel some SRC resources the way of the IAS. Office furniture, a typewriter or two, and some small cash amounts were donated to the IAS as it began setting up offices in downtown Johannesburg. I was also asked to sign the lease for the IAS offices, as the landlord was reluctant to accept a worker advice bureau as a tenant and would not have entered into a lease with anyone who was not white. Apart from racist assumptions about black tenants held by most landlords, the Group Areas Act prohibited the renting of space to black tenants in 'white' areas such as the Johannesburg city centre.

* * *

The immediate impetus for setting up the IAS arose from the work of the Wages Commissions, as well as the new organising initiatives in Durban and Cape Town. However, there was a deeper strategic and analytical basis for this initiative, involving the writings of Rick Turner, the varying intellectual traditions of Marxism and socialism, and the history of South African resistance politics. For those entering the politics of labour for the first time, these elements were being synthesised into an eclectic montage of identity, activism and analysis.

Marxists and socialists argued that the working class was the motor and agent of political, economic and social change. This view diverged dramatically from received wisdom that elites controlled and influenced change, or that the oppression of racial capitalism would be ended through the good intentions of liberal reformers, the rational self-interest of economic development or the gradual but unhindered expansion of market forces.

Rick Turner had set out the importance of utopian thinking, arguing that a first step to any change necessitated a vision of an alternative. It was possible, argued Turner, to conceive of a society based on radically different structures and ways of organising and being. The logic of this was that society could be challenged on the basis of what could be, rather than what existed.

Turner's critique of the way in which capitalist production and consumption were organised, and his argument for participatory democracy in the workplace, strengthened the developing identity of young socialists entering the labour movement for the first time. He was equally influential in pointing out that there were alternatives to capitalism other than the Soviet model of communism: 'Soviet society has done away with private ownership of the means of production. But this is not enough. For there are no political institutions in Soviet society which would enable the people to assert their control over the means of production ... The only real alternative [to capitalism] is to ensure popular participation, based on workers' control, in a context of political freedom.'[16]

Despite this critique of Soviet communism, we studied Lenin's writings carefully, especially in regard to the 'economism' inherent in trade unionism. We reminded ourselves that unions were a reflection of relations between capital and labour, and could not in and of themselves resolve or overcome that contradictory relationship. We were attracted to Lenin's assertion that some form of 'vanguardist' political formation – the political party – was required to counteract the 'reformist' tendency of trade unions. While trade unions could engender a 'trade union consciousness' among the working class, a political party was required for the development of revolutionary class consciousness.

This fitted well with Georg Lukács's analysis of how the proletariat moved from 'false' to 'true' consciousness at certain stages of its development. By linking a selective reading of Lenin with a schematic understanding of Lukács, we were able to conclude that the trade unions we aimed to organise would require political leadership if the organised working class was to avoid the traps of economism and reformism.

There were attempts to understand and integrate the complex relationships between class and race in this analysis. Did apartheid or 'national oppression' render class and race largely identical categories and identities? What was the role of progressive intellectuals – white and black – in relation to trade unionism and working-class organisation? These questions bore some similarity to the challenges Black Consciousness had posed to radical white students at universities, but now extended to a far larger canvas, which included relations between the ruling and working classes.

Just prior to the IAS being set up, I had raised funds from Beyers Naudé at the Christian Institute to employ Barbara Hogan as a literacy co-ordinator on the Wits campus. Deeply influenced by Paulo Freire's model of literacy for political 'conscientisation', she was joined by Susan Brown in the development of a literacy training course which aimed to teach reading, writing and numeracy at the same time as 'raising the consciousness' of 'the oppressed'.

Barbara, Susan, Steven Friedman and I were sharing a house in

Orange Grove at the time, and it was a natural development when the literacy programme offered its services to the IAS as part of the overall worker education initiative. IAS strategy explicitly linked worker education and organisation, and the literacy model being developed by Susan and Barbara complemented this focus on worker education well.

Once the IAS had established offices at Sacta House, 277 Bree Street, Johannesburg, Jeanette agreed to fill the role of administrative organiser. Her early reports to the steering committee provided a window into IAS activities: a complaints and advice service; development of material for worker education courses and literacy; training of trainers for worker education and literacy; training of organisers; proposed legal aid, medical and dental clinics; a fund (15 cents a week contribution) providing death benefits; distribution of pamphlets and a worker newspaper at the gates of factories; factory visits and worker meetings outside the factories and at homes in the townships; development of a library and resource centre; and research into different industrial sectors.[17]

By the end of June 1974, worker education classes were taking place on Saturday mornings and afternoons; and over 30 workers were enrolled in literacy training programmes. Miriam Sithole was producing a fortnightly IAS newsletter for distribution at factories where organisation was taking place. In the next two months, the caseload for worker complaints doubled to 130, and membership increased from 48 to 132. Worker education classes were running for groups from four industrial sectors: iron, steel and engineering; paper and pulp; building; and furniture. On 9 July a special general meeting of the IAS was held, at which 49 factories were represented.

In September, Jeanette indicated that she would have to step down as administrative organiser. She would still be available to participate in IAS activities on a voluntary basis, but could no longer manage the workload of two demanding jobs. When no replacement was forthcoming, Susan and Barbara were asked to assume Jeanette's responsibilities for a month. They agreed. As I had just completed my term as SRC president at Wits, they sought approval from the steering committee for me to assist them. Sue and Barbara argued that, through student leadership roles, I had more experience running and managing organisations than any of our peers, and that I would bring much-needed systematisation and stability to the IAS's procedures and operations.

I agreed to the suggestion immediately, even though I had no experience in worker organisation. During 1974 Wits University had granted me special dispensation to function as a full-time SRC president, exempting me from any courses but maintaining my status as a registered student. I still needed one first-year subject to complete my degree, but had decided to register for that by correspondence in 1975, through the University of South Africa. This left me free to immerse myself in IAS activities.

I had little understanding of relations between the three centres where new forms of worker organisation were developing – Durban, Cape Town and Johannesburg. However, Jeanette's final report to the steering committee for the period ending September 1974 reflected a distinct chill in relations with the Durban-based Tuacc. The IAS declined an invitation to affiliate to the Institute for Industrial Education (IIE), which was running education programmes for the unions being formed under the auspices of Tuacc. The steering committee minutes indicated concerns over the apparent separation between organisation and education, which the IIE represented, and also criticised the IIE's policy of awarding certificates to workers who completed courses.

The report left the door open to some co-operation on future projects and indicated that relations were 'fairly friendly' with some individuals and 'those trade union officials we have met', although Jeanette questioned how this would develop when they moved up to Johannesburg to start organising in sectors where the IAS was already present. At the same time, there was a suggestion that relations between IAS and the Workers Advisory Project in Cape Town should be developed and encouraged, because of greater compatibility in strategy and work.

At its November meeting, the steering committee appointed me as 'temporary administrative organiser', with responsibility for managing other staff, taking minutes at all meetings, implementing decisions of the steering committee, office management and logistics, and financial administration, all on a half-day basis, because that is what the budget allowed for.

As temporary organisers during the month of October, Susan, Barbara and I had prepared a comprehensive report on our month's activities for the steering committee. Office filing systems covering all areas of activity had been created. An average of ten cases a day were being processed through the complaints and advice service during the month. However, the report questioned the strategic value of this service in promoting worker organisation, especially where the issue involved the individual circumstances of a single worker, rather than a group concern. Would it not, asked the authors of the report, make more sense to refer these matters to institutions such as the relevant Industrial Council, the Department of Labour or the Legal Aid Bureau?

IAS finances were in a state of crisis. By the end of the month, an amount of R443.72 would be required to pay salaries (and there was a saving here, because the temporary administrators were not claiming any payment), office rent (R75), rent for the next four months on a photocopy machine (R30), and an accumulated telephone account of R188.72, which had not been paid since its installation in April. The balance in the current account stood at just over R200.

Literacy teaching was developing well. A number of black instructors were being trained. They would be able to take over classes by the beginning of the new year. Literacy classes were increasingly being linked to factory organisation. Sue Brown had drawn up 'a pamphlet on the difference between and uses of works committees, liaison committees and factory committees, and how to set them up'. This pamphlet was being distributed in the various factories by her pupils, and Pindile Mfeti was mandated to make contact with the workers at those factories with a view to incorporating them into IAS organisation.

The report also noted that a number of volunteers had been brought into the IAS to assist in developing materials for worker education classes. These included Wits academics Phil Bonner, Sheldon Leader and Bernie Fanaroff, and Chris Bonner, a school teacher.

Towards the end of February 1975, Jeanette Curtis proposed to the steering committee that I be appointed in a permanent position. This was agreed to, but a dispute arose over salary levels for staff members. The committee accepted that no IAS staff member should be paid more than an 'average worker's factory wage'. However, some committee members argued that, given the multiple skills demanded in the post I was being appointed to, an exception should be made. The minutes read that 'Mr Moss re-entered the meeting and made it clear that he would not accept a salary higher than the organisers', who were on a scale of R100 a month. As my job in the IAS was deemed to be half-time, R50 month was offered and accepted.

IAS activity was steaming ahead. Embryonic worker representative structures were being constituted in more and more factories, and these had to be guided, serviced and assisted. This involved factory and home visits, worker education and literacy classes, investigation and resolution of group grievances against management, meetings, distribution of publications and pamphlets at the factory gates, and research into industries where organisation was taking place.

The back-up required for these activities was functioning fairly efficiently. The demands placed on those involved were considerable, and many of us were working very long days and then meeting late into the evening, six or seven days a week. As the person delegated to convene most meetings, and take and distribute the minutes, what should have been my sleeping hours were increasingly consumed by typing out minutes and compiling background documents and reports. Apart from maintaining and running the office during the day, I found myself in consultations: with lawyers and law students on setting up a workers' law clinic; with doctors from the Alexandra Clinic to see if medical services could be set up for workers; and with state bureaucrats on the registration of the IAS as a benefit society.

I regularly negotiated with institutions such as the Labour Department, Bantu Affairs Administration Board and Industrial

Councils to undertake the implementation and enforcement of those minimal rights that workers had in the system of labour relations. Each of these initiatives, each of these engagements with the state in its various forms, demanded a report, a position paper or a strategic plan.

*　*　*

There was growing international interest in the IAS and its work. A delegation from the Swedish Trade Union Federation (LO) undertook a mission to South Africa, and spent some time in the IAS offices observing our work, asking probing questions about organising strategies and our views on trade unionism. Åke Magnusson, who served as assistant secretary to that mission, recalls that both their visit and recommendations were severely criticised by the ANC and the Swedish solidarity movement for going against the policy of isolating South Africa. In particular, the mission's proposal to support trade union initiatives within South Africa was strongly rejected by Sactu.[18]

Although some veterans of Sactu still active within the country were involved in the new trade union initiatives, Sactu-in-exile initially responded as if these constituted a threat to its position. Stephen Dlamini, president of Sactu, had dismissed the internal organisations as 'yellow or puppet' trade unions at the 1976 ILO conference.[19] Some individuals within the ANC and SACP argued that democratic trade unionism under apartheid was an impossibility, and that new initiatives to organise workers were of their nature 'collaborationist' or involved the discredited form of parallel unionism advocated by the conservative Trade Union Council of South Africa (Tucsa). Some within Sactu criticised international – and particularly Western – union support for the new initiatives within South Africa as being undermining of the struggle for national liberation.

Ray Alexander, founder of the Food and Canning Workers Union in the 1940s and a Sactu stalwart, had argued in 1969 that 'the most urgent task is to rebuild a militant trade union movement in

South Africa ... We must organise under any name – Mutual Benefit Societies, Co-ops. We may even have to consider utilising the "Works Committees".'[20] Yet there were Sactu leaders who dismissed these new unions as 'yellow' or 'puppets', and were campaigning to exclude them from international union solidarity.

Most of those working in the IAS were ill equipped to find a route through these competing claims, which seemed to have more to do with protection of territory and position than organising workers. Following the Swedish mission, the International Confederation of Free Trade Unions (ICFTU), historically antagonistic to Sactu on the basis of Cold War politics, expressed interest in supporting the IAS. There were a number of interactions with its Africa secretary, Andrew Kailembo. The IAS did not have any established policies on international collaboration and liaison. We were aware of the ICFTU's historical pro-West, anti-communist leanings, and its hostility to the communist-aligned World Federation of Trade Unions. To the extent that the IAS considered these issues – and they were not priorities at the time – a cautious non-aligned stance seemed sensible, and funds offered by the ICFTU were gratefully accepted.

At around the same time, security police increased surveillance, and there was at least one forced entry when documents were scrutinised, but nothing stolen. When I reported this as a burglary to police at John Vorster Square the morning after the break-in, the CID officer sent to 'investigate' slipped up, indicating that he knew all about the break-in, even though I had not yet provided details. I suggested that fingerprints should be taken from a window ledge above the door where entry had been forced. No point, explained the officer; the widow frame had been wiped clean – but he had not yet looked at it.

* * *

All of these issues, and the growing daily workload, were just manageable. However, it was the developing conflict with those supporting Tuacc's vision of trade unionism that became increasingly destructive of the progress being made by the IAS as a model of worker organisation.

Over December 1974 and early January 1975, Tuacc efforts to influence the strategic direction of the IAS intensified. It is likely that unionists from Durban cemented an alliance with individuals in the IAS structures over this period and planned to increase their influence in an orchestrated campaign. Some of their newly found allies spent their December holidays in Durban, and this facilitated the formation of these links. Private meetings were held to plan a takeover of the IAS and the marginalisation of those perceived as hostile to Tuacc strategies.

There was a range of political and strategic differences within the IAS, and between the IAS and the equivalent initiatives in Durban and Cape Town. These were by no means absolute or separated by Berlin-type walls. They could best be viewed as part of a search for appropriate strategic and analytical approaches to complex issues of history, politics and worker organisation. The dominant faction in Tuacc sought control over the IAS, rather than engagement over the most appropriate strategies for worker organisation. This intervention was the major factor in the dysfunctional conflict which developed in the IAS over the next few months, rather than any internal differences between Sactu supporters and students over the place of 'the national question' in class organisation.

There were certainly different motives for organising workers within the IAS. One approach was based on adherence to political support for the ANC and its military struggle through MK. Its supporters viewed worker organisation as a tool through which advance-guard workers could be recruited for MK training or other underground activity on behalf of the national liberation movement. This had its adherents both within a pro-ANC faction in Tuacc and within the IAS.

A second and related strategy conceived of worker organisation as a means to strengthen political support for the multi-class politics of national liberation. This was sometimes presented as an attempt to bolster the presence of working-class interests within the broad class alliance on which the ANC was based. The Communist Party's two-stage theory of revolution was compatible with this approach, as was the stated role of Sactu as the trade union wing of a multi-class movement for national liberation.

The role and position of Sactu in these different strategies was itself contested terrain. For some, new initiatives to organise workers at factory or shop level presented an opportunity to revive or strengthen Sactu's 'underground' presence within South Africa, and to enhance the influence of the ANC-led alliance in the country. The critique of this approach was often premised on suggestions that Sactu had historically subordinated working-class interests to those of the multi-class national liberation movement.

Yet another strategic variant viewed worker organisation in strictly 'economistic' terms. On this argument, politics was inevitably the preserve of interests opposed to the working class, and worker organisation needed to be sealed off and protected from political influence emanating from beyond the factory or shopfloor. Worker organisation should focus exclusively on 'point of production' issues and the economic relationship between labour and management. The working class should be insulated from alliances with other interests and classes, because history showed that these inevitably subordinated worker interests.

Another faction viewed worker organisation as just one strategy in the struggle against apartheid and for national liberation, no different from other struggles against racial oppression. Organising workers at their places of employment was part of a general attempt to mobilise oppressed people against apartheid, regardless of whether they were in factories, the communities, at universities or schools, or unemployed.

Adherence to one or other of these positions was both based on, and resulted in, opposing organisational strategies and political loyalties. Different questions being asked of worker organisation logically resulted in different answers. During 1975, these solidified into organisational factions and contending alliances, which formed the basis for the intense disputes between what were loosely called 'workerists' and 'populists' in the union movement of the later 1970s and 1980s.

These schisms also presented themselves in different forms of trade unionism. Those more inclined to support working-class involvement in political, community or anti-apartheid alliances argued that general trade unions, organised across industrial sectors, best facilitated their strategy. Adherents to a narrower form of shopfloor unionism, strongly rooted in 'bread-and-butter' or economic demands, saw industrial unions as the appropriate organisational structure.

A range of other issues cut across these two models. The timing of union formation; the roles and responsibilities of shop stewards and shop steward councils; union democracy and accountability of officials and organisers to membership; and the role of worker education in organisation were among the most contested of these.

The Durban unions being formed under the auspices of Tuacc were explicitly industrial in structure. In the Western Cape, a general workers' union was the chosen model for organisation, as it provided a better vehicle for united worker action across industrial divides. Tuacc proponents argued that unions could be formed on the basis of membership in a few factories, and then expanded as more factories were organised. The dangers of industrial division and narrow sectoral interests could be avoided through strong industrial unions united under a co-ordinating federation of unions.

Some of the foundation members of the IAS steering committee believed that deep organisation and intensive education, especially for worker representatives, should precede union formation. This was seen as a better basis for internal democracy and accountability of worker representatives to members, and as a safeguard against 'economism' and co-optation into 'gradualist reformism'.

Until Tuacc elements started actively intervening in IAS strategies, the majority in the steering committee and those working on the projects were committed to finding strategic and organisational answers to these issues through a synthesis of the Durban and Cape Town positions. There was certainly a greater sympathy for the strategies of the Western Province Workers Advice Bureau and the Workers Advisory Project. Their support for models of general unionism, and efforts to link factory and shopfloor organisation to the wider issues of the communities where workers lived, took account of a political dimension largely absent in the Tuacc model. However, there was also an acceptance that solid industrially based organisation was a fundamental requirement for any viable trade unionism or for unions to assume a sustainable political role.

Differences in approach also related to the timing and circumstances in which industrial unions were constituted, and whether this was best viewed as a means to organise further or as an outcome of organisation. The IAS argued that premature imposition of industrial unions undermined the development of worker democracy, strengthened union tendencies to bureaucratisation and top-down decision-making, and limited the potential for united working-class activity by entrenching industrial divisions.

I had produced a position paper arguing that a cross-industry general shop stewards' council would be an appropriate representative structure pending the formation of any industrial unions. On this model, workers from each factory where the IAS had established a presence would elect representatives. They would be offered intensive education and skills training as a general shop stewards' group, rather than as separate factory or industry representatives. This education programme would have broad historical elements, including discussion of past relationships between trade unions and anti-apartheid politics; a focus on the contemporary place of worker organisation and worker interests; and practical orientation and skills training in respect of democracy, accountability of representatives, legal provisions, membership recruitment, grievance resolution and the like.

Once organisation had penetrated a particular industry sufficiently, and membership had grown, individual industrial unions could be formed. However, the cross-sectoral shop stewards' council would remain, with representation from all industrial sectors being organised. On this model, the council should, over a period of time and in a phased manner, take over responsibility as the decision-making structure for the IAS, replacing the steering committee.

* * *

These ideas were discussed at a meeting of representatives from the steering committee, worker education and literacy groups, and the Wages Commission on 14 January 1975. Johann Maree from the Western Province Workers Advice Bureau was present as an observer, and explained that group's preference for general worker unions over industrial unions. The meeting was conducted in a constructive manner, with serious debate and discussion on different ways forward and their implications. It is apparent from the minutes that the development of a broad cross-industry shop stewards' council, linked to worker education and training, received considerable support, as did the idea of a carefully phased introduction of industrial trade unions in the metal and furniture sectors, where the IAS had its strongest bases.

A minority of representatives from the worker education group remained silent. They had reservations about this approach and were also unhappy that a supporter of general unionism in the Western Cape had addressed the meeting. It is probable that they left the meeting to caucus with other supporters of the Tuacc position and develop a counter-strategy. This group had already initiated a secret caucus with Tuacc representatives during December, but were now galvanised into further action by the IAS's efforts to find its own strategic route independent of what 'Durban' wanted.

The numbers attending the next meeting were swelled by representatives from the worker education group who had not previously attended sessions. One of those who had not been present at the previous meeting put forward a set of counter-proposals, aiming to change the structure of decision-making in the IAS and hasten the formation of industrial unions. Steven Friedman restated the proposals discussed at the previous meeting, including the role of a cross-industry shop stewards' committee and its phased assumption of executive and decision-making power in the IAS. Even though the previous meeting had accepted this approach in broad form, a second endorsement of Friedman's proposals was minuted.

Those who identified with the Tuacc approach were unhappy with this decision, and they used the rest of the meeting to suggest changes in the structure and composition of the steering committee. Their proposal involved dissolving the existing steering committee and replacing it with an expanded executive committee incorporating more worker education and literacy representatives. Although this would dilute the influence of those who had formed the IAS, it did not look in principle problematic, and was accepted. However, it soon became clear that there were now two contending factions in the IAS competing for ascendancy. The Tuacc strategy to gain control of the IAS involved the dissolution of the steering committee, and the insertion of representatives of the worker education group into a self-appointed decision-making executive committee.

In an effort to defuse this increasingly destructive conflict, an IAS delegation travelled to Durban to explain its strategy to Tuacc representatives and to confirm that the differences in approach posed no threat to the Natal-based unions. The IAS, we wanted to assure Tuacc, had no territorial ambitions or demands.

* * *

Jen Curtis, Sipho Kubheka – employed by the IAS after he had been dismissed from Imextra following attempts to organise workers there – and I set off for Durban in my old Volkswagen. Outside Mooi River, the accelerator cable on the vehicle snapped. I was able to effect a makeshift repair by shortening the cable and reattaching it. This left the engine running at very high revs, as if the accelerator was already depressed, and I had little control as we careered along the N3 highway. Slowing down was both difficult and dangerous, as it involving braking at the same time as accelerating – something even a learner driver knows can lead to a vehicle overturning.

We stopped in Mooi River, making enquiries at the local garage about replacing the cable. White mechanics in Mooi River were unaccustomed to dealing with a group made up of a young white woman and two young men, one black and the other white. We were in high spirits, slightly hysterical after the dangerous ride at speed into Mooi River. We were clearly friends. Hostility, tending to aggression, exuded from the mechanic. Initially, he indicated that the cable could not be repaired or replaced. Then he retreated a little, saying that the job would take a day. After I indicated that I would then have to route the cable through the driver's side window and control acceleration and deceleration by hand, he relented, and agreed to replace the cable with another I had found at a spares outlet across the road. We could not sit together in the strictly 'whites only' Mooi River café attached to the garage, so stood outside in the main street, sipping cold drinks and waiting for the mechanic to repair the vehicle. Sipho had found a soccer ball in the back of my car, and we kicked it to each other while we waited.

Back on the road, it soon became clear that the cable had not been fitted correctly. The vehicle roared and over-revved whenever I changed gears or shifted into neutral in an attempt to slow down without braking. Another makeshift adjustment on the side of the road, and we continued our hazardous trip to Durban.

We stayed at the home of Luli Callinicos and Eddie Webster. It must have been difficult for them to host us. We represented a tendency in emerging unionism opposed to the group with which they were working in Durban. In addition, they had recently had a baby, who was occupying much of their time and focus. Yet they were welcoming and engaged us in a probing but constructive manner on the IAS approach to worker organisation. I also recall Luli trying to teach me how to make fluffy omelets, with extremely limited success.

Our welcome was somewhat cooler at the Tuacc offices in Gale Street, and it seemed that organisers had been instructed to keep their distance from the IAS delegation. Neither contending group gained any deeper understanding of the other's position, although a few existing relationships were consolidated.

* * *

The next few months demonstrated the destructive and corrosive effects of factionalism and caucusing. Lack of experience in organising workers, and the absence of any substantial membership base or constituency, allowed both factions to behave with scant regard to worker interests. Positions were attached to individuals, who were then attacked and undermined as an easier route than debating differing approaches. Secret caucuses were formed, plots hatched, strategies to win more power planned. Factionalism and ill-discipline were evident on both sides. Youth (I turned 23 in the midst of this), inexperience in dealing with organisational conflict and difference, naiveté around what the structures of worker organisation entailed, and an increasing physical and emotional exhaustion were all ingredients in this toxic organisational brew.

8
Unravelling the Industrial Aid Society

In little more than a year, the Industrial Aid Society had made some progress in developing an independent model of worker organisation for the Transvaal. This was based on the principles of a strong factory-floor presence, consciousness raising through education programmes, development of a shop stewards' council which cut across sectoral boundaries, and a blend of industrial and general unionism.

This innovative approach tried to take account of the history of relations between trade unions and political organisation, especially in the alliance between the ANC and Sactu. National democratic or liberation politics were necessarily based on an alliance of classes and differed markedly from the more specific rigours of working-class organisation. Defining the relationships between them guided IAS attempts to develop appropriate strategies to challenge employers in the workplace as well as the apartheid state. The developing conflict with the Durban-based Tuacc soon undermined and then destroyed the fragile IAS initiative.

The multiple demands of administering and maintaining the IAS, attending all meetings, implementing mandates and decisions, as well as coping with the gradual fragmentation of what had thus far been a fairly coherent and supportive group, exacted something of a toll. Along with others, I was guilty of over-personalising and individualising the issues. On occasion I threatened to break away from the IAS or resign my position. I became resentful that the Tuacc faction seemed unable to appreciate what the IAS founders had delivered in terms of infrastructure, direction and activity. I was personally angry that the punitive workload I had carried for months seemed unacknowledged, that the efficient manner in which the IAS was running, and the successes Jeanette and I had achieved in putting the organisation on a fairly sound financial footing, were being undermined.

The Tuacc group now openly moved to take control of the IAS. Attacks on individuals became commonplace, and increasingly the immediate battles, rather than the issues and interests that lay beneath them, became the focus of activity.

Some supporters of the Tuacc initiative were being supplied with information of a confidential nature that did not relate to IAS activities. While I was still SRC president at Wits, Beyers Naudé had entrusted me with a source of funds. Initially, it had been used to set up the literacy group and to fund some of Pindile Mfeti's costs when travelling on what I assumed, but did not know for certain, were ANC missions.

Shortly after starting work at the IAS, Jeanette Curtis had taken Steve Friedman and me to see Eli Weinberg. On a few occasions, he had handed over cash amounts for IAS set-up costs. We were aware that these were funds probably channelled from Sactu and the SACP. When the amounts were too large to absorb immediately, we would deposit them into the account used to receive funds from Beyers, gradually releasing them to the IAS as 'donations'. This fund was also used to acquire a kombi, which allowed IAS organisers to transport workers to and from meetings in the evenings and over weekends.

Sometime during the conflict, the Tuacc group in the IAS demanded that I report on the 'literacy' account. I refused, initially for security reasons. I was disinclined to reveal that funds might have been used for underground activities or that one of the sources was a banned member of the Communist Party. Subsequently, and after discussion with Beyers and Eli, I took the position that the account had nothing to do with the IAS, and hence there was no obligation to reveal anything about it to the IAS executive.

Jeanette tried to protect me. She admitted that, as chair of the

IAS finance committee, she had at all times known of the separate account which was now a point of contention, and had approved the gradual release of funds from it into IAS operating accounts. Her assurances did not seem to satisfy those now trying to take control of the IAS, and she tendered her resignation as chair of its finance structure.

Someone must also have informed members of the group supporting Tuacc that I was involved in political initiatives to set up a Movement for Social Democracy and a publishing and printing facility that would function under the name of Counter Information Services. Preparations for these were fairly advanced, and I had obtained in-principle agreement to fund the start-up costs from Lars-Gunnar Eriksson of the International University Exchange Fund (IUEF). He wanted an in-depth briefing on these initiatives. I was unable to travel out of the country legally, as my passport had been withdrawn in 1971, and Susan Brown agreed to travel to Geneva to meet Eriksson on my behalf.

Members of the IAS executive committee obtained access to this information. I was questioned about these initiatives and instructed to report all details – including those of Susan's proposed trip – to its members. Who, asked one member of the committee aligned with the Tuacc group, did Susan intend to visit overseas? What were the funds she was raising intended for? Apart from indicating that the IAS had no authority over this initiative, I refused to discuss the issue.

Finally, I made a strategic error in my dealings with the now-rampant Tuacc-supporting committee. To date, I had only refused to comply with instructions that fell outside the ambit of my employment by the IAS. Then, in a reversal of previous decisions, the committee resolved to constitute a Transvaal branch of the Natal-based Metal and Allied Workers Union (Mawu), and focus all organising efforts on this sector. I strongly opposed this, as I did not think our penetration of the industry in the Transvaal was deep enough to form a union. In addition, I was of the view that this decision had been taken to allow Mawu to claim it had a presence in the Transvaal, something it required in order to strengthen its negotiation of a recognition agreement with an employer who had factories in both Natal and the Transvaal. It seemed a clear case of the interests of the IAS and the workers it represented being subordinated to the requirements of Tuacc and the Natal unions.

A series of long and fractious meetings took place over the next few days. Some convened in the early mornings (one started at 6 a.m.), others ran late into the night. I was instructed to organise the administrative infrastructure required to form a metal union: membership cards, application forms, letterheads – and a rubber stamp. I refused to do this, with one exception: I had the rubber stamp made. I marched into a subsequent meeting. 'Here is your trade union,' I announced. The symbolism of a rubber stamp did not pass everyone by. However, I had refused to implement an instruction from the executive committee and was now more vulnerable to attack.

* * *

While these conflicts were playing themselves out in IAS executive meetings and in caucuses hidden from scrutiny, the daily work of the organisation continued. The initiative to set up a legal aid clinic occupied a considerable amount of my working time, and there was a series of meetings with lawyers who were committed to such a project. They included Felicia Kentridge, who subsequently played a central role in establishing the Legal Resources Centre in 1977; John Myburgh; and Ernie Wentzel, who, despite his public hostility to the Communist Party, showed an admirable commitment to the rights of workers. Students from the Wits Law Faculty Council also became involved in these discussions. By May 1975, it looked as if a regular Saturday clinic, run from IAS offices, supervised by practising lawyers and staffed by legal students, would soon open its doors.

Day-to-day worker issues dealt with in the IAS were often legally complex, and guidance from trained and trainee lawyers would help to resolve them more professionally. Conditions of employment for African workers were administered through a range of state institutions, and subject to a number of different statutes and regulations. As I pointed out in a memorandum to the lawyers and students on the scope of work a clinic would entail, these included the Department of Labour, the Industrial Councils, the Workmen's Compensation commissioner, the West Rand Bantu Affairs Administration Board and the Bantu Affairs commissioner. Through this initiative, the IAS was trying to create a support group of lawyers and aspirant lawyers who would become skilled in understanding this complex set of institutions and laws and using them where possible to assist organising initiatives.

Staff and organisers dealing with individual complaints achieved surprisingly good success rates, despite the hostility of state institutions and the bias of legislation and regulations against employees. Working daily with these sorts of cases showed, over and over again, how employers benefited from the systems of labour control developed as part of racial segregation and apartheid. The way employers took advantage of the weakness of workers was equally clear. In the absence of strong worker organisation, employers were often able to circumvent those very few legal rights and protections which workers did have.

The functional relationship between the capitalist private sector and the apartheid state, which had been theorised by academics, was now given content through daily engagement with the realities of state power, employer conduct and worker oppression.

* * *

My days as an IAS organiser were numbered. I had been targeted as a central opponent of the Tuacc strategy for unionisation in the Transvaal. As a senior member of staff opposed to the Tuacc strategy, I would have to go.

I resolved to throw myself fully into developing the initiatives associated with the Movement for Social Democracy (MSD) and Counter Information Services (CIS). With an assurance from Lars-Gunnar Eriksson that the IUEF would fund start-up costs, I began sourcing litho printing equipment. There was something of a stir when I arrived on my motorcycle at a supplier of printing equipment deep in a white working-class area, and placed an order for a full-colour litho machine, a plate-maker and a supply of chemicals and ink. My youth, hair length and mode of transport clearly worried the salesman, but he eventually took down details of my requirements and became noticeably more enthusiastic when I offered to pay in cash.

I had approached a lithographer whom I knew at Wits to establish whether he would be available to do the printing for MSD and CIS. Simon Behrens had worked through a number of nights to print the publications and pamphlets needed for the 1974 campaign to release all political prisoners, and I was exceptionally pleased when he expressed enthusiasm for these new projects.

In the midst of the IAS conflict and plans for MSD and CIS, a group within Nusas enquired whether I might be willing to re-enter student politics and accept nomination as the next president. It was only nine months since my term as SRC president at Wits had ended, and I was still registered as a student through the University of South Africa, trying to complete the one credit needed for my degree. I remained connected to developments in Nusas through the Wages Commissions and close colleagues working in the student movement, and was a number of years younger than the incumbent president, Karel Tip. Perhaps the suggestion was not as improbable as I initially thought.

I took off a few days from the IAS, and headed for the annual Nusas congress, which was being held at the Durban campus of the University of Natal. There, I was able to discuss plans with a number of trusted colleagues, including Dan O'Meara, who was involved in the MSD initiative, and friends like Gerry Maré and Cedric de Beer, who were still in Nusas leadership positions. It didn't take me long to decide that I was not going to re-enter student politics, and that I would rather throw my energies into developing the MSD and CIS as post-student initiatives.

One evening, a group from the Nusas congress landed up at the home of Eddie Webster and Luli Callinicos. Discussion slowly evolved into a more social evening, and before long there was music and dancing – and copious consumption of Tassenberg, the cheap red wine many of us drank. Two of the left's more promising troubadours – Dan O'Meara and Barry Gilder – were present. They produced guitars and started playing and singing. This certainly did not involve the 'struggle' songs for which Barry subsequently became well known, after he went into exile to avoid military service, joined the ANC and trained as a member of MK. It was the music of the 1950s and 1960s, featuring as much of Elvis Presley as Barry and Dan could recall. There must have been a wildness in the air, because I joined them, singing along and displaying what little remained of my guitar skills. A frenzied, slightly desperate mood took hold of the gathering, as many of those present seemed to understand that we were at the end of the youthful politics that had dominated our lives.

* * *

I did not attend the executive committee meeting which expelled me from the IAS. It may have occurred while I was in Durban or at some other time when I was unable to be present. No record of that meeting seems to have survived, although I do know who proposed and supported my expulsion, and who tried to defend me. Refusing to undertake the administration required to 'form' a metal workers' union (apart from the rubber stamp supplied) constituted one reason for the expulsion. Declining to report on financial matters that had nothing to do with the IAS, including Sue Brown's trip to Geneva on behalf of MSD and CIS, as well as the secret 'literacy account', apparently constituted the other.

This decision could have been challenged. I was an employee of the IAS and could not therefore be 'expelled'. Some sort of disciplinary process would have been required to dismiss an employee, rather than expulsion as a member of a committee. Although this was something one would have expected a group of aspirant trade unionists to be aware of, I decided not to contest the decision. It was clear that the

IAS founded by Jeanette Curtis and Steven Friedman, and strongly supported by the Wits Wages Commission, had changed radically. It was equally obvious that efforts to find a separate path to progressive worker organisation in the Transvaal had been demolished on the altar of Tuacc requirements. Within a short period of time, Jeanette, Steven, most Wages Commission members and the literacy co-ordinators had been expelled from, or left, the IAS.

The early conflicts in the IAS were sometimes incoherent, as contestations over power and control, rather than programme and strategy, often are. Ideologically, there were no insurmountable barriers between the evolving positions on worker organisation and structures of trade unionism, although differences over the relationship between worker organisation and national liberation politics were based on real divergences in approach.

Ideologically and analytically, there were questions whether the ANC, as a multi-class organisation committed to national liberation, would inevitably subordinate the interests of the working class to the popular politics of nationalism. There were questions whether trade unions should avoid political engagement, especially in multi-class, nationalist or populist initiatives, or whether they should engage as a way of asserting working-class interests within alliance politics. If unions eschewed broad anti-apartheid politics, were there other forms of political engagement that emerged from and on the factory floor, separate from the politics of national liberation and the struggle against apartheid?

Taffy Adler, who became involved in IAS activities after this period of intense conflict, characterised the differences between Tuacc and the IAS as 'whether you focused on trying to create a political movement or a trade union movement'.[1] This was a caricature of a far more complex set of issues, both organisationally and ideologically. Operationally, the IAS had been making considerable headway in developing solid factory-based structures and servicing these through legal, educational and administrative services. The model it was developing tried to synthesise the strongest characteristics of both general and industrial unionism as represented in the strategies of

Tuacc and the Western Province Workers Advice Bureau, avoiding what were perceived to be their weaknesses.

At the same time, the IAS model confronted some of the broader political issues of worker organisation. How were unions best to avoid the institutional dangers of narrow economism, in which the immediate material interests of workers excluded engagement with apartheid or 'national oppression'? Did unions operate in the most progressive manner if they had some link to political programmes or organisations? If this was the case, how were they to guard against the interests of their members being subordinated to the interests of other classes forming part of a broad alliance? Was a progressive legal trade unionism even possible under South African conditions of repression? Some elements in Sactu and the Communist Party argued that unionism of African workers was impossible under South African conditions. It was bound either to be smashed or co-opted by employer and state interests.

Johann Maree, who was associated with the organisation of workers in the Western Cape, introduced greater subtlety than Adler in his discussion of general and industrial unionism:

> The argument in favour of a general union approach was that an industrial union would become economistic especially if it followed Tuacc's policy, and that it easily led to bureaucratisation ... It was also feared that a trade union without the guidance of a political party would fall prey to reformism. To overcome this worker education was considered to be of the utmost importance to ensure that an appropriate worker consciousness was developed before trade union structures came into existence.[2]

However, even this more sophisticated analysis misses the point. The contestation between the IAS and Tuacc was not exclusively over a general versus an industrial structure, or whether unions should be 'political' or not. It was the methods of organising, the role of worker education, the depth of factory and shop steward organisation required before unions should be formed, and the nature of working-class politics, that informed the IAS's early efforts to find an independent way.

These were the difficult questions being raised over competing class interests, terrains of organisation and struggle, different identities, and the relationship between short-term economic gains and longer-term political agendas.

Differences in the strategies and tactics of organisation were woven through this tapestry of contending analyses and arguments. Were general worker unions more appropriate for the development of a working-class politics based in the factories and in the communities, or did solid and accountable organisation necessitate tight industrial structures? Should unions be formed as a way of organising workers at the point of economic production, or was democratic practice better entrenched by organising groups of workers across a range of factories first, and only then forming a trade union?

The controlling faction in Tuacc had rigid views on these issues and believed that the imposition of its approach on the IAS was a requirement for its expansion. The forms of worker organisation developing in the Western Cape were based on different socio-economic conditions and political histories and had adopted other strategies and organisational tactics. Early IAS pioneers, setting up in the heartland of the economy, were trying to develop a third way. This took into account aspects of the Cape and Natal 'positions', and welded these into an 'independent' approach that could be implemented in the political, economic, social and ideological conditions of the Transvaal.

* * *

There is little agreement over the role of the organisations of national liberation, represented in the alliance of Sactu, the Communist Party and the ANC, in the new unionism. Individuals owing some allegiance to Congress Alliance organisations in general, and Sactu in particular, were involved in organisational initiatives in Natal, the Western Cape and the Transvaal in the early 1970s. In Natal, this seemed to extend to underground ANC activities, including initiatives to recruit workers for military training under the auspices of MK.[3] In the Western Cape, UCT-linked Wages Commission members made contact with a range of people in the townships who had experience in trade union organisation. These included Sactu stalwarts, who became involved in the new forms of organisation.[4]

Within the IAS, there were at least three different ways in which individuals associated with Congress Alliance organisations influenced developments. The first was on the basis of past experience. The young student group associated with the Wages Commissions had no experience in organising workers or setting up trade unions. Partly through Jeanette Curtis, they sought access to an older generation that had been involved in trade unionism. This is how Miriam Sithole, who had worked in the Sactu office in the early 1960s, serving at one time as acting general secretary, was asked to join the founding IAS steering committee. However, at the same time a trade unionist historically associated with Sactu's rival, the Federation of Free African Trade Unions of South Africa (Fofatusa), was also asked to join the steering committee. This suggests that those forming the IAS were seeking access to past experience in unionism, rather than a specific Sactu involvement or endorsement.

Secondly, there were some individuals involved in the IAS who acted, on a clandestine basis, with others linked to Sactu, the ANC and the Communist Party. I do not know whether this extended to underground cell systems, or whether it involved more informal 'networking' between people of similar history, outlook and loyalty. Certainly, Miriam Sithole was in close contact with people committed to reviving ANC structures within the country. It is probable that she and Pindile Mfeti were part of an ANC cell which included Lindiwe Sisulu and reported, through Swaziland, to Thabo Mbeki. While their ANC allegiances obviously influenced the positions they adopted in the IAS disputes, there is no suggestion that they were undertaking any ANC activities – such as recruiting – through IAS structures.

Thirdly, there were some ANC operatives who saw IAS education programmes as an opportunity for young supporters to develop their political understanding, and possibly as a way of identifying people for recruitment to the ANC and MK. Robert Manci was an ANC veteran who had served a sentence on Robben Island and had been banned. He became a regular visitor to the IAS offices, bringing groups to literacy courses and worker education programmes. As an older man, he was something of a mentor to these youngsters, and worked with Sipho Kubheka at Imextra before he was fired and then employed as an IAS organiser.

Elliot Shabangu, who had been one of the accused in the Suppression of Communism and Terrorism Act trials of 'the 22' in 1969 and 1970, was involved in sending young people to the IAS to participate in education programmes. One of these young protégés was Amos Masondo, at the time a member of the National Youth Organisation (Nayo). A number of Nayo members, including Masondo, were subsequently charged under the Terrorism Act for allegedly making preparations to leave the country and undergoing military training with MK.

One of the youngsters Robert Manci brought to IAS classes on Saturdays was Bafana Mohlayaneng. When 'Sammy', as he called himself in IAS classes, appeared as the fourth accused in a major ANC trial, charged with undergoing MK military training, it became apparent that at least one ANC group was using IAS facilities to recruit and educate potential members for MK.

By 1976, Manci was heading an ANC underground unit, together with Joe Gqabi. Manci and a young MK soldier from Soweto, Tokyo Sexwale, were apprehended by uniformed police shortly after crossing into South Africa from Swaziland. Locked into the back of a police van without being searched, Sexwale was able to throw a grenade into the front cab of the van, and he and Manci escaped.[5]

Sipho Kubheka joined the ANC in 1977. Up until then, he saw himself as a supporter of the ANC, and worked with Manci, Joe Gqabi, Elliot Shabangu and others who were involved in ANC underground activity. Although Manci was guiding a group of young people along a political path, Kubheka says that he did not try to recruit them to the ANC or MK:

What is interesting about Manci is that he did not recruit us to the ANC. He just gave us the basics so that we could find roots ourselves. The accusations which were levelled against the ANC by the ultra-left grouping was that the ANC was only interested in recruiting people to the military and to the ANC. Yet the ANC was introduced to us differently. We were not told to join the ANC when we were still at Imextra. We were taught labour politics, the political history of South Africa and international politics. That is what the ANC–Sactu people did.[6]

* * *

Funds which Eli Weinberg channelled to the IAS probably came via Sactu or the SACP. A small IAS group travelled to Botswana in 1974 or early 1975 to meet with Sactu and ANC representatives, including Ray Alexander, and brief them on emerging organisational initiatives. I was supposed to be part of that delegation, but decided not to join it as I did not have a passport and would have had to cross the border to Botswana illegally. Given the risks involved, I decided not to attend.

This IAS trip to meet Ray Alexander in Botswana was paid for out of IAS funds, and while discretion was certainly advised regarding the initiative, it was not 'secret or clandestine' and had been discussed among members of the IAS steering committee.[7]

By the time the IAS was splintering under pressure of internal disputes, there was no single or coherent 'Sactu' or 'ANC' position. Over time, Pindile and Miriam gravitated towards the Tuacc group, which was highly critical of the Congress Alliance. Jeanette Curtis, who was close to both Sactu and the ANC, lined up against Tuacc efforts to shift IAS strategy, and remained supportive of the general worker initiatives in the Western Cape. Sipho Kubheka, linked to people in the ANC and Sactu underground, became an organiser and then secretary of the Metal and Allied Workers Union in the Transvaal – a strongly 'workerist' union within the Tuacc grouping. He worked closely with Gavin Andersson, who, in 1975, was one of the major proponents of the Tuacc takeover of the IAS, but thereafter linked up with Sactu and ANC structures – to which the Tuacc lobby was implacably opposed.[8]

There was nothing simple about the way in which individuals decided to associate themselves with different and competing tendencies. Those decisions cannot be 'read off' relations with Sactu or the ANC, support for general or industrial unionism or – in the language of the late 1970s and early 1980s – 'workerism', 'economism' or political 'populism'. The positions adopted by individuals in this conflict were more fluid, the boundaries porous, the allegiances and alliances complex. They often related as much to issues of power and control as to ideological coherence and organisational affiliation.

Networks associated with the ANC in Johannesburg saw the IAS as an opportunity to recruit and train members for MK and the ANC underground. However, there was little evidence or indication of efforts to influence or direct IAS strategy and activity on the part of Sactu, the Communist Party or the ANC. The IAS organising strategy, which differed in notable respects from both the Tuacc and Cape-based initiatives, was in many respects 'home-grown'. It evolved as a process, in discussion and study, and from the experience gained trying to recruit workers, organise them, run worker education programmes, and set up cross-industry shop steward councils. Individuals and organisations may have had separate agendas and viewed IAS structures and activities as opportunities for a range of initiatives. However, the central organising strategy was developed in relative autonomy from the influences and requirements of other interests.

The issues which divided the IAS were early indicators of the conflicts that subsequently emerged between 'workerists' and 'populists', 'community' and 'shopfloor' unions, and general and industrial unions in the late 1970s and early 1980s. Fosatu, for instance, held different views from the 'community' and general unions over whether trade unions should involve themselves in class alliances beyond the factory floor and tackle political and community issues. Strongly divergent attitudes were also held about the politics of national liberation in general, and the ANC–Communist Party–Sactu alliance in particular, ranging from active support for the alliance to outright hostility. Partly for these reasons, Fosatu refused to affiliate to or support the United Democratic Front (UDF) when it was formed in 1983. All these schisms were both anticipated and reflected in the factional battles within the IAS in the mid-1970s, in its attitudes to the organisations and politics of national liberation, and in its changing relations with trade union initiatives in Natal and the Western Cape.

9

Unavoidably detained

'Perhaps you have heard of me? My name is Spyker van Wyk.' The notorious security police torturer leered at me from the front seat of a police vehicle, parked in a partially constructed, dark and deserted garage under a building in central Pretoria.

In the weeks following my expulsion from the executive committee of the Industrial Aid Society, I had moved increasingly into the role of full-time political activist. Initiatives to set up the Movement for Social Democracy (MSD) and a publishing and printing unit to be known as Counter Information Services (CIS) were well under way. I had received support for these initiatives from some of those who had left the IAS after my expulsion, Nusas leaders, progressive academics and intellectuals, Beyers Naudé from the Christian Institute, and members of the Congress-aligned Human Rights Committee, with which the Wits SRC had worked in 1973 and 1974. Lars-Gunnar Eriksson of the International University Exchange Fund (IUEF), which was already supporting political research being undertaken by Dan O'Meara and Duncan Innes, also agreed to fund my proposal, including the printing infrastructure required.

There were, at the time, a number of overlapping initiatives aimed at gathering political intelligence useful to anti-apartheid opposition. CIS fitted into this frame, as did the South African Project at Warwick University, run by Martin Legassick, Duncan Innes and Dan O'Meara. The ANC head of research in London, Frene Ginwala, sometimes asked O'Meara and Innes to undertake research on multinationals and the South African economy, although they did not see themselves as working specifically for the ANC.[1] In addition, the organisation

Okhela, supported initially by at least two senior ANC leaders as well as elements within the Dutch anti-apartheid movement and a small group centred around the exiled poet and cultural activist Breyten Breytenbach, had plans for information-gathering and publications.

These projects reflected the broad anti-apartheid movement's growing need for thoughtful and useful political intelligence from within South Africa. The exile movements had been cut off from much of the political organisation, analysis and debate which had been developing internally. The reasons for this included the length of time they had been out of the country, communication and security issues, and distance. Yet information was a critical element in strategic planning, assessment and policy. It was also hard currency in the never-ending battles for ascendancy and position within the factions making up the ANC, Communist Party, Sactu, the various anti-apartheid organisations, governments, non-governmental and support organisations, and donors.

This explained the growing interest in information and political intelligence. Internal opposition politics were changing and becoming subject to the influences of new ideologies, notably Black Consciousness and non-Stalinist forms of Marxism. New structures of worker organisation were developing largely independently of the national liberation movements. Those distant from the country needed to know more of what was shaping internal political opposition, and how it influenced their strategies and operations.

Efforts to develop a 'third way' in politics, beholden to none of the players in the Cold War, were superimposed on this growing need for information from within South Africa. Social democrats from the Scandinavian countries had identified the Black Consciousness initiatives as a possible alternative to the ANC–SACP alliance, which they believed was too influenced by the Soviet Union. This was one of the reasons for Eriksson and the IUEF's strong financial backing of BC projects and organisations.

> The West was in an embarrassed alliance with apartheid South Africa, while the East – in the form of the Soviet Union – backed the ANC

through its alliance with the SACP ... The Scandinavian countries – in particular Sweden, under Prime Minister Olof Palme – shared the anti-Soviet [position] ... of their Western allies. But they were uncomfortable with support for the apartheid regime.

A small 'kitchen cabinet' around Palme welcomed the emergence of anti-apartheid forces which were hostile to the Soviet system and the SACP ... Brent Carlsson, general secretary of the Socialist International, Lars-Gunnar Eriksson, head of the IUEF, and Palme formed the core of this kitchen cabinet.[2]

Eriksson was particularly enthused by the emergence of new forces within South Africa which rejected Soviet-style communism but seemed to embrace democratic forms of socialism and socialist humanism. This included the BC movement as well as the 'new' radical left on the campuses represented through Nusas. The Swedish kitchen cabinet 'resolved to provide as much support as possible to encourage the growth of this perceived new force while ... preserving a non-sectarian façade towards the ANC'.[3]

According to Terry Bell, it was this 'desire to create a third way which helped propel [the apartheid spy] Craig Williamson into the position of IUEF liaison in South Africa through his prominent and responsible position in Nusas'.[4] It also facilitated Williamson's growing contact with representatives of Black Consciousness initiatives through his ability to provide funds. Although I certainly never discussed the MSD (or its proposed publishing wing, the CIS) with Williamson, Bell thinks he was aware of the idea in outline, and presented it to Eriksson in a note that referred to a potential 'national organisation' which would involve 'hand-picked people'. The note 'also casually made use of the names of various activists, including ... Glenn Moss, the student leader who continued to maintain that Williamson was suspicious'.[5] The 'home-grown' political radicalism of the early 1970s had now attracted international attention and become a small player in Cold War politics.

* * *

Dan O'Meara and Duncan Innes, who were visiting South Africa, participated in a number of discussions on the MSD and CIS during the first half of 1975. These meetings included Jeanette Curtis and Gerry Maré, who was a full-time member of the Nusas executive. Cedric de Beer, also a member of the Nusas executive, was briefed on developments whenever he travelled to Johannesburg, as was Gordon Young, a past Nusas leader involved in worker organisation in Cape Town. With a promise of funds from the IUEF, I placed an order for a litho printer and plate-maker, fully expecting to be able to begin printing and distribution of pamphlets and publications within the next few months. I prepared a draft constitution for the MSD, and there was a sense of excitement and anticipation as we began setting up a 'post-student' political organisation based on the experience and lessons of the first half of the 1970s that had formed us.

I was fully aware that these initiatives were moving closer to semi-clandestine or underground activity. During one of our meetings, Duncan and Dan introduced me to some of the techniques used to send coded messages and communications. Jeanette circulated Hugh Lewin's just-released but banned book, *Bandiet*, detailing his experiences as a detainee and political prisoner in both Pretoria Local and Central prisons. She had been advised that this was essential reading for anyone who might be detained or jailed in the future, and I devoured its contents.

Gerry contacted me, asking if I would travel to Cape Town to meet with someone interested in the work I was doing. We assumed that communications were subject to interception by security police or intelligence agencies, and rarely discussed any details telephonically or in writing. It was not unusual to be told that 'someone' wanted to meet and discuss 'something'. Any more information ran the risk of alerting one of the state agencies to what was being planned.

I did not need more detail. A close colleague had asked that I come to Cape Town, and that was enough. However, finances for a flight were an issue, and Gerry indicated that the costs would be covered through the Nusas student travel agency. Early on the morning of 13 August 1975, I flew to Cape Town. When I met up with Gerry, he was disinclined to tell me whom I would be meeting, or for what purposes. Again, this was not particularly unusual. Together with a number of colleagues, I had been spending more and more time in a twilight world between legality and illegality, above-ground activity and clandestine plans and intentions. This was the reality of trying to fashion a political role beyond the structures and constraints of student and campus politics.

We set off from the Nusas head office, with Gerry driving a yellow Volkswagen Beetle used as a run-around by the student organisation. Weaving our way through the city centre, we stopped at an intersection. I got out and moved into the back seat at Gerry's request. A tall bespectacled man, wearing a white trench coat, slipped into the front passenger seat. As we drove off, he spoke to me over his shoulder, introducing himself as 'Christian Galaska'. After a few minutes in which he and Gerry talked to each other in Afrikaans, he turned round and began asking about the publications I intended producing, and how he could get access to them. While I was cautiously explaining that subscription would be possible, with delivery by mail, Gerry suddenly pulled up. The vehicle behind us came close to tail-ending the yellow VW, confirming Gerry's terse statement: 'We are being followed.'

Gerry pulled off slowly, then accelerated, and began a hair-raising drive through the city centre, swinging right across ongoing traffic, turning suddenly left down smaller side streets, and accelerating up wider main roads. It soon became obvious that there was a phalanx of cars following us, no longer making any effort to avoid detection. Gerry speeded up further, onto De Waal Drive at the top of the city, along the M3, and finally cut across traffic to begin the climb up Rhodes Drive past Kirstenbosch.

A massive storm was lashing the Peninsula. Sheets of rain made it difficult to see, and strong gusts of wind threatened to blow us off the road. Conversation had ceased, as Gerry concentrated on keeping the car on the road. I watched through the rear window to see if we were making any headway in losing the line of vehicles behind us.

As we rounded a bend, Gerry braked hard. Lying across the road was a massive tree, uprooted by the high winds. We swung round in a tight turning circle and headed back down Rhodes Drive, passing the line of cars which had been following us. Slowly, they repeated the turning manoeuvre with less ease than the little VW had managed, and the procession made its way down behind us.

Back in the city centre, it was agreed that we would stop suddenly at an intersection, 'Christian' would jump out of the car and run off down a side street, and Gerry would drive off as fast as possible. 'You must leave, get out of South Africa, immediately,' Gerry told 'Christian'. As he left the VW, two men jumped from one of the cars behind us, and followed him down a side street.

Gerry and I drove back to the Nusas head office. I made it clear that I did not want to know any details of the man we had met or his mission. I decided to return to Johannesburg as soon as possible, but did have enough time for a brief discussion with Cedric de Beer. Like everyone else in the Nusas head office, he seemed to know that something dramatic had happened. Without giving any details, I told Cedric that I was worried about the events of the past hours and feared problematic consequences.

If Cedric was aware of unusual activity, then others in the Nusas offices, including Craig Williamson and Karl Edwards, must also have known. Williamson, as Nusas treasurer, would have been aware that an air ticket had been bought for me through the student travel office. Apart from any other leaks in security – and there were in all probability many – these alone made the contact between 'Christian' and people like Gerry compromised from the start.

'Christian', of course, was Breyten Breytenbach, although I did not know this at the time. I did, however, know that there was a move afoot to recruit whites from the left to an organisation which appeared to have some ANC support. I had discussed this in Durban when I visited the Nusas congress held in July. Shortly afterwards, Jeanette Curtis mentioned that she understood that some of the non-communist leaders in the ANC were committed to loosening the influence of the SACP. They were willing to support an initiative to set up a left-wing, but non-communist, organisation, made up predominantly of white intellectuals, who might provide some balance to the centralist and pro-Soviet form of communism represented by the SACP.

Both Jeanette and I had thought the initiative sounded dangerous and ill-conceived, although we did not have any further details about it. She did mention that there was someone in the country from whom she might obtain more information, but I think this referred to Barend Schuitema, who was apparently in Johannesburg, rather than Breytenbach. Jen had been quite ill with a bout of rheumatic fever and was confined to bed. Our discussions about what I later learnt was Okhela were limited, and the main purpose of my visits was to check on her health and establish whether she needed more reading material.

Over the next week, I became aware of some security police surveillance. The most obvious of these incidents involved an early-morning visit to my Bellevue flat, where a group of post office technicians arrived to install a telephone. I had applied for this some months before, but was told that no lines were available. Suddenly my application had been prioritised, and a number of technicians were out and about early in the morning to ensure good service. Two of the group were obviously not telephone technicians. My first call was to a friend telling her that I now had a telephone number, but that I was sure there were people listening in to our conversation.

* * *

The Nusas president, Karel Tip, had sent a message that he would be in Johannesburg, and asked if he could stay over in my flat. It was SRC election time at Wits, and both the campaign and the nature of the candidates standing suggested that there might be a swing away from Nusas. Karel wanted to monitor what was happening and be available when the results were announced. Sometime during the course of the afternoon of 20 August, Karel arrived at the flat and shared some very worrying news. Gerry Maré had been arrested while on a Nusas trip with Barry Gilder and had been taken to

Pietermaritzburg. Karel also mentioned the arrest of a few others, whose names were not familiar to me.

Karel thought that if Gerry had been arrested, his own detention would follow shortly. I wondered whether he should go into hiding, perhaps even leave the country for a while. He had thought about the various options but did not feel that, as Nusas president, he should try to avoid consequences or responsibilities. 'This is something I have to live through,' he explained.

I did not think I was in any particular danger. Even if security police were to arrest me in connection with my visit to Cape Town, I assumed it would be a short-term detention. It would soon emerge under questioning that I did not know whom I had met with, and that nothing of substance had transpired at the meeting.

We took ourselves off to an Italian restaurant in Hillbrow, and I joked with Karel about 'the last supper' as we consumed a decent quantity of red wine with pizzas. Then down the hill to the Wits campus, where SRC election results were being announced. Candidates hostile to Nusas had done well in the polls, indicating the beginnings of a shift in campus sentiment. I invited a number of the younger Nusas activists back to my flat in Bellevue, so that they could talk to Karel, and also to ensure that, if the security police arrived to detain him, there would be a supportive group of friends present. There must have been ten or more crammed into my tiny front room, drinking wine, when there was loud knocking at the door.

'We have been looking for you all night,' announced one of the security police as they entered the flat and saw me. 'And we are looking for Karel Tip.' I was fairly certain I recognised at least one of them from the group of 'technicians' who had installed my telephone.

Karel was in the bath and a policeman tried to open the bathroom door. Shielding a towel-draped Karel from the man's gaze, I told him that the security police wanted to speak to him. 'Then,' said Karel with incredible dignity, 'I had better see them.'

After he had dressed and packed his small satchel, Karel was taken off by one group of police. The others remained and began a systematic search of my flat. Removing every book from my plank-

and-brick bookshelves, they leafed through them, shaking the pages as if expecting to find something hidden. A growing pile of books, magazines and papers were put to one side. There was excitement when police found an expired passport belonging to Sue Brown. 'We thought she was in Geneva,' said one of the searchers. 'What passport is she using?'

During the search, one of the police reminded me how I had refused to give them access to filing cabinets when the SRC offices were raided the previous year, and hidden the keys. 'I hope you are not going to try to obstruct us tonight. You won't get away with it this time.'

Finally, satisfied with the havoc they had created in the flat, and with the pile of books and papers seized, police drove me down the dark and steeply inclined Stewart Drive behind the flat, into Viljoen Street, through Bez Valley and Bertrams, and onwards through the city to John Vorster Square. We turned into a garage through a side entrance, and got into a lift serving only the tenth floor – security police headquarters. I was being marched along a corridor when I saw Jane Lowmass walking towards me. A close friend, she had been part of the group which had returned to my flat earlier that evening. Breaking away from her police escort, she reached out and walked arm-in-arm with me until she was roughly pulled away. Hers was a brave gesture of support and defiance, which I carried with me as I was ushered into one of the security police offices leading off the corridor.

While I was looking at an official list of the documents taken from my flat, Colonel Johann Coetzee, then head of the security police in Johannesburg, entered the office. 'I am detaining you in terms of section 6 of the Terrorism Act,' he told me, adding that he was sure I was aware of the provisions and conditions of detention. Then he leaned forward and, smiling nastily, told me that 'no reasonable requests will be refused ... I am sure you understand what I mean by reasonable requests.'

Section 6. Solitary confinement. Indefinite detention. No access to lawyers, family or friends. No reading material. Ahmed Timol had died while being interrogated under this provision. Salim Essop had been tortured so severely that he was hospitalised. I had faced my first arrest in 1970 while protesting against the continued incarceration of 'the 22' under section 6. In some ways, Coetzee was right: I knew far too much about what happened to detainees held under section 6.

* * *

For the next few days and nights, I was held in a filthy cell at John Vorster Square, toilet overflowing and stinking, thin coir mattress on the floor, police station food pushed in at the door a few times a day. For the rest, I saw no one outside the closed system of control, and had no way of occupying myself except to pace the cell and try to sleep. The process of indefinite detention, in solitary confinement, had begun. On one occasion, a magistrate put his head into the cell and muttered something about *klagtes*. As he was scuttling out, I called after him that I did have complaints, but he hastened away before I managed to express them. At another time I was taken to a nearby district surgeon. He examined me in a cursory manner before handing a note to the attending security policeman, who was present throughout the examination. I wondered what the note confirmed: fit to undergo interrogation? Perhaps it noted a minor heart condition, and warned that I might succumb if subjected to electric shocks. District surgeons were as much part of the closed system of detention as interrogators, jailers and magistrates.

A week later, two security police arrived at my cell door in the late afternoon and told me to pack up. Pack up what? I had nothing with me apart from the clothes I was wearing. I was handcuffed and led up to the tenth floor, after being told that the restraints were for my own protection: 'We don't want you jumping or slipping, and then people claiming we did that to you,' one of them sniggered. Coetzee entered the office, and told me that I was being transferred to Pretoria. His colleagues there wanted to investigate my case, and in any event it would be better if I was out of Johannesburg where 'my friends' were 'causing trouble'.

Only after my release did I realise that he must have been referring to demonstrations against detentions. A university assembly of staff and students, convened by the vice-chancellor and attended by over six thousand people, had called for the release of those detained.[6] Only the fourth time a general assembly had been called in the university's history, it was addressed by the chancellor, vice-chancellor and acting president of Nusas, as well as Professor Phillip Tobias, who told the gathering that the detention of Karel, Gerry and me 'attacked and sought to erode our heritage of freedom of speech, freedom to protest, freedom to strive by all legal means for better conditions of life for the underprivileged and the disadvantaged'.[7]

The university general assembly also endorsed a statement issued by the Wits SRC, to the effect that while our detentions were legal in the strict sense of the term, 'there can be no law unless it is based on the State's respect for individual liberties, basic human rights and the rule of law recognised by all civilised nations of the world. There can be no order while the individual in South Africa remains crushed ruthlessly under a burden of suppressive legislation.'[8] After the meeting, about a thousand students formed a picket line along Jan Smuts Avenue, and then took their protest to various suburbs of Johannesburg.[9]

I was transferred to Pretoria on the day of those university protests. After being taken from the tenth floor of Vorster Square and down to the garage area, I was pushed into the back of the car and handcuffed to one of the arm rests. Driving down Jan Smuts Avenue *en route* to the Pretoria highway, we passed Wits University and saw a demonstration of students calling for the release of Karel, Gerry and me. The police were furious. I should have been jubilant that students were showing such strong support for those detained. But I was already experiencing some of the numbness that sets in after even short periods of solitary confinement, and I felt strangely disconnected from the demonstration and wanted the journey to Pretoria to be over as quickly as possible.

The drive to Pretoria was full of drama. There were armed personnel at various stages along the highway, monitoring our progress and,

I believed, that of others being moved from Johannesburg. What were the police anticipating? Escape attempts led by armed groups? Attacks on the vehicles? The security police must have believed that we were part of a well-organised conspiracy, whose members still at large were capable of mounting armed initiatives to free those in custody.

Driving into Pretoria along Potgieter Street, I assumed I was being taken to the old red-brick Pretoria local prison with its massive iron-studded wooden doors. But we passed that, turned into the city centre and pulled up in a side street running between Pretorius and Schoeman streets. One of the police jumped out of the car and drew his weapon. The other unlocked the back door, removed my handcuffs, and pushed me through a side door. Looking around, I realised I was in Compol, headquarters of the Pretoria security police, and a place where detainees had been tortured since the early 1960s.

It was growing dark outside. I was handed over to two other security policemen, hustled out of the side door of Compol and into a waiting car, although this time not at gunpoint, nor was I handcuffed again. A brief drive along Pretorius Street, and the vehicle turned suddenly into the entrance to a partly built underground parking garage. We drove in semi-darkness through the building works, with piles of bricks, bags of cement and mounds of sand scattered about. Images of being shot and my body dumped, interrogation in the darkness of a building site, or simply being 'softened up' prior to interrogation, terrorised me.

That was when the vehicle stopped, and the driver turned to me. 'Perhaps you have heard of me? My name is Spyker van Wyk.'

* * *

'Spyker' is Afrikaans for 'nail'. He had once used a piece of wood with a protruding nail to interrogate a well-known political activist, striking his penis. The name 'Spyker' stuck. Detainee after detainee had alleged that Van Wyk had been involved in brutal interrogations, and he was widely believed, with his brother Andries, to have been involved in torturing Imam Abdullah Haron to death in Cape Town during 1969.

'Didn't you and your brother kill the Imam?' I asked. Van Wyk was a wiry man, with slicked-back hair, a precise middle path, and a trim military moustache. He looked back and, instead of punching me, which I had expected, responded in a most revealing way: 'Andries had nothing to do with that,' he asserted angrily.

Then he and his colleague – a Sergeant Van Aggenbach, who invariably accompanied Van Wyk – led me through a door, up some half-finished concrete stairs, and into the charge office of the Pretoria Central police station. There I was 'processed' and handed over to the uniformed police, one of whom took me to the second floor and locked me into a cell. There must have been some prior planning around the transfer to Pretoria, because somehow my parents had managed to deliver clean clothes, a toothbrush, toothpaste and a few pieces of fruit, and these were tossed into the cell after me.

For the next three weeks I only left the cell to shower and for a half-hour period of exercise in an enclosed courtyard. I saw no one apart from the uniformed police. Lying on a mat on the floor of a police cell, with no access to reading material or any other forms of distraction, I became increasingly disoriented and restless. I asked without success for a Bible, as I thought this might elicit a sympathetic response. I fantasised more and more about escape, often dreaming of high-speed chases with me speeding along a road on my motorcycle. I could almost feel the wind in my hair, the air on my checks. I found a toilet brush with a wire handle in the cell, and began a slow and painstaking exercise to scrape away the mortar between two bricks. I would flush the dust down the toilet regularly, to avoid detection. I managed to remove the cement around a whole brick to a depth of about two inches before the wire handle finally wore away. I don't think this involved any serious plan to escape. It was an activity designed to deal with boredom, with inactivity, and with the slow and debilitating effects of solitary confinement.

Late one morning the uniformed policeman on cell duty made

an error and let me out into an exercise yard where awaiting-trial prisoners were sunning themselves. I tried to talk to one of them, asking him to call my parents when he was released. It was a fruitless exercise, although he did pass me part of a newspaper, which I took back to the cell and read over and over again until it was found under my mat during a cell search and removed. It was in those pages that I came across a statement from the Transvaal Attorney-General, Percy Yutar, claiming that the recent round of detentions of whites 'was going to lead to the biggest case since Rivonia'.

The uncertainty began playing on my mind. Why was I not being interrogated? What would I be interrogated about? I had very little to reveal regarding my meeting with 'Christian' in Cape Town, which I assumed must be the immediate reason for detention. However, there was a range of other involvements – the IAS and worker organisation, Nusas, MSD and CIS – that I would prefer not to be questioned on. In a bizarre way, part of me began looking forward to interrogation. At least it would involve some human engagement, some break from the tedium of nothingness that was becoming the routine of each hour, each day and night, and that was now stretching to a month.

One morning, while I was lying on my mat, a uniformed policeman arrived: '*Kom, maak gou. Die speurders wag*' (Come on, be quick. The detectives are waiting). I was ushered down to the charge office, where two security police took over and drove the few blocks to Compol. There I was handed a foolscap pad and told to 'write my story'. I asked them what they were expecting me to write about, because I had no idea why I was in custody. I cannot remember who these two were, but I don't think they were very senior, and one of them went off to another office, presumably to obtain further instruction. When he returned, I was told that I had to write the story about the person Gerry had introduced me to in Cape Town.

I wrote out a short statement. I had travelled to Cape Town at the request of Gerry Maré, where we had met a man whose name I did not know. He had asked me about publications I intended producing and how he could receive them regularly. I told him that we would be setting up a subscription system. At that stage, we stopped talking because we had become aware that we were being followed, probably by members of the security police.

To my amazement, the 'interrogators' seemed to accept the statement. They asked no questions. I knew the police's usual response to a detainee's first statement: to tear it up, tell the detainee he or she was talking *kak*, and force them to write a new statement, over and over again, each time including more detail.

There was a moment of drama when a black policeman was brought into the office and asked whether he had ever seen me 'in the camps'. Initially, he responded that he had, but then changed his mind. He must have been an ex-ANC member who had been in exile, captured and then 'turned', and was now working as an early version of what came to be known in the 1980s as an *askari*. The racial hierarchy, however, remained intact within the security police, and he was instructed to make tea for the two 'interrogators'.

An hour or so later, I was taken back to the cells. When I was dropped off at the charge office, the security police looked meaningfully at me and said that they would be back the next day.

Another week or two followed, with no sign of the security police. By then I had been in solitary for around five or six weeks, and the strain was starting to show. One afternoon, I was again taken to Compol. Sitting in an office, I was distressed to see Jeanette Curtis being ushered past. I am sure I was meant to see her, because a few minutes later one of the police came in and said I had been brought in just to confirm information they already had about Eli Weinberg. What did I know about his making donations to the IAS? Jeanette had already made a statement on this, they said, and I just needed to confirm it.

I was not thinking clearly, and should have been more careful about believing what the police said. However, I confirmed that I had been involved in receiving funds from Eli, and that Jen and I had used these for IAS activities. Again, to my surprise, there were no additional questions. This time, an old manual typewriter was brought into the office, and I was told to type out this statement myself. The simple act of typing was a relief, given the absence of any activity for the past weeks.

The security police were being surprisingly amiable. One of them – I think his name was Captain McIntyre – went to buy me a hamburger at the nearby Bill and Wally's, a fast food outlet near Compol, which I recalled as a 'ducktail' hangout when I was growing up in Pretoria. While I ate this, he went through another typed statement, marking every name in it with a coloured highlighter.

Late that afternoon, as I was being taken back to the cell, McIntyre told me that I was being transferred from the police station to a prison. 'You're going to a better home,' said one of the police. The few possessions I had at Pretoria Central police station had been collected, and we drove south up Potgieter Street, passing Pretoria Local. Turning off Potgieter Street a little further on, we approached a more modern building, which I soon learnt was Maximum Security, where the gallows stood. Through numerous gates and clanging doors, accompanied by the rattle of massive keys, I was escorted into a long passageway. Cells ran off the corridor on both sides, and I was marched to its end. All the doors stood open, and the cells were unoccupied. Finally, I arrived at the last cell on the right – number 13 – and became the only occupant of Maximum Security's C Section.

* * *

A small cell, perhaps 4 x 2 metres. A high ceiling, emphasising the narrowness of the space. A bunk bed bolted to the wall. A shelf. A basin and a toilet on the side of the bed. Barred openings in the roof, to enable guards who patrolled along the catwalks above to view prisoners. A small perspex window in the roof above the bed, so that guards could look down on a prisoner even when sleeping. A solid metal door with a small grille. A single-bulb light set high in the roof, controlled from somewhere outside the cell.

The daily routine at Maximum Security was unchanging. Breakfast was brought to the cell early in the morning: brown bread and coffee. Lunch at around 11.30: soup, vegetables, sometimes a stew. Supper at 3.30: more brown bread, peanut butter. On weekends, lunch at 10.30, supper at 2.00. After breakfast, a warder escorted me to the bathroom: '*Kom, 'n bad*' is what he invariably said. The bathroom was always empty, the floor dry, because I was the only prisoner in C Section. Then half an hour's exercise in a yard at the back of the cells, which, although it had very high walls, was open at the top. The sky and sun were something to look forward to each day, as was a space large enough to walk in. Apart from a warder watching, I was always alone in the exercise yard.

Two warders were responsible for me during the day. I never saw the night warders, because the section was locked down after 'supper', and I did not know who was on night duty beyond its doors. One of the warders told me he had 'looked after' Bram Fischer in jail. I do not know if he had. His surname was Arlow, and he boasted that his policeman cousin Nick had killed the alleged serial killer known as 'The Pangaman' at the Fountains gardens just outside Pretoria. I remembered the incident from school days. A masked man had allegedly attacked courting couples at Fountains, killing them with a panga. Arlow was a policeman assigned to the case, and he had apprehended the alleged murderer one night and killed him in an ensuing struggle. My warder was very proud of his cousin. It was something to talk about in the occasional moments of conversation.

There were 'trusties', black prisoners who cleaned the corridor outside my cell most days. They kept their eyes down, polished the cement floor with rags, moved on. Arlow told me they had been threatened with severe punishment if they communicated with me. The guards who patrolled the catwalks above the cells, 24 hours a day, looking down at those in the cells through the high window as they lay on their beds, were also under strict instructions not to talk to detainees.

I know there was an execution one morning, because I could hear singing the previous night, and next morning Arlow told me that someone had been hanged. I do not know how close to the gallows I was. I did not want to know.

Once an official from what I suspected was the Bureau of State Security came to my cell, and asked me if I knew anyone called 'Zak', who had some contact with 'Bruce' at the Australian Embassy.

He must have been trying to establish whether I harboured any suspicions about Karl Edwards, a member of Nusas head office. Edwards, whose middle name was Zachariah, was generally known as Zak. As far as I knew, he was in fairly regular communication with Bruce Haigh at the Australian Embassy. This was a strange enquiry, which worried me the more I thought about it. Were the intelligence agencies concerned I might have correctly identified one or more of their agents? If this was the case, what were the implications?

A Major Baker arrived unannounced on a Saturday morning, and asked about a group of Wits students he had detained and interrogated in 1971. They had included sisters Colleen and Athalie Crawford, Ian Margo, Ben Cousins and Martin Notcutt. Prominent radicals on the Wits campus in 1970, they had been among the organisers of the illegal march to John Vorster calling for the release of 'the 22', which had precipitated my first arrest. Baker wanted to know what had happened to them after their release. I had no idea, but he seemed keen to discuss them, appearing almost nostalgic for the time they had been in custody.

I started experiencing severe migraines while at Maximum, and the prison head – a Captain Harding, who subsequently became officer in charge of Robben Island – agreed that one of the warders could hold a stock of strong painkillers for my use when needed. I used to hoard these, rather than take them when required, and occasionally took more than the regulation dose as a way of getting through the day and sleeping deeply at night.

One day, 'Spyker' van Wyk came to my cell. He had probably brought another detainee back to Maximum, after interrogation at Compol. I asked him how he was, and he confessed that he was suffering from a bad migraine and did not have his medication with him. I found one of my hidden tablets, which he took immediately. A few days later, he arrived at the cell again, asking for another. 'Spyker' van Wyk, security police torturer, killer of Imam Haron, asking a prisoner for a migraine tablet – and the prisoner obliges.

* * *

Conditions improved somewhat towards the end of my time at Maximum Security. My family was permitted to see me on two occasions and hand over some books required for a university course. A warder was authorised to bring me reading material from the prison library. The first few books were Westerns, generally by Zane Grey. This was not my favourite genre, but by that time anything to read was a bonus. Then, one day, the warder dropped off *Tinker, Tailor, Soldier, Spy*, the first in John le Carré's incomparable trilogy on intelligence agencies during the Cold War. I devoured it, and then read it a second time. My mind turned increasingly to spies and 'moles' in my own political world – first as a distraction, and then more seriously.

The more I thought about it, the more convinced I became that there must be at least one informer close to the circles in which I had been active. I was not led to this conclusion by what the security police had asked me or indicated they knew about my activities. The opposite was the case. For close to a year, I had been involved in initiatives to organise workers in Johannesburg, and had worked with some of those doing the same in Natal and the Western Cape. I had interacted with activists close to Sactu, the ANC and the Communist Party. In the recent past, I had been in contact with one of the main funders of radical youth activity in South Africa, the International University Exchange Fund, and had been planning a political and publishing initiative which was explicitly socialist and oppositional in orientation. Prior to that, I had been centrally involved in some of the most radical student campaigns ever to take place on the Nusas campuses, and moved among a group loyal to the Congress Alliance. Yet the security police did not seem particularly interested in delving into these issues. I concluded that they were steering away from these topics to protect one or more undercover sources of information.

I began trying to link people to some of the issues that the security police clearly knew about but had not probed, aiming to establish if there were any common denominators of people involved. Probably over-influenced by the reading of le Carré, I was trying to find a 'mole' through the absences or gaps in interrogation. By now, I had access to pen and paper, sanctioned because I needed to make study notes.

The security police knew about the MSD initiative. When I was asked if I had drawn up a constitution for MSD, I denied this. The questioner must have known I was lying, because I think he had a copy with him, which was in my handwriting. Yet he simply left the matter. I was also asked whether I knew anything about an IAS trip to Botswana to see Ray Alexander of Sactu. Again, I denied knowledge, although I had paid for that trip from IAS funds, and at one stage had intended being part of the delegation myself. Again, the matter was left, although Jen Curtis told me after her release that the police had full details of the trip, including the names of those who had met with Sactu representatives and my involvement in funding the trip.

I was asked nothing of any substance about the IAS or the Wages Commissions. Neither was I questioned about Nusas or the campaign to release all political prisoners. Yet at that very time, security police were preparing a case against Nusas leaders relating to those events.

Like George Smiley in *Tinker, Tailor, Soldier, Spy*, I started trying to work backwards to see if I could establish any common threads, ambiguities or unexplained developments. Together with many others, I already had concerns that Craig Williamson and Karl Edwards might be both more and less than they appeared to be. However, those two would not have had substantial access to information about the IAS and its clandestine funding, the MSD and CIS initiatives, or relations with Congress-aligned individuals in Johannesburg. If these matters were being avoided by security police in order to protect undercover sources, the informants were not Williamson and Edwards.

I ran through names in my mind, becoming obsessed about who might, and who might not, be informers. A long period of solitary confinement is not conducive to a balanced assessment of the reliability of others, and I am sure that paranoia intruded into my 'spy catcher' efforts. I wondered how some members of the IAS executive committee had access to information about the secret fund set up with help from Beyers Naudé, or Sue Brown's funding trip to the IUEF. I became increasingly concerned about whether one of those attending IAS executive meetings might be an informer. I drew up a list of 'suspects', but then destroyed it when I realised that a search of my cell would put it in the hands of the security police or Boss.

The Okhela investigation was headed by a Colonel Broodryk, nick-named 'Kalfie' (little calf), presumably because of his rather bovine appearance. He bragged that he had been part of the force which raided the Lilliesleaf Farm in Rivonia, leading to the arrest of MK's high command. I had little to do with him, possibly because of my limited knowledge of or involvement in Okhela, which was the object of his investigation.

Yet one day I was fetched from Maximum Security and taken to his office. There was another person present, who did not appear to be part of the security police. He did not speak, nor was I told his name. He just observed and listened. Broodryk told me that some of my friends on the outside were turning against me, that they were asking questions about my administration of a secret fund. Some were suggesting I might be an agent for the police. Why, he asked, did I think this might be happening? Who did I think was behind it? I did not understand what Broodryk was doing, what he was looking for, why he was telling me this. Was it possible I was being warned off something? Could he be trying to establish whether I harboured suspicions about the trustworthiness of someone? I was taken back to my cell, distressed at what he had told me, worried about what might be implied – and bewildered as to why he had given me this information, but asked no questions in return.

Around mid-November, I was suddenly told to pack up what I had in my cell, and transferred to Pretoria Local. Warders walking me through one of the courtyards pointed to some marks on a wall. This, they told me, was the spot where Jopie Fourie had been executed by firing squad, having taken up arms in the 1914 Boer rebellion against Prime Minister Louis Botha.

Local was a dark and dank medieval-type prison, dating back to Paul Kruger's Transvaal Republic. Little light entered its corridors, yards or cells. There was no running water in the cells, and a bucket toilet system was in operation for prisoners, who were locked up for most of each day. Each morning started with the cover of the Judas hole in the cell door being pushed back, an eye peering in, and then a command to bring out the bucket as the solid cell door was opened. Although I was still granted the mandatory half-hour exercise period outside the cell, this was no longer in the open and was limited to walking round and round what appeared to be an old hall.

The cell itself had very little light. There was only a small barred window, set up high in the wall, with a number of the small panes broken. Although it was November, the nights were extremely cold. The upside was that I could smell the rain which fell on a number of evenings. The window faced outwards towards the railway bridge, and if I pulled myself up high enough on the ledge, I could see out into Pretoria.

One evening, lying on my mattress, I heard someone whistling. Listening more carefully, I recognised the tune of 'We shall overcome'. This had to be friend, not foe. I whistled back in response, and soon managed to exchange a few words with Gordon Young, who was in a cell opening into the same corridor as my cell. Communication was difficult. It was hard to hear each other, and we were alive to the possibility of being overheard by warders. Nothing of importance was communicated, although Gordon did tell me that Horst Kleinschmidt was a few cells down the corridor, and that they had been able to speak occasionally. We managed a few words, but one morning a highly charged and visibly angry prison official rushed into my cell, shouting that detainees had been speaking to each other, that this was a breach of prison rules and we would be charged.

Nothing resulted from this incident, but I was by now used to my routine and solitary existence, and any disruption, anything out of the ordinary, felt threatening. I stopped trying to make contact with Gordon, although it was helpful to know that he was just a few cells away.

At that time Breyten Breytenbach was charged under the Terrorism Act, pleaded guilty and was sentenced to ten years' imprisonment. Those, like me, who had been detained ostensibly in regard to the Okhela investigation were released.

While I was being driven from Pretoria Local to Compol, where my father was waiting to collect me, one of the security police present in the vehicle suggested that I keep away from people like Breytenbach and Gerry. 'Look at the sort of trouble they have gotten you into,' he commented.

* * *

The lease on my flat had been terminated while I was in jail, and Steven Friedman offered me a bed in his Doornfontein place. Security police tricked my mother into revealing where I was staying by phoning her, claiming they needed to return some of my books confiscated in a raid. Late that night, the telephone rang. Steven answered, but there was silence on the line.

Since my release, anything unusual or sudden precipitated anxiety and disorientation. I lay on the bed in Steven's spare room, feeling anxious, sure that something was wrong, but unable to rouse myself from the lethargy which had overtaken me.

At around 2 a.m, there was a loud knocking at the door. Steven went to open it. 'We're looking for Glenn Moss,' said Lieutenant Andries Struwig of John Vorster Square.

10
Trials and tribulations

Lieutenant Andries Struwig of the security police at John Vorster Square was an enormous man, with the shoulders and neck of a rugby prop, hands like hocks of ham and a badly pockmarked face. What looked like a First World War leather flying cap, complete with side flaps and fur lining, covered his head and ears. He leered at me and thrust his face close to mine. 'Glenn-o,' he murmured, menacingly.

On the drive to Vorster Square, Struwig told me I was again being held under section 6 of the Terrorism Act. I had just been released from months of solitary and was uncertain how I would cope with another extended period of imprisonment and isolation.

I was handed over to the uniformed police at Vorster Square, who managed the formal booking of prisoners and the cells. A fairly elderly sergeant, with white moustache and red face, remembered that I had been brought in a few months previously. What had happened to me after that night, he asked, recalling that he had escorted me to one of the worst cells at Vorster Square? He seemed surprised, almost concerned, when I told them that I had only recently been released from detention, and instructed me to remain in his office while he made some enquiries. When he returned, he told me I was going to be taken to the women's cells, as they had beds rather than sleeping mats. And so I spent what remained of the night in a proper bed in the white women's section of John Vorster Square.

I did not know what to make of this policeman's gesture. He may have been concerned that the return of a just-released section 6 detainee to cells would require him to mount a suicide watch, with regular monitoring. On the other hand, some of the uniformed police resented the security police with their civvies, longer hair and 'attitude', and he might have been showing his disdain for this elite division of 'political' policing. Perhaps he had sensed something of my desperation at the prospect of more months in solitary, and was responding with ordinary human empathy. Or maybe he was not accustomed to dealing with middle-class white prisoners, and his actions were influenced by some form of 'racial' identification.

As anyone who has spent prolonged periods in captivity knows, the relationships between captors and prisoners are infinitely complex and defy efforts at stereotyping or simplistic categorisation. Even within systems of brutality and massive power differentials, there are those whose conduct is not fully explained by their place within the system of which they are part.

* * *

Early the next morning, I was taken upstairs to the offices of Captain Arthur Benoni Cronwright, who had led various security police raids on the Wits campus during 1974. I was instructed to stand opposite him, with a desk in-between us, and prepared myself for interrogation during which I would be forced to remain standing throughout lengthy questioning.

Cronwright began screaming at me, displaying uncontrollable and irrational fury. He raged about an occasion when he had been attacked by students at Wits. This, he claimed, followed incitement by Cedric de Beer and me when he tried to serve a search warrant on us. During this incident, Cronwright was kicked and pushed down the stairs of the Wits Central Block. When he fell, he had broken vertebrae in his back and neck. Did I know, he roared, that he had been in hospital for months and was now on partial disability, in pain every day? I did not know if any of this was true, but assumed that his fury was not a good omen for the interrogation I anticipated. Then, in the midst of this tirade, Cronwright suddenly ordered me to phone my mother. Bewildered, I ask him to repeat what he had said. 'Phone your mother,' he screamed. My mother, it seemed, had been harassing police at Vorster Square all morning to establish where I was and why I was being held. I should call her so that she would stop telephoning them.

I rang my parents' Pretoria flat from the telephone on Cronwright's desk. He told me to advise them that I could receive food parcels, clean clothes, toiletries and even a visit. I was not being held as a section 6 detainee, but had been arrested and would appear in court in due course. This was soon confirmed by Colonel Johann Coetzee, head of the security police on the Witwatersrand, who came into Cronwright's office to tell me that four others had been arrested in different parts of the country and were being transported to Johannesburg. Coetzee indicated that we would be facing serious charges and that police would oppose the granting of bail.

Over the next day or two, Cedric de Beer, Charles Nupen, Karel Tip and Eddie Webster arrived at Vorster Square, and preparations were made for us to appear in court together. Charles and Eddie were the first to appear, and we were housed in a communal cell. This one was in the men's section for awaiting-trial prisoners, without the privilege of the bed I had enjoyed the previous night. I told them that Coetzee had indicated that police would oppose bail. They seemed rather glum at this prospect but, as I explained to them, awaiting trial in custody was not too bad. With food parcels, visits, the company of others, it was far better than detention under the Terrorism Act. They must have thought that my enthusiasm at the prospect of being an awaiting-trial prisoner was strange indeed.

Coetzee, a dapper officer destined to become national head of the security police and then national police commissioner, seemed intent on impressing us. When Eddie Webster arrived at Vorster Square, Coetzee introduced himself as 'Afrikaner aristocracy'. Quick as a flash, Eddie responded with a chuckle: 'We all have our problems, Colonel, we all have our problems.' Coetzee seemed mortified.

Coetzee told us that he was an intellectual, particularly interested in Trotskyite organisations such as the Unity Movement. He claimed to have a PhD from the Rand Afrikaans University on this subject. Subsequent investigation showed that he did, indeed, have a postgraduate degree on Trotskyism in South Africa, although it was a Master's, not a Doctorate.

The ANC had recently expelled a 'group of eight', who were perceived as being part of an anti-communist Africanist faction.[1] Coetzee kept returning to this, reiterating the often-argued position that Afrikaner nationalists could work with African nationalists, if only the ANC would sever its alliance with the Communist Party. In Coetzee's view, the expulsion of the 'Africanists' indicated that anti-communist African nationalist sentiment was strengthening within the ANC, and that the 'Afrikaners' and 'Africanists' would eventually be able to do 'political business' with each other.

Raymond Tucker, who had been retained as our instructing attorney, managed to convince the Deputy Attorney-General that bail should be granted for all of the accused. Cedric and I were released on bail of R2000 each – a substantial amount in 1975 – and had to report to a police station daily. The other three accused's conditions were less onerous: bail of R1000 and twice-weekly reporting to the police.

* * *

Trials, of their nature, deal with past events. The usual aim in a trial is to prove or disprove 'guilt' for specified offences. Political trials differ in some respects, in that efforts are sometimes made to criminalise or delegitimise ideologically or morally motivated actions. Nuance, complexity and commitment to historical accuracy are rarely the main drivers in either the prosecution or defence of those accused in these types of trials.

The proceedings of the Nusas trial, which ran for a year from date of first court appearance to conclusion on 2 December 1976, offered up a pale representation of the radical politics of the first years of the 1970s. In some respects, this was exceedingly frustrating. The charges brought by the state were sufficiently tenuous in nature to open the possibility of acquittal. This dictated a defence strategy to 'soften' some of the politics, although without necessarily compromising the credibility or integrity of the accused and their actions.

This strategy was at the core of the brilliance of our extremely experienced defence team. It was led by Arthur Chaskalson, a senior counsel who had been a member of the defence in both the Rivonia and Bram Fischer trials. He was assisted by George Bizos and Denis Kuny, who, between them, had played a central role in the defence of hundreds of political leaders, activists and foot soldiers over many years. They were instructed by Raymond Tucker, one of the most credible of those few attorneys willing to undertake political defence work in the 1960s and 1970s. He brought his articled clerk Geoffrey Budlender into the defence team. A past SRC president and Nusas leader, Geoff was already developing a reputation as one of the brightest and most competent of a younger group of socially committed lawyers.

Our counsel had defended many of those who featured in the Nusas campaign to release all political prisoners, including Mandela, Sisulu, Mbeki, Fischer and Toivo. Arthur and George had been close to some of those convicted and sentenced to life imprisonment, notably Mandela and Fischer. Denis Kuny had defended a number of the accused in the first Fischer trial under the Suppression of Communism Act. The experience of this team guided us, ensuring that we would not compromise our political commitment in search of acquittal, but also undermining the state's case where possible through careful and incisive cross-examination of the parade of witnesses brought to testify.

While the trial proceedings did provide a partial window into some of the politics of the period, they were more illuminating in reflecting the state's limited understanding of new forms of political opposition. At the outset, the state seemed intent on presenting a major case aimed at discrediting and criminalising internal political opposition and isolating radical politics from its growing constituency.

The charge sheet indicated the seriousness with which the state was taking the trial. It had been drafted by Dennis Rothwell, Deputy Attorney-General for the Transvaal. He was a highly experienced prosecutor, having appeared in numerous political trials, and was expected to lead the prosecution team in a Supreme Court trial. His star was rising as a senior state advocate, and word was out that he would soon succeed the Attorney-General, Percy Yutar, who had headed the prosecution team in the Rivonia trial.

The charges were formulated under the Suppression of Communism and Unlawful Organisations Acts. Alleging a widespread conspiracy between the accused themselves, as well as between them and the ANC and SACP, the state outlined a set of actions and campaigns which it claimed were undertaken to advance these conspiracies and to further the aims and objects of communism, the ANC and SACP.

The charge sheet set out ten acts which allegedly proved the state's case. These related in the main to the planning and implementation of the 1974 campaign to release all political prisoners; a related focus on the history of opposition politics; the activities of the Wages Commissions; support for both Black Consciousness and the Freedom Charter; and the preparation and distribution of a range of publications and pamphlets.

The prosecution faced a number of difficulties in building its case. While these took on legal form, they were in reality the result of the state's inability to comprehend the nature of opposition politics developing during the 1970s. The state was accustomed to viewing political opposition in terms of clandestine or underground activities, conspiracies, sabotage, and armed and other propaganda promoting banned organisations.

The new radicalism which developed within South Africa in the first half of the 1970s showed few of these characteristics. Its politics were largely public and above-ground, and aimed to broaden participation and involvement rather than limit it to conspiratorial activity. It sought to politicise, educate and conscientise participants through linking action to information, analysis and intellectual contestation and confrontation, rather than propaganda and sloganeering. It was critical of the functional relationships between racism, capitalist development and compromised forms of liberalism, rather than exclusively targeting the policies and institutions of apartheid.

The state had great difficulty understanding how white radicals could be supportive of some of the organisational imperatives of Black Consciousness, such as racially separated forms of organisation, yet be critical of the absence of class as a factor in BC's programme and ideology. It struggled with the developing Marxism of a new left that did not seem compatible with the authoritarian and ahistorical rigidity of the Soviet-influenced SACP. It could not grasp how broad support for the Congress Alliance and the principles of the Freedom Charter could be coupled with critical independence, especially in regard to working-class politics and organisation. It seemed bewildered that progressive whites could be unambiguous in their public advocacy of a unitary state based on universal franchise, underpinned by democratic socialist economic principles.

The state had yet to grapple with the development of mass public opposition politics, supportive of but largely independent of the ANC-led alliance. In the mid-1970s, these forms of resistance were still embryonic and had limited organisational presence or impact. However, new and different challenges to apartheid power were developing and strengthening. The state had not yet comprehended these major shifts in the politics of opposition, and its understanding was limited to conspiracies and clandestine politics, armed struggle and the underground. This is what the prosecution in the Nusas trial demonstrated so clearly.

* * *

In the Nusas trial, the state alleged that the five accused had entered into a conspiracy among themselves, and with others, to further the objects of communism and the aims of the ANC; associated themselves with the policies of the ANC and Communist Party; and worked through Nusas and its affiliated SRCs to promote the aims of the ANC and SACP.

The conspiracy, according to the prosecution, was cemented at the Elgin seminar of December 1973, where the idea for a campaign for the release of all political prisoners was conceived. At this seminar, claimed the prosecution, the accused promoted 'theory, ideology and long term goals of student action towards an egalitarian society'; proposed plans for educational reform and reorientation which would 'fit students for their "African" future'; and developed a programme to research and gather information on universities and schools with the goal of changing the educational system and 'politicising' school pupils. The accused were also charged with encouraging industrial action on the part of black workers, while at the same time supporting Black Consciousness as a means of change. A further leg of the charges involved the development of long-term goals for the student movement and political action, with a focus on the Freedom Charter as an example of the sort of society being worked towards.

The build-up to the campaign to release all political prisoners, through a focus on the history of opposition, featured prominently in the charge sheet, as did the events of the campaign itself. These included a series of meetings, seminars and talks arranged particularly on the Wits campus; mass meetings, production of student newspapers, publications and pamphlets; an illegal protest march through Braamfontein in Johannesburg; quotation of political prisoners and others listed as communists, including Bram Fischer, Govan Mbeki and Nelson Mandela; and publication and distribution of the Freedom Charter.

In a final consolidated explanation of the charges it had brought against the five accused, the state set out to prove that, between October 1973 and August 1974, the conspirators 'actively worked towards the organising of ... [the] Black masses ... to take part in mass action for the purposes of bringing about social, political and economical [sic] changes envisaged by the programme of the SACP, the ANC and the Freedom Charter'. This was undertaken by demanding the release of all political prisoners and depicting them as the true leaders of 'the Black population'; suggesting to the 'Black population' that they were the oppressed and that 'Whites are the oppressors'; and promoting worker consciousness 'as a step towards initiating and organising Black workers into worker organisations'.[2]

The charge sheet highlighted some of the elements of the left radicalism which had developed on the campuses in the first half of the

1970s. These included Black Consciousness, the Wages Commissions and 'new left' analytical Marxism. The prosecution then tried to link these, through allegations of a conspiracy, to the promotion of the aims and policies of the ANC and SACP, especially by focusing on political prisoners, the Freedom Charter and the history of opposition to apartheid.

This presented the prosecution with a number of inherent problems. It had to prove a conspiracy that involved support for the SACP and ANC as well as Black Consciousness, notwithstanding ANC and SACP hostility to BC. It needed to demonstrate that the promotion of independent and democratic trade unionism furthered the objects of the ANC and SACP. The state was also required to prove that a critique of liberalism and capitalism necessarily entailed support for communism. In addition, the prosecution had to demonstrate that these activities involved large numbers of students but were at the same time part of a conspiracy. This conspiracy was spearheaded by a small group, through Nusas and its affiliated SRCs, without the knowledge or agreement of thousands of participating students.

That task was, however, relatively simple when compared with the central ambiguity in the state's prosecution of its case. Those of us on trial had developed our radical politics in the absence of direct ANC and SACP influences. The post-Rivonia political vacuum had created the context for a new radical politics, independent of the banned and exiled liberation movements. The accused in the Nusas trial, and large numbers of the student and post-student activists they symbolically represented, might have had growing sympathies for what they perceived to be the Congress tradition. However, their politics and strategies had emerged in the absence of those influences.

* * *

Evidence and argument in political trials generally lack nuance, and the Nusas trial was no exception to this. Court proceedings do not take account of process, complexity and the way in which events develop. Issues are presented in crisp and unambiguous terms, as if their causes are simple, and as if they are the result of individual decisions and intentions. Prosecutors seek to establish individual guilt and culpability, not multiple and complex chains of causation.

The state seemed to have a number of different aims in bringing charges against the Nusas Five. At the simplest level, there was an intention to jail the accused, thereby removing us from political activity and influence, although this could have been achieved more easily through banning and house-arrest orders.

There must also have been some intention of finishing the work of the Schlebusch Commission of Inquiry, which had resulted in the banning of eight Nusas leaders and officials, and the Van Wyk de Vries Commission, which led to Nusas being prohibited from receiving foreign funds. These efforts to weaken Nusas, and drive wedges between it and its student base, had been partially successful. Yet at the same time, Nusas's programmes and public campaigns had become more radical, and with this a growing number of students on the Nusas-affiliated campuses had moved to the political left. In trying to criminalise the sort of public political activity Nusas represented, the state was attempting to weaken the radicalism which was influencing students each year.

By charging Eddie Webster, the state was sending a message that it was aware of the role of critical analysis in dislodging relatively privileged students from their social base. The involvement of students in the Wages Commissions and emerging trade unions, the growing resistance to military conscription, and the interest of students in the ANC and socialist alternatives to liberal anti-apartheid opposition, posed the beginnings of a threat to South Africa's power elite. This would increase when radical influences were felt more strongly among the economically exploited and politically oppressed majority.

Yet the state was a prisoner of its own ideologies. Its strategists believed that growing radicalisation among the majority of South Africans would be the consequence of the influence of a small – usually white – minority. The Nusas trial involved an attempt to weaken or suppress the extension of radicalising influences beyond the campuses.

The ideas and actions the state had put on trial had strong elements of independent socialist radicalism, yet the prosecution was attempting to link them to a conspiracy to further the aims and objects of the ANC and SACP. The ANC had prioritised military struggle in its tactics and strategies, and recruitment for military training outside the country became a major focus of its activity and propaganda. On the other hand, the new radicalism and its socialist underpinnings emphasised political struggle within the country and organisation of workers in the factories and shops. Trying to link these two very different trajectories in a political trial based on a conspiracy would always present problems for the prosecution.

* * *

During the first months of 1976 the state changed tack in its prosecution tactics. The trial would no longer proceed in the Supreme Court, but in the Regional Court. The prosecution would now be led by P.B. 'Flip' Jacobs, a senior prosecutor with little experience in political matters. Perhaps Deputy Attorney-General Rothwell had started to see some of the difficulties in the state's case. It may also have been that the state was now unable to present some of the evidence it had against the accused without compromising one or more of its informers.

The trial would no longer be presided over by a judge, but by a senior regional magistrate, Gert Steyn. He had been part of South Africa's legal team when Ethiopia and Liberia tried to end South Africa's mandate over Namibia through the International Court of Justice in The Hague. Steyn was not one of the magistrates usually selected to hear political matters, and our lawyers cautiously concluded that he might conduct himself with some semblance of judicial independence in the trial ahead.

Bartholomew Hlapane was one of the prosecution's first witnesses. A crucial figure in the case against Bram Fischer, Hlapane had been an ANC member in the 1950s and 1960s, and also served on the central committee of the underground Communist Party. 'Joe Slovo had recruited [Hlapane] in 1955. Appointed a full-time party organizer in 1961, he had joined the central committee in 1962 and had attended several key meetings before being detained in June 1963. Released after 172 days, he had been allowed to resume his place on the central committee in May 1964. Detained once more in September 1964, he had soon "cracked".[3]

Hlapane, who had been present when the Freedom Charter was adopted at Kliptown in 1955, was also an accused in the 1956 Treason Trial of Congress leadership, although charges were subsequently withdrawn against him, along with many others. In the Nusas trial, he focused on the relationship between the ANC and the Communist Party, and claimed that the Freedom Charter was the 'brainchild' of the Communist Party.

It was unclear what the state intended to achieve by calling Hlapane as a witness. As Arthur Chaskalson pointed out to the presiding magistrate, I was three years old at the time of some of the events to which he testified, and could hardly be expected to challenge or accept Hlapane's version of events from my personal knowledge. For that reason, argued Chaskalson, the defence needed to seek advice on Hlapane's evidence from potential witnesses who had been involved in the events he had described. It was on this basis that an application was made for the defence lawyers to consult with three Robben Island prisoners, Nelson Mandela, Walter Sisulu and Govan Mbeki.

This application caught the state unawares. Initially, the Department of Prisons granted approval for the consultation, but soon after withdrew this. However, when the presiding magistrate indicated that he would not allow Hlapane's evidence to stand if the defence was unable to cross-examine him properly, permission was reinstated. Our defence team travelled to Robben Island to consult with some of the prisoners whose release we had called for.

On the basis of information obtained during the Robben Island consultations, and a careful analysis of evidence Hlapane had given in earlier trials, Arthur Chaskalson rose to cross-examine the witness. Gradually, it emerged that there were serious discrepancies between his new evidence and what he had said previously. Hlapane had, on one occasion, indicated that the Communist Party did not have a written constitution, but in recent testimony he had identified a document as the SACP constitution. He had testified that his children had not been looked after while he was in detention, but on another occasion indicated that the Defence and Aid Fund had supported his family. He had testified that 'Bri-Bri' (a code name for the MK leader Wilton Mkwayi) had reported to him about sabotage actions undertaken by Umkhonto we Sizwe at a time when he (Hlapane) could not have received these reports, as he was in detention.

Hlapane acknowledged his earlier testimony that the Freedom Charter was the brainchild of the Communist Party might be open to question. He admitted that, while an accused in the Treason Trial of 1956, he had been told that Professor Z.K. Mathews was the father of the Charter, and that this had been confirmed by Albert Luthuli.

While these discrepancies challenged Hlapane's credibility as a witness, they did not relate in any direct way to the charges we faced. In calling Hlapane, the state was trying to connect the Nusas trial to previous conspiracy trials involving underground ANC, SACP and MK activities. However, unless the state could show a direct relationship between the accused and these organisations, Hlapane's testimony would be tangential to the case.

Although many saw Hlapane as one of the most notorious examples of traitorous behaviour, there was also something tragic about his story. He admitted under cross-examination that he had a terrible fear of being detained again if he did not accede to security police demands to give evidence in political trials. Every time the security police approached him, this fear was his reason for agreeing to be a witness. Much as I understood the hatred for Hlapane as someone in the communist underground who had testified against comrades, I could also see the shadow of a proud and dignified man who had been broken by psychological and physical torture. On one occasion, I recall him listening intently to a question put to him by Arthur Chaskalson. He thought about the question, then set his jaw and drew himself erect to his full height, before answering.

In that moment, I could see traces of the once senior underground communist leader.

Chaskalson's cross-examination of Hlapane was devastating, and we believed that the state would no longer be able to rely on him as a witness in future trials. Although his evidence was not of great relevance to our trial, George and Arthur were trying to ensure that he would never again be called as a witness. There was also a sense that they were settling accounts with Hlapane. As a key witness against Bram Fischer, their close colleague and friend, Hlapane shared responsibility for his sentence of life imprisonment, a sentence which had only ended with Fischer's death the previous year.

* * *

Cecily Palmer, who had been my executive secretary when I was SRC president, was called as a witness by the prosecution. Sitting outside court with her mother, the redoubtable Vesta Smith, a well-known political activist, she indicated that she was not prepared to testify for the state and against me. As the prosecution team prepared to make application to jail her, our defence team came up with a proposal. Would I be prepared to admit her evidence, especially in regard to documents she had typed for me? That would remove the necessity for her either to testify or face jail time. Of course I agreed, and a tearful Cecily retrieved the small bag she intended taking to jail with her, and was able to leave the court building.

Later that day, court adjourned to a small studio in the building to view a film. According to a security police witness, this would show me leading an illegal protest march through the streets of Braamfontein, calling for the release of political prisoners. Imagine my surprise when the witness identified not me in the front row of the marchers, but Alan Fine. As he explained when we were back in court, '*Edele, ek het 'n fout gemaak*' (Your worship, I made a mistake). In fact, the witness made two errors – confusing Alan Fine and me, and not seeing me in the march, just a few metres away from Alan.

* * *

George Bizos had travelled to the Island to consult with Mandela, Sisulu and Mbeki about the evidence given by Hlapane. He came back with surprising news: not only did Mandela know about the trial, but he was willing to testify in our defence to rebut some of the evidence given by Hlapane. 'The three on the Island were pleased to see us', reported George, 'and intrigued by the student publications, newspaper cuttings and other court evidence ... Of course the three were willing to be called as witnesses for the defence and greatly admired the dedication of the young people on trial. I was to thank them for risking their freedom to call for the release of political prisoners.'[4]

Mandela told George that a number of prisoners were suffering from poor morale. Many had been in jail for ten years, ANC activity was at a low ebb, and they had a sense that they and their organisations were being forgotten. Suddenly, a group of white students were running a national campaign, calling for their release and integration into a political process to end apartheid. This activism, he told George, provided an important boost to flagging spirits.

Since his conviction and life sentence at the end of the Rivonia trial, Mandela had not been publicly seen or his voice heard. He now had the opportunity to come to Johannesburg and speak in open court. Nonetheless, our lawyers advised us not to call him as a defence witness. They pointed out that Hlapane's evidence had little to do with the case against us. They also argued that calling Mandela would dramatically alter the atmosphere of our trial. Police would mount substantial security in and around the court, crowds would gather in the hope of catching a glimpse of Mandela, and the possibility of rioting and clashes with armed police was strong. Coils of barbed wire and police dogs would in all probability confront everyone entering and leaving the court, and the presiding magistrate – who until then had generally conducted the case politely and professionally – might become overtly hostile to the accused and their legal representatives. Our chances of acquittal could be prejudiced by a decision to bring

Mandela to Johannesburg. However, as Arthur Chaskalson was at pains to point out, the defence team could only advise us whom to call, and whom not to call, as defence witnesses. The accused had to make the decision.

I argued strongly in favour of calling Mandela. This would focus the sort of attention on prisoners that we had aimed for in running the campaign. Any evidence he gave in court would be reported in the media, and his very presence in the heart of Johannesburg would be an important boost for opposition to apartheid. However, by a narrow margin it was decided that Mandela would not be called as a defence witness. I felt that an important political opportunity had been lost.

* * *

Calling Hlapane as a witness indicated that the state aimed to prove a direct conspiracy between the actions of the accused and the underground ANC and SACP. Using Professor Andrew Murray as an 'expert' witness suggested that the state 'sought in the Nusas trial to recreate a grand political trial involving the ANC, in the style of the 1950s [the Treason Trial] … Thus, it used the same expert … to attack the Freedom Charter as communist.'[5] If Hlapane was meant to establish a conspiratorial link between communism, the ANC and the Freedom Charter, then Murray's role was to prove that the writings, publications and ideas of the accused fell within the ambit of communism and Communist Party strategies.

Murray was a former head of philosophy at the University of Cape Town. He had been the state's expert witness in the Treason Trial, where the defence advocate Vernon Berrangé had led Murray to mistakenly identify some of his own writings as those of a communist.

For the Nusas trial, Murray analysed a number of papers written by the accused, as well as various student publications. He concluded that Nusas had accepted Black Consciousness as a means of establishing 'black domination' over society. Yet, confusingly, he also argued that the Freedom Charter was 'virtually a communist document', and my distribution of it was an indication of support for the aims of the Communist Party. The contradictions between Black Consciousness as a racially based mode of thinking, the non-racial character of the Freedom Charter, the two-stage strategies of the Communist Party and the working-class orientation of the Wages Commissions created considerable difficulties for Murray's interpretations.

Murray had demonstrated in the Treason Trial that he did not grasp the differences between social democratic, communist and liberal policies. In the Nusas trial, he showed his inability to interpret the Black Consciousness challenge to multi-racial liberalism or the contradictions between 'new left' Western Marxism and Soviet-style communist thinking.

As in the Treason Trial, Murray's evidence was gradually eroded under cross-examination. He initially testified that the Freedom Charter was 'virtually a communist document' but, after careful questioning by Chaskalson, conceded that some of its demands were similar to those contained in an early Broederbond charter, which spoke of exploitation and demanded that the riches of the land be developed in the service of the people. Murray agreed further with Arthur that, whenever a political party took up the cause of people under economic domination, it demanded a redistribution of wealth, regardless of whether it was communist, socialist, social democratic or nationalist in orientation. There were, he admitted, substantial similarities between the language used in the Afrikaner struggle for emancipation and Black Consciousness.

In analysing the writings of the accused, Murray testified that some of the documents were Marxist-Leninist in orientation. He made particular reference to my comments about a 'façade of peaceful democracy' in South Africa. Chaskalson pounced. 'You will agree that South Africa is not a peaceful country?' he asked Murray. 'Yes,' responded the witness. 'That South Africa is not a peaceful country is a well-known analysis?' probed Chaskalson. Again Murray answered in the affirmative.

When Chaskalson put it to Murray that 'Many people feel there is violence close to the surface, [and that] ... to pretend there are no conflicts would be incorrect', Murray could hardly contain himself. It would be, he said, 'suicidal'. Murray then stunned the court by stating that paying low wages was a sin 'bigger than a sex sin', and agreed with Chaskalson that his own writings on capitalist exploitation involved a 'more trenchant' critique than the documents the accused had authored.

After this cross-examination, the prosecution's expert evidence lay in tatters. Professor Murray was never again called as an expert witness in a political trial.

* * *

In their attempts to infiltrate the universities and gather information on student activities, the security police had used both student informers and police. One of these was a former law student at the University of Natal, Pietermaritzburg, who had attended Wages Commission meetings. However, J.H. Reynecke was soon identified as a probable informer, and the chairman, Brian Hackland, had asked him not to attend future meetings.

A full-time security policeman, Sergeant Gerhardus Horak, admitted that he posed as a student at Wits for over a year, attending meetings and gathering information. His evidence confirmed that Nusas and the Wits SRC had organised a range of political meetings and seminars during 1974. He testified that speakers from political parties, such as the United Party's Gideon Jacobs and the Progressive Party's Gordon Waddell, had been criticised by students. Although Horak did not seem to realise it, these meetings were part of the History of Opposition build-up to the campaign to release all political prisoners and had been organised to expose students to a critique of political parties contesting the all-white 1974 general election.

A second group of meetings attended by Horak aimed at continuing the political education of students. Speakers included the political science lecturer Michael Nupen, the sociologist Frederik van Zyl Slabbert and the former editor of *The Star* newspaper René de Villiers. Other meetings which Horak attended were addressed by

Peter Randall, an educationalist who was standing as an independent social democrat in the general election, and the political scientist Alf Stadler, who spoke on the inherent and systemic nature of violence in South African society.

Horak did not appear to derive much benefit from his year 'loafing about' the Wits campus. He had not realised that there was a general election in 1974, and admitted that, apart from the meetings on campus, he had never attended a political gathering. He usually tried to position himself close to me, in an effort to hear what I was saying. When asked whether he submitted any reports on this, he candidly admitted that he rarely understood a word I said.

The prosecution's major 'insider' witness was Lieutenant Derek Brune, a security police infiltrator who had slowly worked his way up SRC structures until he became one of my vice-presidents in 1973. In the year before I was elected SRC president, Brune had served on the executive as treasurer. I had discussed with my close colleagues how we were going to deal with him on the new SRC, given that it was inevitable he would be able to secure one of the executive positions again. This was not necessarily because we thought he was an informer, although we had considered that possibility. More important was the absence of any political commitment. He made no attempt to present himself as a political being, and for that reason I did not believe he could make much of a contribution to the year's programme.

A solution presented itself. Brune was administratively competent, committed to bureaucratic efficiency. This was not always the political left's strength. The SRC was a representative structure, not a self-appointed activist group, and if Brune could command sufficient support from students and other SRC members, then he was entitled to a senior position. The post of internal vice-president seemed ideal for him. It involved administrative responsibility for the student canteen, staffing, parking allocations and office routine. He undertook these tasks well. I do not know whether he was trying to ingratiate himself with the left leadership on the SRC through his efficiency or whether he just took pride in being competent at what he did.

It was not a great surprise when Brune was called as a witness by the state. A few weeks previously, I had seen him in a car with known security police and had alerted our defence lawyers to this. More significantly, the state had labelled a range of documentary exhibits as 'DB'. It did not take a great leap of imagination to realise that these were the initials of the witness who would hand them in as evidence.

Brune's evidence-in-chief contained nothing particularly startling. He had not been close to the politics of the SRC or Nusas. Much of his testimony involved innuendo, based on his claim that the radical left was a 'clique' which dominated student politics through manipulation and control. The implication was that this was undertaken with a hidden agenda to further a political conspiracy.

Brune's reports to his security police handlers showed some understanding of the left's politics, especially when compared to the reports and evidence of Sergeant Horak. In one report, he wrote:

> Mr Moss and Mr de Beer had planned a campaign at Wits during 1974. The theme of the campaign was the effect of White political opposition as well as White violence in the South African situation.
>
> Part of the programme was to present speakers from the various [political] parties who would then be attacked for their failure in the hope of exposing their policies as hollow.
>
> Once this had been achieved, students would be presented with an alternative ... When they accepted these ideals the plan was to recruit them into Nusas projects.[6]

Brune understood that the radical left, which he believed had taken control of the SRC, had a 'total project' for questioning society and the institutions that supported and maintained it. This included the university itself, which was seen as part of the 'ideological state apparatus' (to use the concept developed by Louis Althusser, the French Marxist philosopher). What Brune could not do was link this to any conspiracy involving the SACP or the ANC.

His evidence was unable to advance the prosecution case in any major respects, although he did try to establish a relationship between the left's critique of the university and Nusas's programme. This he did by drawing attention to an incident involving the Wits vice-chancellor, Professor Bozzoli, at the beginning of 1974. Traditionally, both the vice-chancellor and SRC president addressed first-years as part of the university's orientation programme. Brune described the event in the following way:

> In his speech, Prof. Bozzoli outlined the type of life the students could expect at university ... This intensely annoyed Accused no. 1 [Moss]. In a speech after the professor, he attacked the professor's views ... and [argued] that the university did not turn out a 'whole' person but rather alienated person [sic] who would function well in terms of white interests in the status quo. He also attacked Prof. Bozzoli ... [for] the manner in which he addressed first year students as children and describing life at university as a combination of work time and play time.[7]

Brune then made reference to an open letter I sent to Professor Bozzoli after this incident, which was published in *Wits Student*. This set out the way radical student leadership viewed the relationship between the university and society as a whole. It reflected a critique of the liberalism which underpinned the university's narrow concept of academic freedom, and its refusal to confront its responsibility for preparing students to fit into an oppressive and exploitative society. Radicals were beginning to challenge the traditional institutions of liberalism and analyse how these reproduced society as it existed.

'Dear Dr Bozzoli,' I wrote as SRC president in February 1974,

> Your basic presupposition is ... that the University is in a healthy state, and is both training students in a rigorous academic manner, and making a meaningful contribution to South Africa ...
>
> [However], our academic environment is stagnant and sterile, the courses biased in favour of the needs of white affluence ... Students do not leave this institution with any clear, critical analytical ability ... The University is slowly rotting, and this is not only because of

Government pressure. Hiding behind a façade of academic neutrality, this University is fast becoming a mirror image of the society it ministers to ...

During the Orientation week, I and many other speakers attempted to jolt the first-years from their potential apathy and acceptance of Wits as they found it ... You, on the other hand, attempted to undermine everything we had said or done by your complacent description of what University life is all about ... You have a certain 'standing' with the 'respectable' white community, which you play on when dealing with new students ...

I do not believe that compromising with the representatives of white capital – the representatives of exploitation and repression – will change our society or our University. This is certainly what your plea to students to be 'respectable' in their endeavours within society seemed to imply.[8]

Brune was right when he claimed that this incident reflected the manner in which radicalism had taken over student leadership. The university itself had become a site of legitimate struggle, and there was value in trying to undermine its relationship with society's economic and political elites.

Arthur Chaskalson's cross-examination of Brune was masterful. Slowly, he undermined the picture Brune had painted. Brune was forced to admit that he was skilled at lying and deception and, by inference, that his evidence should not always be believed. He admitted that he had a personal resentment against me, apparently because of his romantic interest in a woman with whom I had a relationship. At one stage, Arthur – presumably in the rhythm of cross-examining Andrew Murray previously – called Brune 'Professor'. Then he stopped: 'I apologise. You are not a professor, are you?' he said to Brune. 'You are just a lieutenant.'

Brune's destruction as a spy was almost complete when Arthur produced the final nail for his coffin. His exit report to the SRC concluded by stating that 'I must give my most sincere thanks to the members of the executive and especially Glenn. I found my term of office an interesting and enjoyable one largely due to the people that I served with.'

The deep-cover spy had been unable, despite six years of work on campus, to find a link between the leadership of Nusas and the SACP or ANC. The prosecution had established that the accused and their close colleagues were radicals, that they rejected liberalism, that some described themselves as socialists. However, the state was unable to grasp the essentially home-grown nature of the radical politics on the campuses and the development of a radical but democratic socialism that had emerged without external conspiracies.

* * *

Shortly after being charged and released on bail, I took stock of what lay ahead. A long trial seemed inevitable, and I did not want to be a 'full-time' trialist. Wits was about to introduce an experimental interdisciplinary honours course in Development Studies, which would be run with contributions from the departments of Political Studies, African Government, History, Sociology, Economics, Industrial Sociology and Social Anthropology. It was an exciting initiative, attracting many of the best and most progressive lecturers, some of whom I already knew through student events and in nascent worker education and trade union initiatives.

The university seemed reluctant to admit me to the course, and not only because of my mediocre undergraduate degree. One of the co-ordinators of the programme was Eddie Webster. A deputy vice-chancellor was overheard to say that he was concerned that, with Eddie and me involved in the course, the university would be harbouring 'other Raymond Suttners', referring to a Durban law lecturer who had just been sentenced to seven and a half years' imprisonment for underground Communist Party activity.

However, I met the minimum requirements for the programme and, after intervention from some of the lecturers involved, was admitted. Eddie's head of department, Dunbar Moodie, insisted that if the charges he faced did not compromise his ability to teach while on trial, then they should also not inhibit my participation as a student. I enrolled as a Development Studies honours student, together with Gerry Maré and Susan Brown, while Eddie's appointment as a lecturer in the Sociology Department was allowed to stand.

Prosecution documents had taken to describing me as being 'of no permanent abode'. I spent the first few months of the year staying with friends, particularly Jen Curtis and Janet Love in their Yeoville flat. It was there that a group of us who were either on trial or recently released from detention spent far too much time playing a form of poker known as 'lie dice', over quantities of tequila and red wine. It was an anomic and confusing time, in which I found it hard to focus on short-term plans because of the possibility of having to serve jail time at the conclusion of the trial.

I started playing bridge with Steven Friedman and Erica Emdon for relaxation, and they were particularly generous in offering me a spare room in their flat. Both the bridge and the wine which accompanied it were wonderful distractions – so much so that one night, in the middle of a hand, I realised I had forgotten to meet my daily bail-reporting requirements. Steven drove me at great speed to the Hillbrow police station, where I rushed into the charge office and signed the bail book. For a few days, I wondered if my late reporting might lead the state to apply to revoke my bail, all because of a bridge game. However, nothing resulted from this momentary lapse of concentration.

Slowly, some stability developed in an unstable context. I rented a flat in nearby Bellevue and began reading for my honours courses. This was challenging. My concentration was impaired, partly because of the time in solitary confinement. In addition, I had entered a particularly complex area of endeavour. I was studying the writings of a new generation of French Marxists, including Louis Althusser and Etienne Balibar; structural anthropologists influenced by Marxism, such as Maurice Godelier and Claude Meillassoux; the seminal work on politics, power and the state by the Greek political scientist Nicos Poulantzas; and the core methodological texts of Karl Marx, *Capital*, *Theories of Surplus Value* and the *Grundrisse*.

The honours course asked questions of different economic systems and development models. What was the relationship between developed and underdeveloped society? What was the role of mercantilism in the process whereby the developed capitalist world created underdevelopment elsewhere as a condition of its economic growth? How could South Africa's economic and political trajectory best be explained, and what was the relationship between its form of capitalism and segregation and apartheid?

Harry Zarenda, an economics lecturer, agreed to run his part of the course at night, so that I could attend after a day in court. On other evenings, I would try to digest the heavy and complex texts under scrutiny in the honours course. I would read the same paragraph from Althusser and Balibar's *Reading Capital* over and over again, underlining key words in pencil, studying sub-clauses to make sense of them. My concentration and understanding improved as lecturers in the course and my co-students coaxed me out of my post-detention mental lethargy.

In one of the first seminars with Sheldon Leader, one of South Africa's foremost Marxist scholars and someone I had clashed with in the Industrial Aid Society, I learnt a hard lesson. When I erroneously suggested that Marx had stated that 'all property is theft' (it was Proudhon), Sheldon looked up at me and smiled. 'You are charged with being a communist, and you don't even know what communism is,' he joked. In some ways he was correct. Most of the radicals of the early 1970s had been too busy to study the classics of Marxism and socialism in depth or delve into the new forms of Marxist philosophy which had been developing in Europe. I resolved to use my time on trial to develop an understanding of the way societies functioned, their economic and political structures, and the factors that gave rise to fundamental social change.

During one of our early court appearances, I was reading a book by Nicos Poulantzas, arguably the most interesting of the new group of political theorists influenced by the Althusserian school. George Bizos came up to me during a break in proceedings. What, he enquired, was I reading? I set out to explain Poulantzas's analysis of the capitalist state, its relationship to the social classes which made up society, and the ways in which fractions of classes had different forms of political representation within the state. George blinked at me, as I carried on my enthusiastic exposition. 'He must be very good,' he said, cutting off my mid-morning lecture in the Johannesburg magistrate's court, 'he's Greek.' And Bizos was right on both counts.

* * *

Court was in recess on 16 June 1976. I was working in a postgraduate study room in the Wartenweiler Library at Wits when Barbara Hogan rushed in to announce that Soweto was on fire, and that police had shot pupils marching in the streets.

Only Eddie Webster and I of the Nusas accused were on campus, but the other three joined us there, and we held an impromptu meeting to discuss how we should conduct ourselves. It was inevitable that there would be protests from Wits students, possibly leading to clashes with the police. We all agreed that it would be problematic if any of the accused were to become involved. We were trialists, out on bail. Of the five accused, only I was a registered student at Wits. We were older and politically more experienced than most of the students likely to protest, and police might identify us as instigators or leaders of any action.

Richard de Villers, who was SRC president, had also received information about the Soweto protests and police reaction. This had come through cleaning and maintenance staff on campus and from Sheila Sisulu, who worked as a secretary to Nusas in the Students' Union and had been telephoned by other members of the Sisulu family in Soweto. Richard quickly called a mass meeting in the Wits Great Hall. Students were more angry than I had seen before. Police had opened fire, killing school children. The township was on fire, and fury among the youth was spilling over into an orgy of burning and stoning. Pupils and police were engaged in running battles. This was not just another protest, not just another instance of police brutality, which would soon subside into the slow-bubbling discontent which had characterised urban townships for years.

William Kentridge captured the mood well when he argued that students had to protest and confront the police because 'For every cop we keep busy here, that is one less free to shoot children in Soweto'.[9] I joined the students moving from the Great Hall to the university boundary with Jan Smuts Avenue, with the aim of participating in a picket for a short period. However, when a few hundred students led by Kentridge set off down Jan Smuts Avenue, towards Queen Elizabeth Bridge and the city centre, I felt I had to join them. It was just two years since I had been at the front of an illegal march demanding the release of all political prisoners, and six years since my first arrest while calling for the release of 'the 22'. I could not stand by while others marched in protest against police barbarism in Soweto. After all, I rationalised, I was still a student and had a long history of participation in these types of actions.

Halfway along the bridge to town, police baton-charged the march. I did not want to be arrested, as this might lead to withdrawal of bail, and tried to climb over the rails separating the incoming and outgoing sections of Queen Elizabeth Bridge, intending to leave the area. However, I became stuck on the top rail, and a policeman took great pleasure in beating me savagely around the head and shoulders before I fell onto the other side of the railings and made my escape.

That night, Gerry Maré, Sue Brown and I – the three Development Studies honours students – met at a house in Yeoville, where we decided to produce a pamphlet on the day's events. Sue illustrated it and suggested the title: 'Sow the wind, reap the whirlwind.' We went down to Wits late that night and, using the keys I still had for a printing room, cut a wax stencil and soon had the old Gestetner roneo machine working overtime. By early next morning, piles of the pamphlets had been placed neatly at the entrances to most buildings on campus.

Later that morning, we received a message from a Wits student who was in contact with Soweto leaders of the South African Students' Movement's Action Committee, which had organised the 16 June march. Our pamphlet was greatly appreciated. Could we arrange for another hundred thousand to be printed? The numbers were daunting, partly because we were using the manual facility on the roneo machine to avoid the sort of noise which might draw attention to this illicit activity. However, we agreed to do what we could later that night and hand over whatever number had been printed by 4 a.m.

Students marched off campus again the next day, but I did not join them this time. I had been roundly criticised for irresponsibility in joining the first march, and accepted that my involvement in the events of June 1976 would have to be of a low-key and unobtrusive nature. Printing pamphlets for Soweto pupils late at night fitted these criteria well, and over the next few months I assisted SASM, and then the Soweto Students' Representative Council (SSRC), in roneoing various communications, including the call for a stayaway in August 1976. On that occasion, I delivered boxes of pamphlets to a house in Soweto. There was a consequence to this sometime later, when a witness in the sedition trial of Soweto student leaders described the person providing pamphlets to the SSRC as young, white, with long black hair, a beard and sometimes on a motorcycle. I was a member of the defence team in that trial, and Ernie Wentzel, who led the defence, turned round in court and glared at me suspiciously as the witness finished his evidence.

* * *

The events of June 1976 marked a seismic shift in the nature of opposition to apartheid, and it was obvious that the role of radical whites in organisation would have to be reassessed. The continuing Nusas trial was becoming frustrating, because it was dealing with the past, with 'yesterday's politics'. I wanted to move on and start exploring new involvements based on the changed political circumstances. Nonetheless, the trial demanded considerable attention, especially as we began preparing our defence to the state's case.

George Bizos had a way of protecting clients from rash political assessments and statements without compromising fundamental principles. The state had produced a number of editions of *The African Communist*, banned organ of the Communist Party, in an attempt to show similarities between SACP aims and those of the accused. George asked me whether I had ever seen these documents before the trial. 'Yes,' I responded, to his visible unhappiness. Where had I seen them? he enquired. The best answer I could come up with in the moment was that the security police had shown them to me while in detention. George looked at me severely. 'You may believe that your detention under section 6 of the Terrorism Act is a badge of honour,' he announced. 'I doubt the presiding officer in your trial will see things the same way. What I want to know is whether you ever saw these documents while you were involved in Nusas politics.' 'No,' I responded. George looked happier.

The state's case against the Nusas accused was not particularly convincing. However, our defence team wanted to make it as difficult as possible for the presiding magistrate to accept evidence from the state's 'expert', Professor Murray, or from informers like Brune and Reynecke, the Pietermaritzburg student who had spied on the Wages Commission.

Identifying an appropriate academic to debunk Murray's testimony was the most difficult of these tasks. An initial approach was made to Leszek Kołakowski, the Polish political philosopher who had broken with Stalinism to become a leading exponent of Marxist humanism, and who was lecturing at Oxford and Yale universities. Kołakowski was sent an outline of the state's case and samples of writings by the accused. In his initial report, he indicated concerns that my writings might be compatible with communist thinking and strategies. Some people viewed him as increasingly sympathetic to Western interests in the Cold War and this, combined with his ambivalence about my writings, discounted him as a defence witness.

Next we turned to André du Toit, a professor of political philosophy at Stellenbosch University. His assessment of the writings of the accused was that they fell within the scope of liberalism and 'radical liberalism' although he, too, expressed concern that my articles and papers showed some Marxist influence. None of the documents written by any of the accused, stated Du Toit, 'is the work of a Marxist thinker in any serious sense. The only possible exception here is Moss, but there is too little firsthand material from him to be able to form a reliable assessment.'[10]

We obviously wanted to be acquitted, but not at the expense of damaging credibility and political integrity. One of the political themes of the early 1970s had been the critique and rejection of liberalism, and all of the accused were loath to retreat from this as part of a defence strategy. We agreed that Du Toit's well-intentioned agreement to testify in our defence, which might have negative personal and career consequences for him at Stellenbosch University, should be declined.

Finally, we resolved that the accused themselves would challenge those parts of Murray's interpretation that were damaging. However, to strengthen this, Lawrie Schlemmer, director of the Centre for Applied Social Sciences at the University of Natal, agreed to give expert evidence on trade unions as a constructive channel for the institutionalisation and management of conflict. In addition, he testified about the results of surveys he had undertaken, which indicated that the vast majority of black people in South Africa felt bitter, frustrated and discriminated against, and did not require Black Consciousness ideology or university students to tell them of this.

Two ex-student leaders – Laurine Platzky, who had been SRC president at the University of Cape Town, and Brian Hackland, who had led the Wages Commission in Pietermaritzburg – immediately agreed to testify for the defence when approached. Laurine set out to demolish the idea that the political prisoners campaign had been conceived as a result of a conspiracy. The state had not claimed she was part of any 'radical clique' or conspiracy, yet she testified how she and the SRC that she led had promoted the idea of the campaign and participated in it.

Hackland explained the rationale behind the Wages Commissions, setting out how they operated and what they aimed to achieve. Like Laurine, he was an impressive witness. He was firm, uncompromising and straightforward about the imbalance of power between workers and employers, and the necessity for institutions like the Wages Commissions and trade unions to organise and strengthen workers in an effort to change deeply exploitative conditions.

Both these student witnesses gave evidence in a way that supported the approach of the accused: no apologies, no compromises. We were proud of what students had achieved and, if this rendered us guilty of political offences against an oppressive state representative of a racial minority, then we would face the consequences.

* * *

The evidence which I was to give as part of the defence case was critical. Our lawyers agreed that I was the accused most in danger of being convicted. I could damage the defence case for all of the accused by giving unconvincing evidence, and would have to be particularly careful not to allow the prosecution to strengthen its conspiracy approach by linking the other accused to my own actions. If, in the view of the presiding magistrate, my evidence was not credible, he might use that to question the evidence of the other accused.

I would have to walk a tightrope with extreme caution. I could not take on all responsibility myself, because then I might well be convicted and also undermine the credibility of the other accused. On the other hand, I could not claim my actions were part of a general programme which included all of the accused, because then they might be convicted on the basis of a conspiracy. I would have to take responsibility for what I could as an individual. Where I could safely claim that my role had been part of general Nusas and SRC activity, I would do so. I would deny that anything I had done or written was on behalf of the ANC or the SACP or to further the interests of communism. I would proudly assert that I was a socialist in orientation, found little to disagree with in the Freedom Charter and believed that the most credible leaders of the majority of South Africans were in prison or in exile. I understood and had supported the progressive role of Black Consciousness, especially in the student movement, but was also critical of some of its elements. Finally, I would assert that I saw the organisation of black workers into trade unions as one of the most important preconditions for radically changing South African society.

George Bizos was delegated responsibility for preparing me to give evidence. Over a period of six weeks, we met many nights at his home after long and sometimes tedious days in court. On some evenings I had to attend honours seminars, which were being run by Eddie Webster. It was a strange disconnect: sitting with Eddie in the dock during the day, and debating the role of the working class in Africa in the evenings. During one seminar, we disagreed strongly on the position of workers in post-colonial societies. Did they form part of a labour aristocracy, with interests aligned to the comprador bourgeoisie which ran the economy and state? What was their relationship to the peasantry and urban lumpen-proletariat which formed the majority in most African countries? Our dispute became heated at one stage. Eddie questioned whether I was willing to learn anything from him. Could we not, I responded, learn from each other? Next morning, we were back in court, facing charges of furthering the aims of communism.

George often found our defence preparations difficult. I had a tendency to default into debates over political theory and strategy, rather than deal with the evidence I would give. George enjoyed these discussions and participated with enthusiasm. However, his job was to defend his clients. He developed an interesting technique. He would play the role of prosecutor, asking me questions, cross-examining me on my responses. If he felt that my response was problematic, he would look at me severely: 'That cannot be right,' he would say. 'Why not?' I would counter, ready for an argument. 'Because you have pleaded not guilty, and your answer puts that plea in question.' Then I would understand that I needed to polish my answer to a finer finish.

'Ideas' had become increasingly important in the trial, as the prosecution's efforts to prove a conspiracy with the ANC and SACP floundered in the absence of hard evidence. George explained to me that the state would have to try to infer that a conspiracy existed, and the way I set out my political ideas and identity would be important in countering that. This led to a long and sometimes heated engagement. Surely, suggested George, my approach fell within the ambit of liberalism or at least radical liberalism? No, I countered, it is informed by democratic socialism, to be distinguished from communism. Then, said George, you are a social democrat in the style of the European social democracies. No, I explained, there is a world of difference between social democracy and democratic socialism. Yes, said George, that might be the difference between you being acquitted and being found guilty and taking your co-accused down with you.

We could not resolve this, and George finally advised me to deal with the issue as best as I could, bearing in mind my responsibility to both myself and others. In the 200 pages which my evidence covered when transcribed, the prosecution did not once ask me whether I was a liberal, a radical liberal, a social democrat or a socialist. The distinction between these positions, and the strategies which flowed from them, was not something occupying state prosecutors at the time, who probably believed that these could all be reduced to 'communism'.

The prosecution found it hard to reconcile my approach to Black Consciousness with my support for non-racialism. Explaining that Steve Biko had made a major impression on me when I first met him in April 1970, and that I had engaged with him on a number of times subsequently, I told the court that 'I consider Mr Biko to be a very fine man'.[11] I also told the court that 'I agree ... that there is a possibility in South African society for violence. I don't think this has been caused by the emergence of Black Consciousness. I think Black Consciousness is a positive and responsible step.'[12]

I explained that I considered myself a 'committed radical who has a commitment to a non-racial South Africa'.[13] This posed no contradiction to my support for the principles of the Freedom Charter: 'There is nothing strange about the beliefs of democrats ... being compatible ... with the Freedom Charter.'[14] This was one of the occasions on which the prosecutor, P.B. Jacobs, looked up at me threateningly. 'We'll come back to that,' he warned. Slowly I began to understand that this meant he was giving up on that particular line of attack. By the end of my cross-examination, the spectators in the gallery and some of my co-accused had started to giggle every time Jacobs promised to 'come back to that'.

Explaining my support for the release of all political prisoners, I argued that a solution to South Africa's political conflict could only be 'peacefully effected through full participation of all the people and freely chosen representatives in a process of extended negotiations ... The release of more than 400 South Africans banned, banished, detained and imprisoned ... would constitute the first step towards a new political dispensation.'[15]

Jacobs and I clashed over the question of security police torture of detainees and deaths in detention. I had written a number of articles on this. A piece entitled 'Torture', which appeared in *Wits Student*, seemed to infuriate Jacobs. He queried how I could know that the police treated detainees in this manner. When I began citing evidence and affidavits proving this, and indicated that these issues would be of grave concern to any democrat, Jacobs threatened that he would 'come back to this'.[16] He did not.

In October, the magistrate adjourned the case until the beginning of December, for judgment. I was relieved at this development, as I was due to write my final honours examinations during November and needed time to study. Exhausted, I also made application for a variation of my bail conditions, so that I could spend a few days in the Drakensberg trying to walk the tension and exhaustion out of my system. Although this was agreed to, the security police insisted that I continue reporting to a police station while away. I drove between the campsite and the Bergville police station each day to sign the *borgboek*.

As the beginning of December drew closer, I raised an academic but real problem with the defence team. Although I would be finished exams by the time of judgment, I still had to write a dissertation, which was due at the end of February 1977. If I was convicted and sentenced, it would mean I could not complete my honours degree.

Arthur agreed that this was a concern, but undertook to prepare a bail application pending an appeal if I was convicted and sentenced to a term of imprisonment. He would have it with him in court, and be ready to argue immediately should that be necessary.

Ray Tucker advised me to pack a small case with toiletries and a few other essentials, just in case there was a guilty verdict and the magistrate withdrew bail pending sentence. And so I arrived at the Johannesburg regional court on 1 December 1976, carrying a bag which held a toothbrush and toothpaste, soap, pyjamas, underwear – and an impenetrable volume on transition from pre-capitalist to capitalist modes of production, which I was trying to read at the time.

Judgment took nearly two days for the magistrate to deliver. He was not impressed with the evidence of the three police informers. On the other hand, he said, I had stated with great clarity that I opposed the government and aimed for a change in the system. My evidence had not been shaken despite lengthy cross-examination, and my version of events and explanations, he said, 'could not be disbelieved'.[17]

During the tea break, Geoff Budlender took me aside. The fact that the magistrate had not rejected my evidence, and that he was not distinguishing between my role and actions and those of the other accused, was promising. Perhaps I would not need my emergency suitcase after all.

The final verdict was reached very suddenly. The state's case, said the magistrate, rested on proving a conspiracy between the accused. However, the prosecution had failed to establish that the accused's actions had been calculated to further the objects of communism, the SACP or ANC. In those circumstances, said the magistrate, the 'existence or otherwise of a conspiracy is irrelevant. The accused are acquitted and discharged.'

11
Bookends

Political history has no natural beginning or end. Neither do the stories and memories which give texture and depth to interpretation. There are no real conclusions to what is a never-ending narrative, a process in which the past, present and future influence, and in turn are influenced by, each other. There is only background to provide context, and elaboration on how matters developed. And then there are questions about trust and betrayal, thoughts about responsibility and consequence, and reflections on loyalty and comradeship. These are the bookends which frame history and make it more understandable.

* * *

The presiding magistrate Gert Steyn had not been particularly impressed by the evidence of the three police informers[1] who testified in the Nusas trial. Derek Brune, the most senior of the group, had not been part of the student left, nor presented himself as a political radical. He had not attempted to influence the trajectory of student politics. Presumably his role was to compile regular reports on campus activities and hand over documents and publications to his security police handlers.

Most of this was in the public domain, and Brune was unable to uncover anything clandestine or that linked student leaders and their organisations to underground activities. I had suspected, during 1974, that Brune might be connected to either the security police or Boss. Sometime during the year, another SRC member reported that he had followed Brune to a building in Auckland Park, which housed a recording studio trading under the name 'Brigadeurs'. The studio was headed by the son of a former head of the security police, Brigadier 'Tiny' Venter, and I concluded that if Brune was a spy, this was where he delivered his reports and received his payments.

However, I decided not to act on this information. I was not certain that its source was reliable, and this caution was proved accurate when, a few years later, he too was exposed as an informer, although working for Boss rather than the security police. I do not know whether this strange set of circumstances was a reflection of internecine conflict between Boss and the security police, or whether the Boss agent – Arthur McGiven – was trying to enhance his own credibility by exposing an informer from another agency. In any event, I was disinclined to trust either McGiven or Brune with anything outside normal SRC administration business.

More importantly, I was not persuaded that McGiven or Brune posed any particular danger to student government. If they were informers, I reasoned, then their role was to pass on publicly available information to their handlers. This was something just about any student or staff member at the university could do. Neither made efforts to present themselves as being part of the left or to 'infiltrate' its activities. Nor was there any indication that they were acting as *agents provocateurs*, inciting students to undertake dangerous or illegal political activities.

Allegations that this one or that one was a 'spy' were fairly common. This sometimes reflected paranoia, but also self-aggrandisement. If someone was spying on you, this must indicate political relevance. Young and politically inexperienced students could easily inflate their sense of importance, and create excitement and drama, by accusing others of being spies. Allegations of spying could also be the result of petty jealousies and conflicts. On a number of occasions I had been approached with accusations that someone was an informer for the police. Sometimes this happened after romantic relations had broken down or over perceived or real slights. On other occasions, it emerged when individuals were competing against each other for positions of power. These sorts of claims had to be treated with caution. People's reputations and lives could be destroyed through allegations of this nature, and for every informer who was correctly suspected, many others were accused without foundation. I can certainly recall most of those who were correctly identified as spies. In a number of cases, I had suspected them of working for the police or other state agencies. However, I can also remember others on whom suspicion fell but about whom nothing damning was ever established. Many of them were accused of spying on the flimsiest of grounds, and it was important not to let allegations of spying tear organisations apart or destroy individuals.

The position of Craig Williamson was somewhat different. Like Brune, he was a serving member of the security police. However, he could be characterised as an infiltrator, rather than an informer. He became associated with the radical left, assumed a prominent role as a leader, and participated in political activities.

Williamson had been arrested during demonstrations and charged in 1972. He had led the surge of protesters into Anglo American's head offices in the 1973 action following the shooting of mineworkers at Western Deep Levels, using his considerable bulk to force the front doors as Anglo security tried to lock them.

He developed a personal relationship with a number of those in the student left. I often shared long-distance driving with him when we transported students by kombi to Nusas seminars and conferences, and he had been the passenger who noticed that I lost direction *en route* to the December 1973 Nusas seminar, driving to Cape Town through both Bloemfontein *and* Kimberley.

It is too easy to claim that I was suspicious about Williamson's security status from the time of his arrival at university in 1972. A number of people, including me, were at times concerned that he might be an agent for the security police, and at other times accepted his bona fides. However, by the time of the Nusas trial, I had built up sufficient suspicion to advise caution in dealing with him, even though I had no evidence of his dual life.

George Bizos has recalled that the defence team considered

consulting Williamson as a potential defence witness, 'but Glenn Moss warned us off, and claimed Williamson was a police spy'.[2] Terry Bell suggests that a few student leaders were suspicious of Williamson. According to him, Cedric de Beer was 'vocal' in his concerns. 'Another leading student activist, Glenn Moss, also refused to accept that Williamson could be trusted. Both were to be harassed, detained and dragged before the courts ... They did, in those early years, pose a threat to Williamson and the whole security operation.'[3]

This is substantially accurate, although there were moments of uncertainty. During his infiltration of Nusas, I had hovered between suspicion and acceptance of Williamson. His competence and geniality made it difficult to hold a consistent view on whether he was an informer or not, although it was an issue which I discussed often with close political colleagues. However, when Williamson left South Africa for Geneva, I was part of a group that contacted the IUEF head, Lars-Gunnar Eriksson, to raise our concerns. We had no proof that Williamson was an agent for the state, but advised Eriksson that there was sufficient suspicion to block his access to the sort of sensitive information which passed through IUEF offices.

Eriksson must have shown this communication to Williamson, because he wrote to me a few weeks later asking what Phil Bonner – who had acted as courier for the communication with Eriksson – had against him. When Phil was arrested pending deportation – an order which was subsequently rescinded – I wondered whether this was Williamson taking his revenge.

Our representations to Eriksson and to the ANC, channelled through Dan O'Meara and Duncan Innes, were not given credibility, and over the next few years Williamson operated as a successful security police agent abroad.

I am convinced that, when charges were formulated in the Nusas trial, the prosecution intended using Williamson as its key witness. Sometime thereafter, I suspect that a decision was taken not to expose Williamson as an informer, but to extend his infiltration beyond the ambit of the student left. This might explain the apparent 'downgrading' of the Nusas trial from a Supreme Court matter prosecuted by the Deputy Attorney-General to a Regional Court matter with a public prosecutor leading the state's case. As Michael Lobban argued,

> Proof of a direct link between the students and the ANC was likeliest to come from the potential evidence of Craig Williamson ... He would be able to give colour to discussion and ideas the students had, to give information from the inside regarding documents and material possessed by the accused that might at least suggest ANC sympathies ... The downgrading of the case may thus be linked to the state's decision not to call him as a witness ... Instead he was sent to Geneva to work for the IUEF and through the organisation to infiltrate the ANC ... The decision not to use Williamson left the state case in some difficulties.[4]

This may explain, at least in part, some of the 'absences' or 'silences' in the Nusas trial. The prosecution did not lead evidence about my involvement in the Industrial Aid Society and the involvement of Sactu and ANC supporters in those activities. Links between Nusas leaders and Okhela were not revealed during the trial, and neither was my involvement in discussions to set up Counter Information Services and the Movement for Social Democracy. There was almost no evidence presented about my involvement with Congress- and Communist Party-aligned individuals such as Eli and Sheila Weinberg, Mohammed Timol, the Naidoo brothers, Pindile Mfeti, Lilian Ngoyi, Shirish Nanabhai and Reggie Vandayar.

Arthur Chaskalson made reference to this in his closing argument on behalf of the defence. He was particularly irritated by the state's heads of arguments, in which 'Flip' Jacobs, the prosecutor, had made allegations against me that had no basis in evidence. For example, he claimed that I had spent considerable time at the homes of 'known' ANC and SACP supporters some of whom were banned at the time. As Arthur pointed out acerbically, 'My learned friend [Jacobs] has presented argument about the case he hoped to present, not the case he did present.'

Was it the state's initial intention to lead all this evidence through Williamson, and did his absence from the trial fully explain all these 'silences' in the prosecution's case? That is doubtful. While Williamson would have known about some of these matters, he would not have been privy to all of them. For example, he knew little if anything about the IAS and involvement with Eli Weinberg, or regular discussions with the Naidoo family in their Doornfontein home. Perhaps the state decided to suppress this evidence for tactical reasons, not wanting to overemphasise any relationships between young white opposition and an older, Congress-aligned tradition. But why, then, charge us in the first place? Perhaps there were other informers the state feared revealing if evidence of these connections was presented. Perhaps these absences and silences are simply explained by the way in which different sections of the security apparatuses and prosecuting authorities worked in silos, with information and investigations in one area being kept separate from those in others.

Bartholomew Hlapane fell into a different category of state witnesses. He was neither an informer nor a spy. A senior underground leader of both MK and the Communist Party, he had been subject to successive periods of detention, and finally agreed to testify against Bram Fischer in his trial under the Sabotage Act, and thereafter in various other trials of ANC and SACP members.

Arthur Chaskalson's cross-examination of Hlapane in the Nusas trial was devastating. It was widely assumed that Hlapane had been totally discredited as a witness and would not again be called by the state. However, later in 1976 he was used as a witness against Harry Gwala and others accused of reviving ANC structures in Natal and recruiting trainees for MK.

A few years later, in 1982, Hlapane testified before the Denton Committee, a United States Senate Committee looking into 'terrorism' in South Africa. There he claimed that the ANC was dominated and controlled by the Communist Party. This was particularly damaging for ANC efforts to gain support in the US, and the West more generally. On 16 December 1982, Hlapane was assassinated at his Soweto house. MK accepted responsibility for this act.

* * *

Apartheid-supporting newspapers, anonymous pamphlets distributed around the Wits campus, the security police and the state in its subsequent prosecution of student leadership all claimed that the campaign to release political prisoners was the outcome of a conspiracy involving the ANC, 'London-based communists', the South African Communist Party and the British Anti-Apartheid Movement (AAM).

Anti-apartheid organisations in and around London had certainly been campaigning for the release of Mandela with increasing intensity in the early 1970s. Mike Terry, who became general secretary of the AAM in England, has written of a meeting he had with Neville Curtis and Paul Pretorius, then president and deputy president of Nusas, in London towards the end of 1971. Terry, who was at the time national secretary of the British National Union of Students, recalls that the two Nusas leaders were working on a plan to initiate a campaign to mark ten years since the arrest of Mandela. I have no recollection of such discussions within Nusas, but in any event nothing came of the idea at the time.

By 1973, Terry had become involved with the national office of the AAM, and he recalls that, in December 1973, he played

> a small role in a major new initiative by the AAM together with Idaf (the International Defence and Aid Fund) and a number of other organisations. Ethel de Keyser, who was then executive secretary of the AAM, together with Hugh Lewin, then at Idaf, had the imagination to convene a major conference at University College, London, on the theme Southern Africa: The Imprisoned Society. And it was the SATIS Committee, which was set up as a result of the conference, that became the framework through which most of the campaigning against political repression in southern Africa was to be organised in Britain. The conference and the subsequent SATIS campaign helped put the struggle of South Africa's political prisoners firmly back on the campaigning agenda. The AAM Annual Report for 1973–4

comments that prior to the SATIS initiative ... 'many such as Nelson Mandela, have now been in prison for more than ten years – there has been little sustained campaigning [on their behalf]'.[5]

How did the idea and impetus for a South African-based campaign for the release of all political prisoners develop? Were there any 'conspiracies' between student leadership on the Nusas campuses and organisations and individuals associated with the ANC, SACP, AAM and Idaf to launch such a campaign? Was it coincidence, conspiracy or some greater 'strategic synchronicity' that led to a London-based conference and a Western Cape-based Nusas seminar both resolving to foreground political prisoners in the following year's campaigns?

It is possible that individuals from within Nusas or South Africa's broader student left did discuss these ideas in London. I do not know. It is also possible that some of those associated with the London initiatives hoped to encourage similar campaigns within South Africa. Again, I have no knowledge of that. I am, however, certain that the form and strategies for the campaign, at least in Johannesburg, were unambiguously 'home-grown'. These arose from ongoing discussions by a group of radical Wits students who had become prominent within student leadership structures. The political prisoners campaign was the outcome of our own analysis of the political situation, of a critique of liberalism and the state of anti-apartheid opposition, of the successes and failures of previous student actions, and of the actual and potential place of relatively privileged students in society.

The student campaign was, in important respects, very different from the campaigns developing in London. Ours was not a 'Release Mandela' campaign, but a demand to release all political prisoners so that they could participate in a political process to end apartheid. Our campaign tackled the potentially divisive issues of communists in the struggle, violence as political strategy and a critique of political liberalism. We aimed to challenge alliances where they weakened the left's radicalism. International solidarity campaigns generally emphasised unity, a commonality of interests and purpose, and alliances between potentially hostile groups. Ours did not. We aimed to confront and, where necessary, alienate some of the support that would only endorse a weaker demand.

Campaign ideas and strategies were discussed and canvassed with individuals associated with the various Congress organisations and the Communist Party. Tony Holiday of the *Rand Daily Mail* was a regular part of late-night political discussions, often over many drinks for which he usually paid. He was an underground operative for the SACP. There was a growing group of Congress-aligned individuals with whom we shared information and discussed political strategies: Helen Joseph; the Naidoo family of Doornfontein, and Indres in particular, who had recently been released from Robben Island after serving ten years; Mohammed Timol, brother of Ahmed, who had been so brutally killed in detention; Sheila Weinberg, who had been one of the youngest political prisoners in the 1960s, and whose parents were stalwarts and veterans of Congress Alliance politics in general and Communist Party politics in particular. We also knew Winnie Mandela, Lilian Ngoyi, Rookie Saloojee (wife of 'Babla', one of the first to die under security police interrogation while being detained under the 90-day clause). Of course these relationships had an influence on our thinking, as they may have had on theirs.

There is also no doubt that, as a group, we were gravitating increasingly towards a left-oriented, yet critical and independent, Congress identity and way of thinking. This was unsurprising. For us as non-racialists committed to democracy, as radicals influenced by socialist and Marxist ways of analysing society, and as activists seeking ways to act, there were few other organisational allegiances that approximated our worldview.

This identity as left and radical, as non-racial and democratic, emphasising class location over racial identity, had developed within the cauldron of South African experience. The search for appropriate political strategies and actions took place through interaction with other histories and traditions, including Black Consciousness, liberalism, nationalism, socialism and communism. However, the outcome was a development of our own strategies and initiatives.

All historical 'truths' are at best partial and subject to different 'stories' and memories. This is the closest I can come to a 'truth' about what was probably the student left's most controversial and daring political campaign. It evolved in a context of multiple and varied influences and agendas. However, it was crystallised, initiated and driven by a young and independent-minded group of left student activists who were doing their best to advance a politics of radical opposition.

* * *

A few days before our acquittal in the Nusas trial, the state moved against a number of individuals involved in worker organisation in the Western Cape, Natal and Transvaal. About 27 of those active in the Wages Commissions and newly formed trade unions and worker advisory and education bodies were banned. Many of them were close colleagues of the accused in the Nusas trial. If any reminder was needed that acquittal after a trial was no cause for celebration, no great victory, the bannings of so many served that purpose well.

They were also a timely reminder that the world of South African opposition politics had changed dramatically while we were on trial. The urban student-led rebellions of June 1976 and after, and the growing importance of trade union initiatives of various types, were indicators that the politics we had been tried for belonged to a past period. Radical opposition politics of the first half of the 1970s developed at a time of internal quiescence and disorganisation, especially in townships and the workplace. This was now changing, and the sort of role which we had tried to play in that context had been incorporated into more developed and potentially more powerful politics.

The year in which I had been on trial had created the space to reflect and undertake the focused studying and reading required for a more analytical and thoughtful approach to political engagement. It also allowed for an assessment and consideration of the sort of progressive roles which could be undertaken in the changing terrain of South African opposition politics.

This created the context for a range of new activities, generally focusing on information gathering and dissemination, political analysis and education, and publishing. It included *Work in Progress*, the political magazine I co-founded in 1977, and of which I remained editor until 1988. It also involved the *South African Review* series, which ran from 1983 through to 1994, as well as a range of publications linked to the Development Studies Group – which grew out of the honours course I had done while on trial – and the Southern African Research Service.

Some of the material used for the special editions of *Wits Student* and published as part of the political prisoners campaign had been sourced from legal proceedings such as trials and inquests. This stimulated my interest in the way in which material extracted from trials could be used to present information on banned organisations and their activities without courting prosecution. From its foundation until 1989, *Work in Progress* published regular articles and features based on a political reading of trial records to chronicle military and political campaigns against the apartheid state.

Being defended by one of the most talented legal defence teams imaginable, I had learnt a considerable amount about political trials. With the growing number of trials following June 1976, I became increasingly involved as a paralegal consultant in the defence of those accused. These included the sedition trial in which the leadership of the Soweto Students' Representative Council was charged for the events of June 1976 and after; the treason trial involving ANC guerrilla attacks on a bank in Silverton and a police station in Soekmekaar; and a number of trials of other MK guerrillas. The knowledge I gained as a result enabled me to use political trials as one indicator of the developing tempo and nature of anti-apartheid struggle, and I was able to provide some insight as to why ANC operatives were being apprehended with such regularity when they entered the country.

It was also through my involvement in defence of political trialists that I again met up with Mewa Ramgobin, whose 1971 plea for clemency for political prisoners was a brave precursor to Nusas's more radical focus on imprisoned political leadership. Mewa was the first accused in the UDF treason trial in Pietermaritzburg, where I was part of the legal defence team through my association with Priscilla Jana's legal office.

* * *

Relations between Helen Suzman, the Progressive Party's sole MP until 1974, and the student left, were never good. However, they deteriorated further as politics on the Nusas-affiliated campuses radicalised and criticism of Progressive Party policies and practice deepened. This went beyond the obvious rejection of the party's endorsement of a qualified franchise. Its free market economic policies could never address the issues of poverty, a low-wage economy and the exclusion of the majority from society's benefits.

Helen knew I had been one of the motivators for the Nusas communiqué calling on white students to carefully consider how and whether to vote in the 1974 election. She had interpreted this – not totally incorrectly – as an attempt to dissuade students on the Nusas campuses from campaigning or voting for the Progs.

Our relations were generally hostile, although she did not let this influence her when I was detained in 1975. She spoke out publicly in opposition to this set of detentions and in support of the student and ex-student leaders being held under the Terrorism Act.

When Helen spoke at Wits in the run-up to the 1974 general election, Steven Friedman had attacked her pro-capitalist and free market economics. A few years later, he interviewed her in his capacity as a journalist. 'You are the one who called me a racist imperialist [at the Wits meeting], aren't you?' Steven responded that she was mistaken. He had, in fact, called her a 'handmaiden of international capital'. 'Ah, yes,' responded Helen, and they got on quite well after that. When the government withdrew Steven's passport, she made representations for it to be returned to him.

* * *

Students had occupied Anglo American's head offices in August 1973, following the shooting of miners at the Western Deep Levels near Carletonville. A number of the participants subsequently joined the Wages Commission, citing their experiences in this action as a reason for becoming involved in worker organisation. Johnny Clegg's fluency in Zulu made him a particularly valuable new member, and he undertook translation of articles for *Umsebenzi/Abasebenzi*, the worker newspaper distributed by the Wages Commission at factory gates.

One of those present at the Anglo sit-in, Alan Fine, resigned as chair of the East Rand Young Progressives that day and joined the Wages Commission. This was a significant step in his journey of radicalisation, trade unionism, underground work for the exiled Sactu, and detention and trial under the Terrorism Act.

In the aftermath of these events, Steven Friedman and Jeanette Curtis – subsequently killed by a letter bomb sent by Craig Williamson – intervened on behalf of a group of Western Deep mineworkers in jail awaiting trial following the conflict on the mine. The attorney Ismail Ayob was acting for them and had managed to raise bail. Jeanette and Steven were temporarily 'appointed' to the staff of Ayob & Associates for the day and went to Carletonville to try to bail out the workers. 'Of course,' recalled Friedman,

> we knew that they were all migrants and that, if they were given bail, they would go home and never return. I remember us, however, giving the police solemn assurances that, as employees of a responsible legal practice, we would ensure that our clients would appear [in court] if they were given bail. The police fell for it and I can still remember waving to the strikers as they walked away across the veld. I remember telling Jeanette that neither we nor the cops would ever see them again and so it turned out.[6]

* * *

During 1974, Beyers Naudé had assisted me in setting up a discretionary bank account. The funds deposited into this were initially used to finance a literacy programme run by Barbara Hogan and Susan Brown, which later joined up with the Industrial Aid Society (IAS) as part of its worker education initiative.

The administration of this account became a point of contestation during the internecine warfare which broke out in 1975 over Tuacc interference in IAS activities. By then, the account was also being used to fund some semi-clandestine trips between Johannesburg and the Transkei. The Tuacc-supporting group within the IAS had demanded that I report on the fund to the IAS executive, which I refused to do.

When I was detained in August 1975, some of the Tuacc group now rampant in the IAS used my absence to claim that I had refused to report on the account because I had misused some of the funds. Somehow they had found evidence of two withdrawals, each for R200, which they claimed were irregular.

There is an intriguing aside to this. In Mark Gevisser's biography of Thabo Mbeki, he makes mention of an incident in which an amount of R400 intended for Lindiwe Sisulu's underground work was mistakenly sent to Mbeki's sister, Linda Jiba. She assumed this was for family support, and passed it on to her mother, Epainette Mbeki.

It must have been around that time that Pindile – nephew of Mrs Mbeki, and cousin of Thabo and his sister – told me he had to undertake an urgent trip to the Transkei and needed R400 from the special fund immediately. Was that, I wonder, repayment of the R400 which the Mbeki family had thought was a contribution from a brother and son in exile, but was required for underground political activity?[7]

In May 1976, security police detained Pindile, as well as Lindiwe Sisulu and Miriam Sithole (who was part of IAS leadership and may have been part of the same ANC cell as Pindile). Despite intensive interrogation, including torture, Pindile did not reveal any details about the discretionary account set up by Beyers, and as far as I know security police never became aware of its use.

Following his release from detention, Pindile was banned and then banished to Butterworth in the Transkei. He subsequently disappeared while in Natal and is believed to have been assassinated by a South African or Transkei hit squad.

* * *

While my release from detention was being processed at Compol, a Pretoria security policeman warned me to stay away from people like Breytenbach and Gerry Maré, who, he said, had 'got me into trouble'.

My detention was certainly the immediate result of the Okhela initiative and Gerry's request that I meet Breytenbach on his clandestine trip to South Africa. The suggestion, however, that others can be held accountable for the political consequences of one's own decisions and commitments is something that I rejected at the time and continue to discount.

I was detained as a 'terrorist' because I was involved in a set of political struggles against the existing social order. That had been the core of my identity and existence for at least six years. As I had matured from student politics to other forms of activity, the lines between public and clandestine identities, between what was legal and illegal, began to blur, and the stakes and potential consequences rose accordingly.

I had willingly and consciously placed myself in that position. Had I not done so, Gerry Maré would not have been a close political colleague and would therefore not have asked me to meet Breytenbach. He, in turn, would not have been interested in learning more about my work.

I did not support the Okhela initiative. I had some knowledge of it, but no active involvement. If I had not been caught up in the consequences of Breytenbach's ill-advised mission, I would not have been detained at that time. However, I had committed my youth to a form of politics that carried consequences, including detention, trial and imprisonment.

Gerry and I continued to be close colleagues as postgraduate students, as co-editors of *Work in Progress* and the *South African*

Review, and as individuals who have debated the political past, present and future for 40 years.

I have little sympathy for those who consciously take decisions, knowing the risks, and then hold others accountable for the consequences. During the 1970s and 1980s, the dangers of high-profile opposition to the system of apartheid were obvious and apparent. The potential dangers for anyone who put themselves within the ambit of the semi-clandestine or illegal were obvious. For those rejecting the basis of a class- and race-riven society from a position of relative privilege, this might involve rejection, harassment, arrest, banning, detention, torture, imprisonment. For others, death became a real possibility. Some of those I met through the politics of the time were killed by apartheid's security forces – Rick Turner, Steve Biko, Jenny Curtis, Pindile Mfeti, Neil Aggett and, some years later, David Webster. I had worked extensively with some of this group, and a number of them were particularly close friends.

At every turn, there were choices to be made. If consequences followed, this was the result of those choices. I accept, and accepted at the time, that being detained as a 'terrorist' was a consequence of decisions I made as part of a radical political community. I continue to have, however, many unresolved questions about the Okhela operation and the way in which the imperatives of international and exile politics damaged independent left radicalism within the country.

Johnny Makatini, the ANC's North African and subsequently United Nations representative, supported the formation of Okhela and knew of Breytenbach's clandestine mission into South Africa. 'Breytenbach was living in Paris in 1972 when Johnny Makatini ... encouraged him, presumably with the approval of Tambo, to join with a few other non-Communist white exiles to form a secret support group.'[8] In some versions, Oliver Tambo initially approved of the idea of Okhela as a counter-balance to the influence of the Communist Party and its particular brand of Marxism, only to distance himself under pressure from the SACP.[9]

Henri Curiel, who provided Breytenbach with a forged passport bearing the name 'Christian Galaska', may have been linked to a

European intelligence agency. In this murky world of deceit and espionage, Breytenbach may have been betrayed to South African intelligence – possibly by elements within the ANC itself – even before he left on his mission.

Those responsible for the 'Cold War' organisational politics which lay behind the formation of Okhela were most culpable for the consequences of Breytenbach's clandestine mission. Okhela damaged the lives of a number of committed political activists, came close to destroying Nusas, and undermined independent left-wing political initiatives developing within South Africa.

* * *

Several of those I met at university in the early 1970s faced detention and interrogation under section 6 of the Terrorism Act. Campaigns against detention without trial and the human rights abuses that were a common and regular feature of the system became more frequent. Support for detainees, and exposure of torture and brutalisation and abuse, became the basis for organisation rather than just protest. When friends, colleagues and co-workers were detained in a massive police investigation into non-racial opposition in 1981, I was among those who formed the Detainees' Parents Support Committee (DPSC). This initiative forced the state to pay a higher political price for its system of detention without trial than had ever been extracted before.

* * *

The radical challenge mounted on the campuses initially seemed limited, perhaps even marginal. Yet the ideas that underpinned this new radicalism, and its challenge to liberalism as the leading ideology in opposition to apartheid, had a longer-term significance. As Steven Friedman has noted,

> ideas do have an impact, although the influence of radical intellectuals on social movements is always indirect and incomplete. This is entirely

appropriate for ... movements flourish most when they are controlled by those who participate in them rather than those who impart ideas to them. But this is not to say that ideas and those who communicate them are irrelevant. They often have an important impact, creating possibilities while foreclosing others ... The worker movement which developed after 1973 would have been significantly different had the radical academic work of the early 1970s and beyond not influenced a generation of middle-class radicals.[10]

The ideas and organisational approaches which developed in and around the universities in the early 1970s had an important influence not only in the emerging union movement, but also well beyond it. They framed and shaped community politics and organisation, influencing the relationships between the different constituencies which, in the early 1980s, came to form the United Democratic Front and the smaller National Forum. 'The new radicalism of the early 1970s ... [has] been refracted through social realities and movement choices ... [and still has] an impact today. And that is surely the most that [radical] intellectuals who seek to change the world can reasonably expect.'[11]

Some of the new 'home-grown' radicals from the Nusas campuses subsequently went into exile. However, most were committed to remaining in South Africa, rather than relocating to other countries and continents. Many experienced a kind of 'internal exile', a state of being away from 'home' and unable or unwilling to 'return' because of choices made. This was most acute among progressive intellectuals, writers and journalists, students who extended their radical political activism beyond university days, and white intellectuals who went into the new trade union movement.

These individuals cut themselves off from the society that had formed them. They severed relationships with ruling-class elites and those with access to power in business, the bureaucracy, government, and even the universities from which many of them had emerged. They declined to follow the professional and commercial career paths mapped out for them. In developing a critique of liberalism and

English business in the 'apartheid–capitalist complex', they separated themselves from the world that had created them.

The rise of Black Consciousness isolated them further, largely cutting off access to black students, intellectuals, and cultural and political activists who would otherwise have formed part of their natural 'community'. As a consequence, the new radicals had to 'create' their own community and sense of belonging, rather than integrating into social and support structures that already existed.[12] This found expression in shared houses and flats, often clustered in the poorer suburbs such as Yeoville, Crown Mines and Mayfair in Johannesburg; Woodstock, Mowbray and Observatory in Cape Town; and Bellair, Mayville and Overport in Durban. It explains the intensity of shared social experience, which often became an extension of political activity. And it sheds light on why members of this manufactured 'community' sought their closest relationships – with friends, lovers, confidants and political comrades – from within the relatively small circle of radical activists and intellectuals, and why so many of these bonds endured – politically, socially and personally – over four decades and more.

* * *

Sometime during 1996, a few of those who had been involved in the Nusas trial began discussing whether we should hold a gathering to note 20 years since our acquittal. George Bizos reminded us that Mandela had often said how important the campaign to release political prisoners had been for morale, and that one day he wanted to thank its leaders.

This had been confirmed when I met Walter Sisulu and Ahmed Kathrada shortly after their release from prison in October 1989. Sitting in the tiny lounge of the Sisulus' home in Orlando West, they told me how the Nusas campaign had energised flagging morale on Robben Island at a time when prisoners began fearing they had been forgotten.

And so it was that, early in December 1996, South Africa's first democratically elected president was guest of honour at my home.

Many of those associated with the 1974 campaign and the trial of the student leadership in 1976 were gathered there for lunch. So, too, were some who had been imprisoned at the time, or whose close family members had been jailed and whose life stories formed one focus of the campaign.

It was at this gathering that Mandela confirmed that the message Helen Joseph had delivered during the campaign had indeed been smuggled out of jail, for transmission to the student leadership. He had not known that Helen had read it out at a public meeting, in defiance of a number of laws.

Mandela spoke at the lunch, held in the garden. He told the assembled group how much he, and other prisoners, had appreciated and admired the efforts of the student leaders who had campaigned for their release in 1974. Mandela made mention of the importance of those white South Africans who, at the high point of apartheid and the low point of resistance, took a stand.

Presidential security ringed the perimeter of the property as Mandela arrived. Accompanied by one of his young granddaughters, he showed his usual interest in the young people present. Mandela absolutely charmed my two sons, then aged five and three. He accepted drawings they had done for him. 'Very good, very good,' he commented, in that characteristic voice of gravel. He signed a popular version of his autobiography for them, which they both still treasure. Then he explained to them that he had come to our home so that, when he retired and became a pensioner, he would still know 'people of influence, like your father'. A new generation of committed South Africans was being formed, under the influence of the best of the elders.

Notes

Chapter 1
1 'Intimidated freshers crawl in sewers', *Wits Student*, 22 (6), 1970.
2 This background is largely derived from 'A brief history of student action in South Africa', Nusas archives, UCT Libraries, A3.
3 Neville Curtis and Clive Keegan, 'The aspiration to a just society', in Hendrik W. van der Merwe and David Welsh (eds.), *Student Perspectives on South Africa*, David Philip Publishers, Cape Town, 1972, p. 95.
4 Curtis and Keegan, 'The aspiration to a just society', p. 95.
5 Barry Streek, 'Skeletons in the Rhodes cupboard: What should be done about them?', *African Sociological Review*, 9 (1), 2005, p. 162.
6 'History of Redacres', *www.redacres.org.za*.
7 Neville Curtis, 'A new realism, a new idealism', address to the 1970 Nusas national seminar held at Redacres, April 1970, Nusas archives, UCT Libraries, A3.
8 Tony Stirling, 'Conscience will bother me if I testify – Shanti Naidoo', *Rand Daily Mail*, 16 December 1969.
9 Desmond Blow, 'Detainees allege police torture', *Sunday Times*, 20 February 1970.
10 I am indebted to Elaine Unterhalter for sharing her memories of this march, including Ian Thompson's eating of his lecture notes.
11 *Convocation Commentary*, 3, December 1970, p. 1.

Chapter 2
1 Quoted in Xolela Mangcu, *Biko: A Biography*, Tafelberg, Cape Town, 2012, p. 161.
2 Ibid., pp. 129, 133.
3 Quoted in Mangcu, *Biko*, p. 141.
4 Turner's intellectual importance and influence is well captured in Andrew Nash, 'The moment of Western Marxism in South Africa', *Comparative Studies of South Asia, Africa and the Middle East*, 19 (1), 1999, pp. 68–71.
5 Steve Biko, *I Write What I Like*, quoted in Mangcu, *Biko*, p. 282.
6 Steven Friedman, 'From class room to class struggle: Radical academics and the rebirth of trade unionism in the 1970s', paper prepared for a conference on The Durban Moment: Revisiting Politics, Labour, Youth and Resistance in the 1970s, Rhodes University, 21–23 February 2013, p. 2.
7 Ibid.
8 Quoted in Sifiso Mxolisi Ndlovu, 'The Soweto Uprising', in South African Democracy Education Trust, *The Road to Democracy in South Africa*, volume 2 (1970–1980), Unisa Press, Pretoria, 2006, p. 336.
9 Thomas G. Karis and Gail M. Gerhart, *From Protest to Challenge: A Documentary History of African Politics in South Africa, 1882–1990*, volume 5: *Nadir and Resurgence, 1964–1975*, Unisa Press, Pretoria, 1997, p. 51.

10 Ibid., p. 65
11 Ibid., p. 17.
12 Biko, *I Write What I Like*, quoted in Mangcu, *Biko*, p. 279.
13 Mangcu, *Biko*, p. 289.
14 Ben Turok, *Strategic Problems in South Africa's Liberation Struggle: A Critical Analysis*, LSM Information Centre, Canada, 1974, p. 10.
15 Background on ANC–BC relations is drawn from Mark Gevisser, *Thabo Mbeki: The Dream Deferred*, Jonathan Ball Publishers, Johannesburg, 2007, pp. 314–319.
16 See Karis and Gerhart, *From Protest to Challenge*, volume 5, pp. 50–55, for a more detailed discussion of these issues.
17 Stephen Ellis, *External Mission: The ANC in Exile*, Jonathan Ball Publishers, Johannesburg, 2012, p. 37.
18 Ibid., p. 38.
19 Letter from Randolph Vigne to Magnus Gunther, 15 December 2002, quoted in Magnus Gunther, 'The National Committee of Liberation (NCL)/African Resistance Movement (ARM)', in South African Democracy Trust, *The Road to Democracy in South Africa*, volume 1 (1960–1970), Zebra Press, Cape Town, 2004, p. 239.
20 Ibid., p. 241.
21 Ibid., p. 243.
22 Horst Kleinschmidt (ed.), *White Liberation: A Collection of Essays*, Sprocas 2, Johannesburg, 1972. Also see Eddie Webster, 'Black Consciousness and the White Left', Appendix 2, 'Report on Nusas December Seminar 1973, Friday 30 November – Tuesday 4 December 1973, Elgin, Cape'. Nusas archives, UCT Libraries, A3.
23 Tom Meisenhelder, 'Amilcar Cabral's theory of class suicide and revolutionary socialism', *Monthly Review*, 45 (6), November 1993.
24 Georg Lukács, *History and Class Consciousness*, in particular 'Class consciousness', 'What is orthodox Marxism?', and 'Reification and the consciousness of the proletariat'; V.I. Lenin, *What Is to Be Done?*; and Antonio Gramsci, *Prison Notebooks*.
25 South African Institute of Race Relations, *A Survey of Race Relations in South Africa, 1973*, Johannesburg, 1974, p. 284.

Chapter 3

1 Neville Curtis, 'Republic Day: What is there to celebrate', 10 November 1970, Nusas archives, UCT Libraries, A3.
2 Letter from Neville Curtis, 21 May 1971, Nusas archives, UCT Libraries, A3.
3 Curtis, 'Republic Day'.
4 Neville Curtis, 'Compulsory call up of students for parades over the period of the celebration of the 10th anniversary of the Republic', letter to P.W. Botha, Minister of Defence, 1971, Nusas archives, UCT Libraries. A3.
5 James Byron, *Fields of Air*, 2nd edition, Covos-Day, Johannesburg, 2001.
6 South African Institute of Race Relations, *A Survey of Race Relations in South Africa, 1972*, Johannesburg, 1973, pp. 373–374.
7 'What Republic Day is all about', pamphlet issued by Students' Representative Council, Milner Park, Johannesburg.
8 Taffy Adler, 'Report on the Republic Day activities', pp. 3–4, University of the Witwatersrand archives and registry.
9 'Report back', official annual bulletin of the SRC, University of Witwatersrand, n.d., University of the Witwatersrand archives and registry.
10 Letter from the office of the Prime Minister to Mr N. Curtis, 2 June 1971, Nusas archives, UCT Libraries, A3.
11 Alan Fine, unpublished manuscript, chapter 7.
12 Heather Dugmore, 'Defending the "open university": The origins of student protest at

Wits', *Wits Review*, April 2012, p. 22.
13 'Academic Freedom Lecture', *Wits Student*, 30 July 1971.
14 'Academic Freedom Lecture', *Wits Student*, 13 August 1971.
15 Ibid.

Chapter 4

1 Charles A. Reich, *The Greening of America*, Random House, New York, 1970.
2 'Today is Sharpeville Day', pamphlet issued by C. de Beer and A. Orkin, University of the Witwatersrand archives.
3 Dale White, 'Sharpeville, the Great Rift Valley of the South African conscience', memorial service, University of the Witwatersrand, 21 March 1972.
4 'Wits mourns Sharpeville', *Wits Student*, 24 March 1972.
5 In a poem about his church's silence in the face of the progression of Nazi evil, often quoted at anti-apartheid gatherings in the 1970s, Pastor Martin Niemöller warned:
First they came for the Socialists, and I did not speak out
Because I was not a Socialist.
Then they came for the Trade Unionists, and I did not speak out
Because I was not a Trade Unionist.
Then they came for the Jews, and I did not speak out
Because I was not a Jew.
Then they came for me – and there was no one left to speak for me.
6 Quoted in South African Institute of Race Relations, *A Survey of Race Relations in South Africa, 1973*, South African Institute of Race Relations, Johannesburg, 1974, p. 243.
7 Ibid.
8 Ibid.
9 Ibid., p. 244.
10 Ibid., p. 245.
11 Ibid., p. 242.
12 Ibid., pp. 243–244.
13 Ibid., p. 244.
14 'Report of the commission set up to examine the establishment of Wages and Economics Commissions at affiliated centres', Nusas national congress, July 1971, Nusas archives, UCT Libraries, B1 Congress, p. 1.
15 Dan O'Meara, 'The 1946 African mine workers' strike and the political economy of South Africa', *Journal of Commonwealth and Comparative Politics*, 13 (2), 1975.
16 Gregory Houston and Bernard Magubane, 'The ANC political underground in the 1970s', in South African Democracy Education Trust, *The Road to Democracy in South Africa*, volume 2, Unisa Press, Pretoria, 2006, p. 376.
17 John D'Oliveira, 'Timol rally hit by 14-day ban', *Star*, 19 October 1973.
18 'Meeting on Wits campus is legal', *Sunday Times*, 21 October 1973.
19 'Meeting ban – but Wits SRC offers hall', *Rand Daily Mail*, 20 October 1973.
20 'Report on Nusas December Seminar 1973', Friday 30 November – Tuesday 4 December 1973, Elgin, Cape, Nusas archives, UCT Libraries, A3.
21 Geoff Budlender, 'An historical perspective of student action', Appendix 1, 'Report on Nusas December Seminar 1973', Friday 30 November – Tuesday 4 December 1973, Elgin, Cape, Nusas archives, UCT Libraries, G1.3.
22 Eddie Webster, 'Black Consciousness and the white left', Appendix 2, 'Report on Nusas December Seminar 1973, Friday 30 November – Tuesday 4 December 1973, Elgin, Cape', Nusas archives, UCT Libraries, G1.3.
23 N. Chabani Manganyi, *Being-Black-in-the-World*, Ravan Press, Johannesburg, 1973, quoted in Webster, 'Black Consciousness', p. 3.

24 Karel Tip, 'Whites and the dynamics of change', Appendix 3, 'Report on Nusas December Seminar 1973, Friday 30 November – Tuesday 4 December 1973, Elgin, Cape', Nusas archives, UCT Libraries, G1.3.
25 Charles Nupen, 'Guidelines for student action in 1974', Appendix 4, 'Report on Nusas December Seminar 1973, Friday 30 November – Tuesday 4 December 1973, Elgin, Cape', Nusas archives, UCT Libraries, G1.3.

Chapter 5

1 The most influential texts in our efforts to grapple with the relationship between 'intellectuals' and the working class were Georg Lukács's 'Class consciousness' and 'Reification and consciousness of the proletariat'; Lenin's, 'What is to be done? Burning questions of our movement'; Cabral's *Revolution in Guinea: An African People's Struggle*; and Antonio Gramsci's *Prison Notebooks*.
2 Martin Legassick, 'Nusas in the 1970s', in South African Democracy Education Trust, *The Road to Democracy in South Africa*, volume 2: (1970–1980), Unisa Press, Pretoria, 2006, pp. 856–857.
3 'The aims and principles of the United Party: SRC comments', pamphlet issued by the Students' Representative Council, University of the Witwatersrand.
4 'SRC comments on the Democratic Party', pamphlet issued by the SRC, University of the Witwatersrand.
5 'SRC comments on Progressive Party policy', pamphlet issued by the SRC, University of the Witwatersrand, 4 March 1974.
6 'Gordon Waddell – a beacon of humanity', pamphlet issued by the Good Fairies of Braamfontein.
7 *Wits Student*, 15 March 1974.
8 John Dugard (ed.), *The South West Africa/Namibia Dispute: Documents and Scholarly Writings on the Controversy between South Africa and the United Nations*, University of California Press, London, 1973, p. 416.

Chapter 6

1 South African Institute of Race Relations, *Survey of Race Relation, 1971*, Johannesburg, 1972, p. 76. See also Thomas G. Karis and Gail M. Gerhart, *From Protest to Challenge: A Documentary History of African Politics in South Africa, 1882–1990*, volume 5: *Nadir and Resurgence, 1964–1975*, Unisa Press, Pretoria, 1997, p. 45.
2 Anthony Holiday, 'Nusas starts campaign to free prisoners', *Rand Daily Mail*, 24 May 1974.
3 Political reporter, 'International support for freedom call', *Rand Daily Mail*, 25 May 1974.
4 'Campaign '74: Release political prisoners', pamphlet issued by Students' Representative Council, University of the Witwatersrand, 27 May 1974.
5 Glenn Moss, 'Report of the Nusas/SRC campaign for the release of all political prisoners, as implemented at the University of the Witwatersrand, May 27th – 30th', p. 2.
6 'SA has banned 1240 says institute report', *Rand Daily Mail*, 28 May 1974.
7 'Banned men to fast', *Rand Daily Mail*, 28 May 1974.
8 Document 29: Speech by Helen Joseph at Nusas rally, University of the Witwatersrand, 28 May 1974, in Karis and Gerhart, *From Protest to Challenge*, volume 5, pp. 434–435.
9 Pamphlet issued by the Students' Representative Council, University of the Witwatersrand.
10 Moss, 'Report of the Nusas/SRC campaign', p. 3.
11 Anthony Holiday, 'Magistrate bans march by students', *Rand Daily Mail*, 29 May 1974.
12 'Police grab students on campus', *Rand Daily Mail*, 30 May 1974.

13 Ibid.
14 Charles Nupen, 'This is a NUSAS campaign', *Wits Student*, 28 May 1974.
15 'Namibia: a "terrorist" speaks', *Wits Student*, 30 May 1974.
16 *Wits Student*, 30 May 1974.
17 'An eye on the campaign', *Wits Student*, 7 June 1974.
18 'Thus spake the editor', *Wits Student*, 7 June 1974.

Chapter 7

1 Tony Morphet, '"Brushing history against the grain": Oppositional discourse in South Africa', *Theoria*, 76, October 1990, p. 92.
2 Ibid., pp. 92–93.
3 Ibid., p. 93.
4 Sipho Kubheka, '"The struggle to be reborn": Twenty years of the labour movement', based on an interview by Luli Callinicos, *South African Labour Bulletin*, 18 (5), November 1994, p. 26.
5 Jabulani Sithole and Sifiso Ndlovu, 'The revival of the labour movement, 1970–1980', in South African Democracy Education Trust, *The Road to Democracy in South Africa*, volume 2 (1970–1980), Unisa Press, Pretoria, 2006, p. 202.
6 Ibid.
7 Martin Legassick, 'Nusas in the 1970s', in South African Democracy Education Trust, *The Road to Democracy*, volume 2, p. 862.
8 Ibid., p. 862.
9 Richard Turner, 'Black Consciousness and white liberals', *Reality*, July 1972, p. 22.
10 David Hemson, Martin Legassick and Nicole Ulrich, 'White activists and the revival of the workers' movement', in South African Democracy Education Trust, *The Road to Democracy*, volume 2, p. 267.
11 'Report of the commission set up to examine the establishment of Wages and Economics Commissions at affiliated centres', Nusas archives, University of Cape Town, B1 Congress 1971 (ii), p. 1.
12 Ibid., Appendix B: Model analysis.
13 South African Institute of Race Relations, *A Survey of Race Relations in South Africa, 1973*, Johannesburg, 1974, pp. 197–201.
14 Ibid., p. 234.
15 Personal e-mail communication from Steven Friedman. Adam Raphael was *The Guardian*'s foreign correspondent for South Africa between 1969 and 1973. During March 1973, *The Guardian* published a series of influential articles by Raphael exposing the wage levels paid by British companies in South Africa. These ignited outrage in Britain, and intensified pressure on companies to improve wages in South Africa. The Wages Commissions had assisted Raphael in some of his research, and their work benefited from intensified international pressure over wage levels. See James Sanders, *South Africa and the International Media: A Struggle for Representation*, Routledge, Oxford, 1999, especially chapter 5, 'Starvation wages'.
16 Richard Turner, *The Eye of the Needle: An Essay on Participatory Democracy*, Spro-cas 2, Johannesburg, 1972, p. 58.
17 All IAS documents referred to in this chapter were accessed from 'Industrial Aid Society, Records, 1973–1977', Historical Papers, University of the Witwatersrand, AH 1585. This is a small and incomplete, but invaluable, collection of minutes and reports from the first years of the IAS.
18 Interview with Åke Magnusson, chairman of the Student Development Fund, secretary to the 1977 Swedish committee on sanctions against South Africa, www.liberationafrica.se/intervstories/interviews/magnusson/Magnusson.pdf.
19 Sithole and Ndlovu, 'The revival of the labour movement', p. 232.

20 Ray Alexander, letter to ANC Consultative Conference, 22 April 1969, quoted in Hemson, Legassick and Ulrich, 'White activists', p. 248.

Chapter 8
1 David Hemson, Martin Legassick and Nicole Ulrich, 'White activists and the revival of the workers' movement', in South African Democracy Education Trust, *The Road to Democracy in South Africa*, volume 2 (1970–1980), Unisa Press, Pretoria, 2006, p. 273.
2 Johann Maree, 'An analysis of the independent trade unions in South Africa in the 1970s', PhD thesis, Faculty of Social Science and Humanities, University of Cape Town, 1986, quoted in Hemson, Legassick and Ulrich, 'White activists', p. 273.
3 See Jabulani Sithole and Sifiso Ndlovu, 'The revival of the labour movement, 1970–1980', in South African Democracy Education Trust, *The Road to Democracy in South Africa*, volume 2, p. 205 on the proceedings of *State* vs *H.T. Gwala and 9 others*.
4 Hemson, Legassick and Ulrich, 'White activists', p. 253.
5 Gregory Houston and Bernard Magubane, 'The ANC's armed struggle in the 1970s', in South African Democracy Education Trust, *The Road to Democracy in South Africa*, volume 2, p. 465.
6 Sipho Kubheka, '"The struggle to be reborn": Twenty years of the labour movement', based on an interview by Luli Callincos, *South African Labour Bulletin*, 18 (5), November 1994, pp. 32–34.
7 Beverley Naidoo is mistaken when she characterises this trip as clandestine. A number of those involved in the IAS knew about it in advance, and its purpose and the composition of the delegation were discussed in the offices. See Beverley Naidoo, *Death of an Idealist: In Search of Neil Aggett*, Jonathan Ball Publishers, Johannesburg, 2012, pp. 84–85.
8 Ibid.

Chapter 9
1 E-mail communication from Duncan Innes, 21 January 2013.
2 Terry Bell in collaboration with Dumisa Buhle Ntsebeza, *Unfinished Business: South Africa Apartheid and Truth*, Redworks, Observatory, Cape Town, 2001, p. 86.
3 Ibid., p. 87.
4 Ibid.
5 Ibid., p. 88.
6 Martin Legassick, 'Nusas in the 1970s', in South African Democracy Education Trust, *The Road to Democracy in South Africa*, volume 2 (1970–1980), Unisa Press, Pretoria, 2006, p. 868.
7 Quoted in Mervyn Shear, *WITS: A University in the Apartheid Era*, Witwatersrand University Press, Johannesburg, 1996, p. 53.
8 Quoted in ibid., pp. 53–54.
9 Ibid., p. 54.

Chapter 10
1 Some of the 'group of eight' had held senior positions in the SACP, and this factional dispute within the ANC cannot be reduced to 'communists versus nationalists'. See Stephen Ellis, *External Mission: The ANC in Exile,* Jonathan Ball Publishers, Johannesburg, 2012, pp. 92–93.
2 Charge sheet, *S* vs *Glenn Moss and four others*, case 41/5474/758, p. 14. A copy of the trial record is held by the Historical Papers archive at Wits University, AD 1718.
3 Martin Meredith, *Fischer's Choice: A Life of Bram Fischer*, Jonathan Ball Publishers, Johannesburg, 2002, p. 138.
4 George Bizos, *Odyssey to Freedom*, Random House, Johannesburg, 2007, pp. 388–389.
5 Michael Lobban, 'White students on trial', *White Man's Justice: South African Political*

Trials in the Black Consciousness Era, Oxford University Press, Oxford, 1996, pp. 107–108.
6 'Campaign by Nusas alleged', *The Star*, 28 July 1976.
7 *S vs Moss*, pp. 1300–1301.
8 Glenn Moss, 'Open letter to the vice-chancellor', *Wits Student*, 22 February 1974, p. 9.
9 Personal e-mail communications with Richard de Villiers, 22 and 23 April 2013.
10 André du Toit, 'Some preliminary comments on the Nusas-seminar documents in the light of Prof. Murray's evidence', unpublished report, personal papers, 1976, p. 11.
11 *S vs Moss*, p. 2366.
12 Ibid., p. 2466.
13 Ibid.
14 Ibid., p. 2493.
15 'Nusas not a Red front, court told', *Rand Daily Mail*, 8 September 1976.
16 'Moss talks of death and torture', *Rand Daily Mail*, 9 September 1976.
17 'Clapping fills court as Nusas five acquitted', *Rand Daily Mail*, 3 December 1976.

Chapter 11

1 Strictly speaking, only Reynecke was an informer. Brune and Horak were employed policemen sent into the university environment to provide information on the political activities of students and their organisations. However, from the viewpoint of those being spied on, this distinction is of little importance.
2 George Bizos, *Odyssey to Freedom*, Random House, Johannesburg, 2007, p. 391. It is probable that I was less definitive than this, warning that there were sufficient concerns about Williamson to avoid dealing with him on anything sensitive. This was certainly my position by the time he left South Africa at the end of 1976 and was employed as information officer at the International University Exchange Fund in Geneva.
3 Terry Bell, in collaboration with Dumisa Buhle Ntsebeza, *Unfinished Business: South Africa Apartheid and Truth*, Redworks, Observatory, 2001, p. 75.
4 Michael Lobban, *White Man's Justice: South African Political Trials in the Black Consciousness Era*, Oxford University Press, Oxford, 1996, pp. 88–89.
5 Mike Terry, 'Some personal recollections of the Free Nelson Mandela Campaign', ANC website, *www.anc.org*.
6 Personal e-mail communication with Steven Friedman, 31 May 2012.
7 Mark Gevisser, *Thabo Mbeki: The Dream Deferred*, Jonathan Ball Publishers, Johannesburg , 2007, pp. 352–353.
8 Thomas G. Karis and Gail M. Gerhart, *From Protest to Challenge: A Documentary History of African Politics in South Africa, 1882–1990*, volume 5: *Nadir and Resurgence, 1964–1975*, Unisa Press, Pretoria, 1997, p. 40.
9 'Makatini assured Okhela members that they had the approval of top elements in the ANC ... At one point, Tambo himself came to address them secretly'. Karis and Carter, *From Protest to Challenge*, volume 5, p. 58 n62. See also Lawrence Weschler, 'An Afrikaner Dante', *The New Yorker*, 8 November 1993, p. 84.
10 Steven Friedman, 'From class room to class struggle: Radical academics and the rebirth of trade unionism in the 1970s', paper presented to a conference on The Durban Moment: Revisiting Politics, Labour, Youth and Resistance in the 1970s, Rhodes University, 21–23 February 2013, p. 22.
11 Ibid.
12 Elaine Unterhalter, in a discussion during 2012, reminded me of this important element in the creation of a coherent and supportive radical community.

Index

A
Abernethy, Desmond 5
Abrahams, Lionel 9
academic freedom 10, 61, 63, 64, 65, 95, 232
Academic Freedom Committee 61, 62, 64
Adler, Taffy 55, 56, 58, 62, 64, 70, 181, 182, 268
African National Congress (ANC) 13, 29, 66, 89, 90, 151, 157, 167, 174, 175, 180, 181, 203, 219, 221, 226, 231, 234, 250, 251, 253, 257, 263, 268, 269, 272, 273
   and Black Consciousness 41, 220
   and Communist Party 40, 41, 43, 164, 183, 188, 190, 191, 194, 215, 217, 218, 223, 243, 246, 252, 254
   and PAC 39, 42, 106, 124
   and Sactu 164, 167, 174, 183, 188, 207
   armed struggle 43, 44, 106, 107, 120, 141, 142, 218
   banning 39, 42, 43, 47, 123, 124
   detainees 18, 19, 21, 22, 24, 33
   exile 41, 42, 123, 203, 220, 242, 260, 262
   leaders 125, 126, 132, 144
   recruitment 42, 184, 185, 186, 222
   Sechaba 41
   underground activities 67, 166, 187, 218, 224, 227
African People's Democratic Union of Southern Africa (Apdusa) 140, 141
African Resistance Movement (ARM) 44, 106, 268
Afrikaanse Nasionale Studentebond 10
Afrikaner Studentebond (ASB) 10
Aggett, Neil 19, 262, 272
Ahmed Timol Memorial Committee 88

Alexander, Neville 41
Alexander, Ray 164, 186, 208, 272
Alliance for Radical Change (ARC) 116
Althusser, Louis 231, 235, 236
Andersson, Gavin 186
Anglo American 82–7, 92, 109, 110, 113, 115, 116, 146, 156, 249, 259
Anti-Apartheid Movement (AAM) 63, 64, 74, 190, 253
Aquarius 55, 112
askari 203
Asvat, Farouk 65
Ayob, Ismail 259

B
Baker, Trevor 206
Bantu Affairs Administration Board 163, 178
bantustans 38, 54, 141, 155
Barker, Anthony 56, 65
Barker, Maggie 65
Behrens, Simon 138, 179
Bell, Terry 191, 250, 272, 273
Berrangé, Vernon 227
Biko, Steve 1, 11, 12, 14, 19, 32, 40, 81, 126, 244, 262, 267, 268
   and Black Consciousness 34, 38, 81, 147
   and Nusas 1, 11, 12, 14–18, 32, 34, 36, 81, 130, 149, 244
   and Saso 34, 81, 130, 148
Bizos, George 216, 226, 236, 239, 243, 249, 265, 273
Black Consciousness (BC) 17, 38, 40, 41, 46, 49, 54, 84, 91, 96, 126, 127, 159, 191, 217–20, 228, 242, 255, 265, 268–71, 273
   and Nusas 11, 14, 16, 18, 32, 33, 65, 97, 98, 99, 101–5, 108, 143, 227, 244

and Saso 11, 15, 16, 34, 36, 148, 149
  ideology 45, 102, 103, 147, 150, 190, 241
Black Sash 54, 55, 56, 70, 95
Bloom, Tony 109
Bonner, Philip 120
Bookholane, Fats 9
Boraine, Alex 87
Botha, P.W. 55, 268
Boustred, Graham 86
Bozzoli, G.R. 7, 64, 69, 70, 79, 108, 109, 232
Breytenbach, Breyten 194, 195, 210, 211, 261, 262, 263
British Labour Party 62
British National Union of Students 253
British Young Socialists 63
Broodryk, 'Kalfie' 209
Brown, Susan 26, 159, 176, 235, 260
Brune, Derek 124, 230, 247
Budlender, Geoffrey 83, 96, 97, 101, 216, 246, 269
Bureau of State Security (Boss) 72, 205
Buthelezi, Gatsha 123, 128
Buthelezi, Manas 131

C
Cabral, Amilcar 14, 45, 105, 268
Callinicos, Luli 172, 179
Carlson, Joel 22, 23, 54, 128
Castro, Fidel 42
Charles Johnson Memorial Hospital 56, 65
Chaskalson, Arthur 216, 223, 224, 225, 227, 228, 229, 233, 251, 252
Cheadle, Halton 153
Christian Institute 54, 55, 70, 74, 80, 95, 131, 159, 189
Christie, Renfrew 13
Clark, Ramsey 54
Clegg, Johnny 259
Coetzee, Johann 197, 198, 214, 215
Cold War 165, 190, 191, 207, 240, 263
Coloured Labour Party 54, 55, 65, 123, 127
Coloured Persons' Representative Council 123, 144
Committee for Clemency 121
Commonwealth of Nations 50
Community of the Resurrection 130
Compol 200, 202, 203, 204, 206, 211, 261
Congress Alliance 8, 19, 43, 48, 63, 125, 126, 130, 183, 184, 186, 207, 218, 255

Congress of South African Trade Unions (Cosatu) 88
Congress of the People 106, 126
Cooper, Saths 148
Costa, Ken 7, 23, 77
Council of Non-European Trade Unions (Cnetu) 106
Counter Information Services (CIS) 176, 178, 179, 180, 189, 191, 192, 202, 208, 251
Cousins, Ben 206
Couzens, Tim 9
Craig, Graham 80
Crawford, Athalie 206
Crawford, Colleen 206
Cronwright, Arthur Benoni 107, 108, 134, 136, 213, 214
Crosland, Anthony 62, 63
Cunningham, Jenny 73, 80
Curtis, Jeanette (Jen) 88, 89, 156, 157, 195, 203, 208, 235, 259, 262
  and IAS 151, 156, 163, 171, 175, 181, 184, 186
  and Nusas 15, 153, 192, 194
Curtis, Neville 15, 17, 18, 21, 55, 58, 130, 157, 267, 268
  and Nusas 1, 11, 13, 14, 35, 51–4, 81, 253
Cuthsela, Mthayeni 141

D
Dangor, Achmat 65
Daniel, John 11, 32
Daniels, Eddie 44
Davis, David 153
deaths in detention 19, 22, 35, 68, 69, 70, 89, 90, 141, 245
De Beer, Cedric 77, 90, 124, 136, 137, 146, 179, 192, 194, 213, 214, 231, 250, 269
De Kadt, Raphael 148
De Villiers, René 120, 229
De Villiers, Richard 237, 273
Defiance Campaign 24, 106
Denton Committee 252
Department of Labour 154, 162, 178
Desai, Amina 144
Desmond, Cosmas 62, 63
Detainees' Parents Support Committee (DPSC) 263
Dlamini, Stephen 164
Dorkay House 9, 10
Douglas-Home, Mark 137
Driver, Jonty 11

Du Toit, André 240, 241, 273
Dugard, John 118, 120, 270
Durban moment 147, 267, 273

E
Edwards, Karl Zachariah (Zak) 194, 206, 208
Emdon, Erica 235
Ensor, Paula 33, 153
Eriksson, Lars-Gunnar 176, 178, 189, 190, 191, 250
Essop, Mohammed Salim 65, 66, 67, 68, 69, 70, 71, 72, 198
Etheredge, Dennis 86
Extension of University Education Act (1959) 61

F
Fanaroff, Bernie 163
Fanon, Frantz 45, 100
Federal Seminary 126
Federation of Free African Trade Unions of South Africa (Fofatusa) 184
Federation of South African Trade Unions (Fosatu) 88
Fine, Alan 85, 136, 225, 259, 268
Fischer, Bram 44, 126, 129, 131, 139, 141, 144, 205, 216, 219, 222, 225, 252, 272
Food and Canning Workers Union 164
Fort Hare 10
Fourie, Jopie 209
Free Education Campaign 79
Freedom Charter 48, 65, 108, 122, 139, 142, 217–20, 223, 224, 227, 228, 242, 244
Freire, Paulo 87, 159
Frescura, Franco 137
Friedman, Steven 66, 73, 74, 81, 159, 211, 235, 258, 263, 267, 271, 273
  and IAS 151, 157, 159, 170, 175
  and Wages Commission 85, 156, 181, 259
  and Wits Student 85, 106, 107, 137
Fugard, Athol 9, 10

G
Galaska, Christian 193, 262
General Factory Workers Benefit Fund 88, 157
Gerdener, Theo 113
Gilder, Barry 180, 195
Ginwala, Frene 189
Goldberg, Denis 131

Gordimer, Nadine 9
Gottschalk, Keith 95
Goudstad College 57
Gqabi, Joe 185
Graaff, De Villiers 83, 116
Gramsci, Antonio 47, 102, 105, 268, 270
Grossman, Jonathan 90, 137
Group Areas Act 157
guerrilla attacks 257
  fighters 29, 43, 257
  warfare 42, 43
guerrilla theatre 54, 112
Gunther, Magnus 268

H
Hackland, Brian 229, 241
Haigh, Bruce 206
Hain, Peter 2, 3, 64
Haron, Imam Abdullah 19, 22, 23, 70, 201, 206
Harris, Anne 2
Harris, John 2, 3
Harrop-Allin, Clinton 2
Hayes, Steven 131
headquarters of the Pretoria security police *see* Compol
Heinke, Rex 7
Hemson, David 95, 151, 153, 271, 272
Hertzog, Albert 2
Heunis, Chris 146
Higgs, Dennis 2
History of Opposition in South Africa campaign 106, 107, 111, 117, 127, 229
Hlapane, Bartholomew 222–7, 252
Hoffenberg, Raymond 11
Hoffman, Abbie 76
Hogan, Barbara 26, 159, 237, 260
Holiday, Anthony (Tony) 6, 68, 73, 127, 133, 255, 270
Horn, Pat 26
Horak, Gerhardus 229, 230, 231, 273
Horwood, O.F.P. 58
Human Rights Committee 89, 90, 189
Hurley, Denis 121

I
Industrial Aid Society (IAS) 88, 202, 203, 208, 236, 251, 252, 260, 271, 272
  and Wages Commission 148, 149, 150, 151, 156
  formation and early history 157–66, 168–72, 174–89

Industrial and Commercial Union (ICU) 106
Industrial Councils 152, 155, 178
Innes, Duncan 32, 189, 192, 250, 272
Institute for Industrial Education (IIE) 161
Institute of Race Relations *see* South African Institute of Race Relations
International Confederation of Free Trade Unions (ICFTU) 165
International Court of Justice 118, 222
International Defence and Aid Fund (Idaf) 253
International University Exchange Fund (IUEF) 176, 178, 189–92, 207, 208, 250, 251, 273

J

Jackson, Stanley 30
Jacobs, Gideon 111, 112, 229
Jacobs, P.B. 'Flip' 222, 244, 245, 251
James, Tim 137, 143, 145
Jana, Priscilla 258
Jiba, Linda 260
Johannesburg College of Education 90, 117
John Vorster Square 24, 26, 58, 68, 107, 108, 128, 145, 165, 197, 198, 206, 211, 212
Jonathan, Leabua 83
Joseph, Helen 88, 89, 125, 126, 130, 131, 132, 255, 266, 270

K

Kailembo, Andrew 165
Kane-Berman, John 63
Kapuuo, Clemens 118, 119, 127
Kathrada, Ahmed 'Kathy' 132, 265
Kennedy, Captain 66, 70, 71
Kentridge, Felicia 177
Kentridge, Sydney 29, 30
Kentridge, William 238
Khubeka, Abigail 9
Kirkwood, Mike 147, 148
Klaasen, Thandi 9
Kleinschmidt, Horst 117, 210, 268
Kołakowski, Leszek 240
Kool Look Wigs 155, 156
Kotane, Moses 43, 44
Krok, Abe 155, 156
Krok, Sol 155, 156
Kruger Commission 80
Kruger, Jimmy 81
Kubheka, Sipho 148, 171, 185, 186, 271, 272

Kuny, Denis 216

L

Le Carré, John 207, 208
Le Grange, Louis 81
Leader, Sheldon 163, 236
Leftwich, Adrian 11
Legal Resources Centre 177
Legassick, Martin 32, 149, 151, 189, 270, 271, 272
Lenin, V.I. 47, 102, 105, 159, 268, 270
Lenkoe, James 19, 22, 23, 141
Leon, Sonny 121, 123, 127, 128, 129, 136, 144
Lestor, Joan 63, 64, 65, 71, 72, 74
Lewin, Hugh 44, 192, 253
Liberal Party 114, 120, 130
liberals 12, 18, 32, 33, 37, 38, 41, 43, 45, 97, 99, 100, 114, 142, 271
  white 12, 16, 38, 41, 49, 98
liberalism 14, 15, 16, 23, 33, 34, 37, 38, 75, 98, 103, 115, 120, 217, 220, 232, 234, 240, 241, 244, 254, 255, 263, 264
  established 105, 111, 149
  moderate 86
  multi-racial 1, 17, 32, 150, 228
  religious 78
  radical 240, 244
  white 36, 97, 150
Lilliesleaf Farm 209
Louw, Derek 137
Lowmass, Jane 197
Ludorf, Joe 118
Lukács, Georg 47, 102, 105, 159, 268, 270
Luthuli, Albert 224
Luthuli Detachment 29

M

MacCrone, I.D. 61
Mafeje, Archie 2
Magnusson, Åke 164, 271
Magubane, Peter 19
Maharaj, 'Mac' 41
Makatini, Johnny 262, 273
Malan, Etienne 111, 112
Manci, Robert 185, 186
Mandela, Nelson 19, 125, 253, 254, 265, 266, 273
  and Nusas trial 216, 219, 223, 226, 227

and Release all Political Prisoners campaign 126, 127, 129, 131, 132, 133, 139, 141, 144
Mandela, Winnie 19, 20, 21, 144, 255
Mangcu, Xolela 41, 267, 277
Maré, Gerry 179, 192, 195, 202, 235, 238, 261
Maree, Johann 170, 182, 272
Margo, Cecil 69
Margo, Ian 25, 26, 206
Margolis, Athol 72, 79, 113
Marx, Karl 235, 236
Marxism 15, 34, 37, 45, 47, 49, 120, 158, 190, 218, 220, 235, 236, 262, 268
   Soviet 35
   Western 35, 148, 150, 228, 267
Masondo, Amos 185
Mattera, Don 65
Matthews, Z.K. 224
Mbeki, Epainette 260
Mbeki, Govan 125, 126, 129, 130, 131, 132, 133, 139, 141, 144, 157, 216, 219, 223, 226
Mbeki, Thabo 41, 157, 184, 260, 268, 273
McGiven, Arthur 248
McIntyre, Captain 204
Meillassoux, Claude 235
Metal and Allied Workers Union (Mawu) 176, 186
Mfeti, Pindile 151, 156, 157, 162, 175, 184, 251, 262
migrant labour 38, 56, 78, 85, 86
military service 4, 55, 117, 180
Mkwayi, Wilton 'Bri-Bri' 224
Mohlayaneng, Bafana 'Sammy' 185
Moodie, Dunbar 147, 148, 234
Moodley, Strini 148
Morphet, Tony 147, 148, 271
Moss, Sam 146
Movement for Social Democracy (MSD) 176, 178, 179, 180, 189, 191, 192, 202, 208, 251
Mvubelo, Lucy 83
Myburgh, John 177

N
Nabarro, Frank 65
Naidoo, Indres 88, 90, 131, 251, 252, 255
Naidoo, Murthi 88
Naidoo, Prema 88
Naidoo, Shanti 19, 20, 27, 28, 90, 251, 252, 267

Namibia 107, 117–20, 127, 131, 139, 143, 222, 270, 271
Nanabhai, Shirish 90, 251
National Committee of Liberation (NCL) 43, 106, 268
National Party 2, 5, 9, 10, 16, 45, 51, 58, 112, 113, 146
National Union of South African Students (Nusas) 1, 5, 9–18, 21, 22, 23, 32–6, 46–9, 51–5, 57, 59, 60, 61, 72, 73, 75, 77, 79, 80, 82, 85, 87, 88, 90, 92, 93–7, 99, 101–6, 108–12, 116, 117, 121, 122, 125–8, 130, 136, 137, 138, 143, 145, 146, 148, 149, 150, 152, 153, 154, 156, 157, 179, 189, 191–6, 199, 202, 206, 207, 208, 215, 216, 218, 220, 221, 223, 224, 227, 228, 229, 231, 232, 234, 237, 239–46, 247, 249–54, 256, 257, 258, 263, 264, 265, 267–73
   and Black Consciousness 11, 14, 15, 16, 18, 32, 33, 36, 49, 54, 65, 84, 91, 96–9, 101–5, 108, 143, 191, 218, 227, 228, 244
   and Steve Biko 1, 11, 12, 14–18, 32, 34, 36, 81, 130, 149, 244
   campaigns
      anti-Republic Day (1971) 54, 57, 59
      Release All Political Prisoners 33, 89, 92, 122, 123, 128, 129, 132, 133, 135, 136, 139, 142, 144, 146, 179, 208, 216, 217, 219, 225, 226, 254
      Twenty-two, The (the 22) 21–4, 134, 135, 206
   history 10–13, 17, 32, 33, 47
   National Council 53, 83, 110
   presidents 21, 35, 73, 196, 199
      Budlender, Geoffrey 83, 96, 97, 101, 216, 246, 269
      Curtis, Neville 1, 11, 13, 14, 15, 17, 18, 21, 35, 51–5, 58, 81, 130, 253, 267, 268
      Daniel, John 11, 32
      Innes, Duncan 32, 189, 192, 250, 272
      Nupen, Charles 103, 104, 214, 270, 271
      Pretorius, Paul 81, 130, 253
      Robertson, Ian 11
   trial 215–34, 239–46, 247, 249–52, 256, 265
National Unity Democratic Organisation (Nudo) 118
National Youth Organisation (Nayo) 185

Naudé, Beyers 55, 74, 159, 175, 189, 208, 259
Ndaba, Queeneth 9
Ndou, Samson 19
Ndzanga, Lawrence 19
Ndzanga, Rita 19
Ngoyi, Lilian 125, 126, 251, 255
Ngudle, Solwandle 'Looksmart' 141
Notcutt, Martin 206
Ntsebeza, Dumisa Buhle 272, 273
Nupen, Charles 103, 104, 214, 270, 271
Nupen, Michael 102, 120, 138, 148, 153, 229
Nuswel 102, 154, 156
Nyembe, Dorothy 144
Nyerere, Julius 100

O
O'Dowd, Michael 87
Okhela 190, 195, 209, 210, 251, 261, 262, 263, 273
O'Meara, Dan 87, 179, 180, 189, 192, 250, 269
Operation Mayibuye 42
Oppenheimer, Harry 83, 84, 87, 113
Orkin, Andy 76, 77
Orkin, Mark 56

P
Palme, Olof 191
Palmer, Cecily 225
Pan Africanist Congress (PAC) 39, 42, 43, 47, 106, 120, 124, 139
Parker, Aida 145
Perold, Helene 71
Phatudi, Cedric 124, 125, 128–32, 143, 144
Piliso, Ntemi 9
Pityana, Barney 81, 130
Platzky, Laurine 241
Pogrund, Benjamin 139
political detainees 18, 19, 21, 22, 33
  Twenty-two, The (the 22) 18, 20–3
  inquests into deaths in detention 22, 70, 141
political prisoners 88, 89, 92, 105, 112, 118, 119, 121–4, 126–33, 135, 136, 137, 139, 142–6, 179, 208, 216–20, 225, 226, 229, 238, 241, 245, 253, 254, 255, 257, 265, 270
  campaign for the release of 121–46, 208, 216

plea for clemency 121, 127, 128, 142, 257
solitary confinement/torture see solitary confinement
Poqo 120
Poulantzas, Nicos 235, 236
Pretoria Boys High 2, 3
Pretorius, Paul 81, 130, 253
Prinsloo, G.L. 89
Progressive Party 3, 5, 8, 9, 18, 30, 109, 110, 111, 113, 114, 115, 229, 258, 270

R
Ragaven, Rogers 11
Ramgobin, Mewa 15, 54, 95, 121, 127, 257
Ramotse, Benjamin 29, 30
Ramusi, Collins 123, 124, 128
Rand Afrikaans University 9, 57, 214
radicals 23, 25, 26, 32, 38, 75, 87, 100, 101, 102, 104, 206, 232, 234, 236, 255
  emerging 47
  middle-class 264
  new 36, 45, 48, 265
  political 82
  progressive 99
  student 75, 98, 150
  white 38, 59, 217
radicalism 30, 32, 35, 37, 40, 46, 48, 49, 91, 92, 100, 150, 217, 221, 233, 254, 263, 264
  anti-apartheid 33
  anti-institutional 23
  left 219, 262
  political 2, 100, 191
  socialist 222
  student 76
Randall, Peter 116, 117, 230
Raphael, Adam 148, 156, 271
Rathebe, Dolly 9
Redacres Mission 1, 13, 14
Rees, John 74
Reich, Charles A. 76, 269
Reynecke, J.H. 229, 240, 273
Rhodes University 11, 12, 267, 273
Rhodesia 29, 30
Richard Feetham Academic Freedom Lecture 60, 62, 269
Riotous Assemblies Act 107, 133
Rivonia Trial 39, 126, 131, 139, 141, 217, 226
Robben Island 19, 90, 112, 126, 127, 131, 132, 140, 142, 185, 206, 223, 255, 265

Robertson, Ian 11
Ronge, Barry 9
Rothwell, Dennis 216, 222
Rubin, Jerry 76

S
Sabotage Act 11, 131, 252
Saloojee, Rokaya 'Rookie' 89, 255
Saloojee, Suliman 'Babla' 19, 89
Satyagraha 15
Schlebusch, Alwyn 81
Schlebusch Commision of Inquiry 81, 111, 116, 221
Schlemmer, Lawrie 241
Schuitema, Barend 195
Selvan, David 7
Sexwale, Tokyo 185
Shabangu, Elliot 19, 185
Sharpeville massacre 7, 8, 42, 43, 77, 78
Sikhakhane, Joyce 19, 20
Simon, Barney 9
Sipolilo campaign 43
Sisulu, Albertina 144
Sisulu, Lindiwe 184, 260
Sisulu, Sheila 237
Sisulu, Walter 126, 127, 129, 131, 132, 133, 139, 144, 216, 223, 226, 265
Sithole, Miriam 151, 157, 160, 184, 260
Slabbert, Frederik van Zyl 229
Slovo, Joe 222
Smith, Clive 7
Smith, Vesta 225
Sobukwe, Robert 127, 131, 139
Soggot, David 22
solitary confinement/torture 40, 128, 140, 141, 189, 213, 224, 245, 260, 262, 263, 267, 273
    Ahmed Timol and Mohammed Salim Essop 68–74
    personal experience of 197–206, 208, 212
    Twenty-two, The (the 22) 18–23, 28, 29
South African Communist Party (SACP) 39, 41, 43, 47, 48, 67, 106, 157, 190, 191, 194, 195, 234, 242, 262, 272
    and IAS 164, 175, 186
    and Nusas trial 217–20, 222, 224, 227, 231, 240, 242, 243, 246, 251, 252, 254–6
South African Congress of Trade Unions (Sactu) 43, 47, 48, 59, 106, 151, 157, 164–7, 174, 175, 182, 183, 184, 186, 187, 188, 190, 207, 208, 251, 259
South African Council of Churches 54, 74, 95
South African Institute of Race Relations 54, 55, 56, 80, 95, 130, 157, 268, 269, 270, 271
South African Students' Organisation (Saso) 1, 11, 12, 15, 16, 34, 36, 41, 79, 80, 81, 84, 97, 99, 130, 143, 148, 149, 150
South West Africa National Union (Swano) 118, 127, 144
South West Africa People's Organisation (Swapo) 118, 139, 144
Soviet Union 148, 190
Soweto Students' Representative Council (SSRC) 239
Sprack, John 11
Stadler, Alf, 120, 230
Steyn, Gert 222, 247
Streek, Barry 267
Struwig, Andries 211, 212
Stubbs, Aelred 126, 130, 131
Suppression of Communism Act (1950) 107, 125, 130, 185, 216, 217
Suttner, Raymond 234
Suzman, Helen 8, 9, 18, 87, 110, 111, 258
Swanepoel, Theuns 'Rooi Rus' 19, 22, 29, 135, 141
Swedish Trade Union Federation (LO) 164

T
Tambo, Oliver 39, 41, 262, 273
Terrorism Act 13, 18, 21–5, 29, 68, 118, 139, 144, 184, 197, 210, 212, 214, 240, 258, 259, 263
Terry, Mike 253, 273
Thebehali, David 54
Thompson, Douglas 90
Thompson, Ian 26, 27, 267
Timol, Ahmed 19, 66–72, 88, 89, 197
Timol, Mohammed 88, 90, 251, 255, 269
Tip, Karel 102, 153, 179, 195, 196, 214, 270
Tiro, Abram Onkgopotse 79
Tober, Karl 79
Tobias, Phillip 199
Toivo, Herman Andimba Toivo ja 118, 119, 129, 139, 140, 216
Trade Union Advisory Co-ordinating Council (Tuacc) 88, 151, 161, 165, 166, 168–72, 174, 175, 176, 177, 178, 181, 182, 183, 186, 187

Trade Union Council of South Africa (Tucsa) 164
trade unions 5, 8, 35, 39, 43, 44, 46, 48, 59, 83, 85, 87, 88, 106, 157, 159, 161, 164, 167, 168, 169, 170, 174, 177, 180–4, 187, 188, 221, 234, 241, 242, 243, 256, 264, 269, 272
trade unionism 84, 106, 107, 110, 120, 159, 164, 165, 168, 169, 181, 182, 184, 220, 259, 267, 269, 273
Treason Trial 90, 125, 126, 223, 224, 227, 228, 257, 258
Tucker, Raymond 27, 215, 216, 246
Turner, Rick 1, 15, 18, 35, 36, 81, 95, 101, 102, 121, 147–50, 153, 158, 262, 267, 271
Turok, Ben 41, 268
Twenty-two, The (the 22) 18–24, 26, 27, 29, 90, 134, 185, 198, 206, 238
    Magubane, Peter 19
    Mandela, Winnie 19, 20, 21, 144, 255
    Naidoo, Shanti 19, 20, 27, 28, 90, 252, 267
    Ndou, Samson 19
    Ndzanga, Lawrence 19
    Ndzanga, Rita 19
    Ramotse, Benjamin 29, 30
    Shabangu, Elliot 19, 185
    Sikhakhane, Joyce 19, 20
    Zikalala, 'Snuki' 19
Twins Pharmaceuticals 155

U
Umkhonto we Sizwe (MK) 29, 39, 42, 43, 126, 141, 144, 151, 157, 166, 180, 184, 185, 187, 209, 224, 252, 257
Umsebenzi/Abasebenzi 156, 259
United Democratic Front (UDF) 188, 258, 264
United Nations (UN) 11, 21, 83, 118, 119, 128, 262, 270
United Nations Special Committee on Apartheid 138
United Nations Universal Declaration of Human Rights 11
United Party 18, 24, 56, 83, 111, 116, 145, 146, 229, 270
Unity Movement 47, 130, 140, 141, 214
University Christian Movement 54, 57, 80
University of Cape Town (UCT) 2, 10, 11, 61, 80, 84, 96, 126, 184, 227, 241, 267, 268, 269, 270, 271, 272
University of Durban-Westville 84, 184
University of Natal 1, 10, 13, 35, 58, 84, 97, 102, 121, 147, 148, 179, 229, 241
University of Pretoria 1
University of South Africa 161, 179
University of the North (Turfloop) 79, 80, 84
University of the Witwatersrand (Wits) 16, 66, 68, 69, 90, 117, 118, 161, 163, 206, 234, 267, 268, 270, 272
    campaigns 25, 54, 56, 57, 58, 92, 93, 124, 130, 143, 144, 219, 229, 231
    campus 23, 55, 73, 80, 124, 125, 159, 196, 206, 213, 219, 253, 269
    demonstrations 24, 26, 57, 70, 80, 89, 199, 238
    mass meetings 55, 56, 219, 237
    Nusas 7, 9, 10, 11, 13, 18, 21, 22, 54, 55, 73, 81, 92, 105, 116, 126, 137, 232, 258
    orientation 232, 233
    police raids 107, 129, 146, 213
    protests 25, 26, 27, 30, 31, 32, 58, 62, 77, 199, 237
    radicals 47, 82, 206, 254
    SRC 55, 61, 73, 82, 85, 114, 129, 143, 157, 160, 175, 179, 189, 195, 199, 229, 230, 231
    student politics 1, 5, 23, 32, 60, 78, 96, 103
    Wages Commission 84, 149, 150, 154, 156, 181
Unlawful Organisations Act 107, 217
Unterhalter, Beryl 119
Unterhalter, Elaine 26, 71, 267, 273
Unterhalter, Jack 20, 27, 119
Urban Bantu Council (UBC) 54, 55, 123

V
Van Aggenbach, Sergeant 201
Van den Bergh, H.J. 72
Van Niekerk, 'Tiny' 134, 136
Van Wyk de Vries Commission 221
Van Wyk, Andries 23, 200, 201
Van Wyk, Fred 55
Van Wyk, 'Spyker' 19, 23, 189, 200, 201, 206
Vandayar, Reggie 90, 251
Veii, Gerson 126, 127, 134, 144
Venter, 'Tiny' 248
Vigne, Randolph 44, 268
Von Brandis constituency 116, 117
Vorster, John 58, 59, 72, 73, 74, 80, 82, 83, 146, 268

W

Waddell, Gordon 86, 109, 113, 115, 229, 270
Wage Determination Boards 84, 155
Wages Commission 35, 84, 85, 87, 88, 92, 101, 102, 110, 115, 152, 153, 154, 158, 179, 208, 217, 220, 221, 228, 229, 240, 241, 242, 256, 259, 271
   and IAS 147–50, 156, 157, 170, 181, 184
Wankie campaign 29, 43
Webster, Eddie 97, 98, 99, 102, 105, 108, 148, 172, 179, 214, 221, 234, 237, 243, 268, 269, 270
Weinberg, Eli 157, 186, 203, 251, 252
Weinberg, Sheila 88, 251, 255
Weiner, Danny 60
Wentzel, Ernie 177, 239
West Rand Bantu Affairs Administration Board 178
Western Deep Levels Mine 82, 83, 85, 87, 88, 92, 93, 156, 249, 259
Western Province Workers Advice Bureau (WPWAB) 88, 151, 157, 168, 170, 182
White, Dale 78, 269
Wilgespruit Fellowship Centre 78
Williamson, Craig 86, 191, 194, 208, 249, 250, 251, 252, 259, 273
Wilson, Tim 65
Wits Student 6, 63, 85, 106, 107, 115, 137, 141, 143, 232, 245, 257, 267, 269, 270, 271, 273
Wolffe, Mark 95
Wood, Chris 116
Workers Advisory Project 88, 157, 161, 169
Workmen's Compensation 178
World Confederation of Labour 128
World Federation of Trade Unions 165
World Union of Jewish Students 128
Wrankmore, Bernie 70

Y

Young Progressive Party 3, 259
Young, Gordon 210
Youth Awareness 57
Yutar, Percy 202, 217

Z

Zarenda, Harry 236
Zikalala, 'Snuki' 19

Picture credits

Photographs from the Historical Papers Research Archive, the Library, University of the Witwatersrand, Johannesburg, were sourced from the following collection: AD1718 State vs Glenn Moss and four others; on charges of contravening Suppression of Communism Act (Act 44, 1950).

The publisher and author have made every effort to identify and acknowledge the sources of photographs reproduced in this book. If there are any errors or omissions, these will be gladly corrected in subsequent editions.

Diana Wall of Museum Africa, Elizabeth Marima from the archives at the University of the Witwatersrand, Robyn Keet of Africa Media Online, Gabriele Mohale of Historical Papers, University of the Witwatersrand, and Michelle Leon of Library and Information Services at Times Media provided invaluable assistance in photographic research. Fritz Schoon, Joyce Curtis-Rouse, David Curtis, Sherry McLean, Jann Turner, Foszia Turner-Stylianou, David Hemson, Gerhard Maré, Omar Badsha, Jeeva Rajgopaul and Alan Fine were all very generous in giving access to their private photographic collections, and with their time and assistance.

Front cover photograph: courtesy Museum Africa (PH2014). From left to right: Glenn Moss, Charles Nupen, Eddie Webster, Cedric de Beer, Karel Tip.

Back cover photographs: (left) courtesy University of the Witwatersrand Historical Papers (AD1718-A6-12); (right) courtesy Wits University archives (Ph/77-17b).